PLAYWRITING MASTER CLASS

The Personality of Process
and
the Art of Rewriting

Edited by
Michael Wright

HEINEMANN
PORTSMOUTH, NH

Heinemann
A division of Reed Elsevier Inc.
361 Hanover Street
Portsmouth, NH 03801–3912
www.heinemann.com

Offices and agents throughout the world

Library of Congress Cataloging-in-Publication Data
Playwriting master class : the personality of process and the art of
rewriting / edited by Michael Wright.
p. cm.
ISBN 0-325-00169-3 (alk. paper)
1. Playwriting. 2. Drama—Technique. I. Wright, Michael.
PN1661 .P63 2000
808.2—dc21
00-057234

Editor: Lisa Barnett
Production coordinator: Sonja S. Chapman
Production service: Colophon
Cover design: Darci Mehall, Aureo Design
Manufacturing: Louise Richardson

Printed in the United States of America on acid-free paper
04 03 02 01 00 DA 1 2 3 4 5

to the memory and legacy of
David Mark Cohen

CONTENTS

CONTENTS

FOREWORD

"THERE IS NO ONE RIGHT WAY TO WRITE A PLAY." SO WE were all told back in Playwriting 101, and, for better or for worse, this basic dictum continues to be professed today in writing programs across the country. All too often, however, this assertion is immediately followed up with one or another of the classic cookbook approaches to play construction: for example, conflict + resolution = audience satisfaction. Or the ancient favorite: rising action, reversal, climax, denouement. Or you may even get the avant-garde gloss on all this: $x \cdot x \cdot x = x3$, at least where $x = x$.

In effect, such structural approaches to play-making, which are meant to expose the scaffolding that effective plays can be built upon, have only served to mystify the creative process even more. Of course we can and do read the high watermarks of dramatic literature; we dissect the structures that supported all that wonderful dialogue—and with any luck this is somewhat instructive. But so what? What we want to know is how these dramatists arrived at those finished works. Surely their manuscripts were not borne fully realized; there must have been false starts, alternate endings, perhaps entire scenes that ultimately were consigned to oblivion. But in most cases, we will never know; those cagey writers have assigned their tell-tale ur-versions to the trash heap. Or, in more current practice, to the computer's trash bin.

Until now. Michael Wright's latest contribution to the art of playwriting—the book that you now hold in your hands—offers us the most illuminating foray to date into the delicate process of a new script's evolution. With the advent of this unique examination of works-in-progress by seven very different artists—examinations of scripts while they are still in progress, mind you—we are privileged to watch the work of masterful writers while they cope with dead ends and unlooked-for left turns as well as sudden, piercing moments of breakthrough and insight. We look over their shoulders as they allow us into that most interior of processes—that of artistic ferment—as they write and rewrite.

Through the artists we meet in this book, we see how truly idiosyncratic the growth of a creative undertaking can be. Michael kick-starts *Playwriting Master Class* by giving all of its participants the same simple task: to write a short play, starting from the same basic image ("there is a key in a drawer"), and chart the development of whatever evolves out of that original stimulus.

Naturally, it progresses differently for each artist. One writer evolves her work associatively, gradually spinning her fable out of dreams, portents, and even the chance comments of friends and relations. Another seems to have conceived of his play wholly from the start; for him, rewriting amounts to a continual tinkering with subtextual matters, carefully adjusting shades of characterization to control the impact of his dialogue. And yet another playwright begins with one play, only to have another intrude upon it, demanding to be written first. Especially amusing is that one of the writers manages to cheat that ultimate palimpsest—the word processor—at its own game by using the computer's ability to track changes for her as her writing metamorphoses from sketch to first draft to stageworthy script.

Thus, Michael's remarkable new book is also a felicitous investigation of the craft of playwriting, because it takes us through the entire endeavor of playwriting without privileging one aspect over another. Each artist begins by summoning his or her muse, and each goes on to plunge into rewriting with just as much relish. All of them, without exception, view the work of perfecting their pieces not as drudgery (as revisions are so frequently characterized elsewhere), but rather as a great pleasure—an adventure, in fact.

Empowering as this is, it is my fervent hope that this remarkable book will encourage you to think of the process of playwriting—your own process of playwriting, I mean—as an adventure, too. After all, composing a script is not merely a means to an end, not just a hurdle to surmount on the way to production. Each successive draft represents a fresh avenue of communication between your creation and yourself. And as *Playwriting Master Class* manifestly demonstrates, being along for the ride in the embryonic life of a new work is an extraordinary journey.

Bon voyage.

Mead K. Hunter
A.S.K. Theater Projects

PREFACE

THE ACT OF PLAYWRITING IS VERY PERSONAL, AS MY subtitle implies. It is generally a quiet undertaking, occurring in solitude. The writer makes a thousand choices the public never sees in order to move from inception to finished work. This is as it should be, of course. Virtually all artists create in private.

Much of my work in recent years has been to contribute what I can to making this personal act a bit more public. My hope has been to open up the inner process in order to provide a means of comparison and learning for other writers.

Part of my aim is to de-mystify the nature of the playwright's craft. We have access to films and TV shows that show painters in process, musicians developing a piece, and so on, but never, in my experience, anything that shows the writer actively at work. Because of the isolated nature of the writer's work, there are numerous unanswered questions: What does the writer do with a new idea? Where does the writer start? What if the play isn't working? How does the writer decide what form the play should take? These are just a handful of the questions students and professionals have raised over the years. *Playwriting Master Class* addresses many of these questions through virtually direct observation of the playwright at work.

My other ambition is to encourage more people to write plays, especially those who feel marginalized because their ideas seem too out of the mainstream, or whose working methods don't seem like those of other writers. Every voice that is silenced because the writer felt *wrong* is a voice lost, and that is regrettable.

When I first began writing plays, I emulated those I admired, both living and dead. These writers were from different worlds than mine, however. It was not until I wrote a play that was in my "native" language, so to speak (I'm from Baltimore, which has a truly unique accent and rhythms), that I felt connected to the real possibilities of theatre as a mode of expression. Years later, I realized that I had become a conduit between this native language and the theatre itself. I had given voice to a few people whose lives would not have been dramatized otherwise. And I had articulated my own vision of the world.

From that point, the next thing I wanted to do was codify various ways of working that I had observed in the processes of other writers, and which I used myself. This resulted in *Playwriting in Process*, a book of exercises for exploration and craft development. *Playwriting in Process* approaches playwriting from a theatrical methodology, not on a how-to basis—it is based on work done by Viola Spolin, Keith Johnstone, Augusto Boal, and others, using theatre games. For instance, if you want to know what a character is like, instead of making lists or writing prose biographies, write scenes for him that examine his home life, his job, his private concerns. Putting the exploration for a play into a playwriting form keeps the work dramatic and not narrative; it inherently theatricalizes the process.

Based on the success of *Playwriting in Process*, I wanted to look at the playwright's work from another angle: the nature of creative choices as a work evolves. And that is where the idea for *Playwriting Master Class* came from.

The playwrights you are about to encounter in this book have opened up their processes, work methods, and thinking for us. They have allowed us to experience an unusual situation as we virtually look over their shoulders while they work. In addition, the playwrights span various generations, backgrounds, styles, and points of view. My hope is that at least one playwright will serve as a model for a reader who shares some portion of the writer's perspective, style, or background, to encourage the reader to pursue their own vision. I have included contact information for each playwright as a way of helping to facilitate communication, should a reader wish to follow up further with a given writer. I can't promise that the writers will write back, of course—they're under no obligation. My goal is to open the door and see what comes of it. My wish is that dialogues will begin, and that every writer will grow in their work.

I have provided my own contact information as well. I have been very fortunate that people from around the world have sought me out because of my other books. Each has brought a new perspective into my life and work. This sharing, this community, is vital to me personally, and to the work we all do in the theatre. My permanent email address is: myquagga@yahoo.com. I welcome all contacts.

A quagga, by the way, is an extinct form of the zebra. Let's hope that there is never a dictionary entry that reads: "Playwright—an extinct form of writer." Instead, let's see to it that process evolves, the theatre flourishes, and the unique voice of each playwright finds expression, acceptance—and productions.

ACKNOWLEDGMENTS

THE PEOPLE WHO DESERVE THE GREATEST THANKS, OF course, are the playwrights who contributed so generously to this book. I also want to thank my family—Judy, Hannah, and Eli—who gave me love, encouragement, and the space to work.

INTRODUCTION

I always begin my playwriting classes with a discussion on the spelling of the term *playwright*. My emphasis is on the "wright" portion of the word. I want to make certain my students understand that there is a history and a resonance to the term. I think it's important for them to have a sense of entering into a tradition.

My *Webster's Ninth New Collegiate Dictionary* gives the etymology of wright as from "Middle English 'wyrhta' or 'wryhta,' worker or work; akin to the Old English 'weorc,' for work (approximately 12th Century)," and defines it as "a worker, especially in wood. Usually used in combination: shipwright, wheelwright." There are two elements of this that I love: first, the playwright as worker—because, let's face it, writing a play *is* work, and certainly no occupation for prima donnas or slackers. The second element is comprised of the images evoked by the definition: the playwright as someone fashioning something as hard yet delicate as wood into a new form—a ship, a wheel, a play—that carries us to new places, new worlds.

Both elements dovetail into what we call process these days in the theatre, referring to the steps needed to move a play from concept to finished product. But process is a term that often gets tossed around easily, as if it has a single, simple meaning. In fact, it encompasses an incredible range of meanings. It is the secret soul and sweat of each work of art, the underwater mass of the iceberg supporting the tip that is the play in performance—most of which the public glimpses only on the rarest occasions—and it is, as this book's subtitle implies, a reflection of the personality of the playwright as well.

Process is a highly individual matter. How one gets from inspiration to completion is as unique as our DNA. Process is something each artist must come to terms with on a variety of levels if she is going to succeed in producing a meaningful body of work. For some writers, process means contemplation and waiting for clear images until they feel compelled to put words on the page. For others, it's a careful procedure involving explorations, plot outlines, event charts, and other means of approaching the play. For still others, process is a matter of research and investigation until the world of the story is known thoroughly and can be fashioned into a plot.

Like all other elements of creative endeavor, however, there is no fixed process for any individual. Plays come to life in a multitude of ways. Every play is an entirely unique endeavor requiring new, or at least altered, methods. Each play represents a learning process: to say what I need in play B, I cannot simply refashion play A; I must find a different approach in order to create play B. There is no single formula.

Process has a dual nature: it is intuitive, yet purposeful. It is the means by which a playwright finds the trail from the initial idea to the finished product, knowing that the trail is often elusive, and even prone to vanish without warning. In this regard, process is also a way to survive the disappearance of a trail. All writers need a bag of tricks, so to speak, which will help the writer find her way out of an unexpected wilderness. My first book, Playwriting in Process, is designed for this purpose, among others. Playwriting Master Class approaches the work from yet another perspective.

The purpose of Playwriting Master Class is to open a window on the working methods of others—on the "personality of process." It is intended to provide playwrights at all levels with something seldom experienced: looking over another playwright's shoulder while they work to see how another person approaches a new play—what is rejected, what is kept, and why. Anyone who has ever had the experience of working in an ongoing playwrights' workshop probably has had some of these insights, though usually one only gets to observe the product and not the steps along the way. My interest is in how we create: why we make the choices we do. If I could have a time machine, I'd go back to watch Sophocles or Shakespeare make their choices, adjustments, rewrites (this was, after all, part of the fantasy of *Shakespeare in Love*), to see how each writer worked. Given the unlikelihood of this option, the alternative is to observe our contemporaries, and discover useful elements from their work.

Another reason for creating this book was to provide a counterbalance to the "having written" perspective we're exposed to for the most part. I have found it very frustrating over the years to read articles and interviews in journals and magazines in which the playwright talks about what they did to make their hit play a success. That's important, but it teaches virtually nothing because the commentary tends to dwell only on what worked. I want to know about *what didn't work*, and how they fixed it. I want to know about their process from the very beginning, including false starts, bad drafts, and all the other things that were not successful but that served to inform the playwright about the true path of the work.

I once had the opportunity to tell Tony Kushner how much I appreciated the acknowledgement in the published version of his *Angels in America* plays of the workshops and productions prior to the Broadway production. I praised this because it's an important tribute to the many creative people who helped him find the play and supported his efforts, but also because it helps my students understand how long a journey such a work can take. An even better step, in my view, would have been to publish all the drafts and fragments written from start to finish, just to see how the play evolved, and to get a sense of Kushner's work as the piece revealed itself to him. What a service to the playwriting community that would be! *Master Playwriting Class* is aimed at providing such a service.

The main portion of the book covers the work of a group of playwrights, each responding individually to a specific prompt. The prompt and the parameters they were given is described below. Each playwright has provided an astonishingly open look into their process and thinking. Each has allowed us to enter into their working methods to see how they went from A to Z. Editing this book allowed me to examine my own playwriting process by way of comparison and contrast to what the writers had provided. This is the aim of *Playwriting Master Class*: to reveal the private steps and struggles normally made by a writer in solitude. The ultimate ambition is for each person—playwright, dramaturg, director, actor, student, playwriting instructor—who encounters the work in this book to have a new concept of process, both as it is used by others and as it will be utilized by the writer herself.

* * *

There were a number of choices involved in starting work on this book. It will be of value to the reader to know what those steps were.

The main concept for the book was to provide a group of writers with the same "prompt" from which each would write a short play, keeping all drafts and explorations, plus a work journal, which they would give to me. The prompt was clearly the element to be most careful about. I did not want to influence the writers with my ideas or values. After some deliberation, I drew the prompt from one used by a friend, Kevin Kling.

Kevin is an actor and playwright whose solo pieces have been performed in many professional venues, and aired on National Public Radio. I first met Kevin at the WordBRIDGE Playwrights Lab in St. Petersburg, Florida, when we were part of the annual workshop there (WordBRIDGE is a two-week developmental program for student playwrights). Later, I was able to bring Kevin to my school to do some workshops.

One of his workshops involved writing from one's intuition. For the workshop, Kevin used this prompt: "write a piece based on the idea that there is a key in an envelope in a drawer." The concept was to work from layers of mystery and possibility, to see what was sparked in the minds of the participants. I found the prompt very effective for the workshop. It was an excellent catalyst for a wide range of creative responses. When I began looking for a prompt for *Playwriting Master Class*, I asked Kevin if I could use his, and he generously gave his permission.

I felt that this prompt would work well for the group of writers I had invited to participate in this project. The writers were selected on the basis of the quality of their work, but also because of their uniqueness from one another in terms of style and point of view. They represent a broad cross section of America. There was no effort to be "politically correct" in the selection, but to offer as wide a range of backgrounds as possible for the benefit of the book's audience. If a given reader finds that the background and/or methods of a given writer validate and inspire her or his own voice, then the book has achieved one of my missions.

It is my hope that there is enough variation in *Playwriting Master Class* to be of value to playwrights, theatre practitioners, and students/teachers of playwriting at all levels, as well as to other writers. If a reader encounters a way of working or thinking they've never considered, or decides to take on the prompt in their own fashion, or if the contents invite further considerations of process (i.e., the *Angels in America* progressive drafts get published), then another aspect of the book will be fulfilled.

The playwrights in this book are artists I admire and have worked with in various capacities. They represent a variety of ages, ethnicities, and backgrounds. Each represents a unique approach to process that will be of value to the reader in a variety of ways. The writers I invited to participate are, in alphabetical order, Elena Carrillo, David Crespy, Gary Garrison, Velina Hasu Houston, Julie Jensen, John Olive,

Guillermo Reyes, and Elizabeth Wong. (Unfortunately, John Olive had too many prior commitments to stay with the project. I feel that John is one of the finest playwrights in the United States, and though I'm sorry he couldn't be part of this book, I hope that readers will seek out his work and get to know him through such plays as *The Summer Moon*, *Careless Love*, or *Standing on My Knees*.)

Once I had contacted the writers and gained their participation, I sent out the following letter (via e-mail; much of this book has been developed through the Internet, a fabulous resource for writers):

> Dear [Playwright],
>
> As you know, you've been asked to participate in the creation of a new book I am editing, titled *Playwriting Master Class*. This book will be published by Heinemann in early 2000. Your part in this will be to write a short five- to ten-minute play, and document every step of your writing process. The following material provides specifics to help guide your work. Please feel free to contact me at any point with any and all questions or concerns.
>
> 1) THE PURPOSE OF THIS BOOK
>
> Our focus is to provide students, teachers, and both emerging and established professionals with a collection of writings that will demonstrate the essence of process. Most books deal with hindsight views on "having written," in which the playwright with a hit play talks about what they did to make the play so wonderful. I believe this hindsight perspective is not helpful. *Playwriting Master Class* is designed to show a playwright's work as it happened—warts, false-starts, breakthroughs, and all. The sense the reader should have is that they're looking over your shoulder as you work from start to finish. My job will be to amplify and annotate your process in anticipation of reader questions and curiosities.
>
> 2) YOUR PROCESS
>
> Because of this book's mission, I urge you to exaggerate your process a bit in order to reveal your steps along the way as clearly as possible. Even if you don't do character studies most of the time (or other explorations) it will be helpful if you did some for this exercise in order to reveal how you think about character (or plot, structure, etc.) as you are developing

a new work. You want to show the reader those little invisible elements that most people wouldn't notice—in the same way that slow-motion reveals the last-second shift in the magician's fingers. In this book we are going to blow the trick on purpose, and show how the rabbit got into the hat. Hopefully, this will encourage others to build from these insights and make their own magic.

Finally, I urge you to err on the side of making too many notes and/or doing too many explorations. My job as editor will be to select the most salient elements of each playwright's work. You will make my job much easier by providing me with a range of material to choose from.

3) THE "ASSIGNMENT"

Each playwright will write a five- to ten-minute play based on this prompt:

"There is a key in an envelope in a drawer."

Please note: I have taken this prompt from an exercise done by playwright and actor Kevin Kling. My intention is to avoid any bias on my part in the selection of the prompt.

The idea of the prompt is to have everyone start from the same catalyst, so that comparisons and contrasts can be made in the resultant work. This prompt can be included as the inciting incident before the play, the future result of the play's events, or appear in the beginning, middle or end of your piece—go with what works best for you.

You are to write your piece based on any idea you have that starts from this stimulus—whether taken literally or not—in any style, structure, or manner which suits your writing best. There are no limitations on language, philosophy, cultural perspectives, etc., because this must be your original work without barriers. As editor I will make selections based on my assessment of what will best serve the intended reading population of this book.

From the first moment you begin working on this assignment, please do two things:

a) keep all drafts (even the really bad ones or dead-ends), explorations, and notes, which you will forward to me in an organized way (in other words, date everything you do so I can follow the evolution of your work),

b) keep a thorough journal of your process as it evolves from start to finish. In your journal I want you to discuss the nature of your choices and any problems you're having as openly as possible. This will ask you to be far more analytical about your work than normal. Again, the idea is to exaggerate your usual methods a bit in order to teach and inform the readers.

4) THE INTERVIEW

When I receive the material, I will go through it and make careful notes on what you've sent. Then we'll talk about your work, so I can ask questions which will help amplify particularly interesting aspects of your process. Telephone interviews are possible, but I hope to do this via e-mail so you don't have to cope with being spontaneous, and I won't have to transcribe. This interview will provide additional material for my commentary in your chapter, and allow me to be certain I'm perceiving and reflecting your process, choices, journal comments, etc., as clearly as possible.

The writers were given a deadline, and commenced working on their pieces. Most of the writers finished in one to two months, depending on other obligations (the majority are also teachers, and several had commissions to fulfill). Some of the writers were invited to participate later than others because I wanted to expand the range and scope of the book.

When the material started coming in, I was staggered and thrilled by the wonderful variety of the work. The range I had hoped for was present in more ways than I could have anticipated. What you will see as you read through each chapter are the selections I've made of each writer's most revealing steps toward a final draft, plus their commentaries, and mine, on their work processes.

The original plan was to have work ready during the summer of 1999, and the manuscript finished by early winter, but schedules are difficult to maintain with this many creative people involved, and with my decision to add additional writers. The plays ended up arriving at various points throughout the year, with some final drafts and additional "final-final" drafts submitted in December 1999 and early January 2000. It turned out to be for the best, however, because the longer I lived with the plays, the further I was able to delve into them and try to understand each writer's process.

Each playwright provided me with his or her interpretation of the prompt, and with his or her own perspectives on process. I followed up with all of them via e-mail to ask additional questions and seek clarification. Bit by bit, each playwright's methods and thinking became clear to me, and I made decisions about the shape of each chapter. In time, I made choices about various links between the writers.

As you will note, the writers are organized into groupings. These groupings occurred naturally—they were not preordained by me or the writers. Once all the material was in, I read through every playwright's work numerous times, and talked to the playwrights—and that is when these groupings made themselves clear. The groupings are: "Dreams"—writers who arrive at their plays from highly intuitive approaches, "Journeys"—writers who complete their plays through a roundabout method, and "Cut from Whole Cloth"—writers whose work appears to emerge in a complete form from the very beginning. This is not to say that there isn't overlap in the ways the writers work, or that writer A works exclusively in the methods described in "Dreams." Writers must be chameleon-like in their approach to each new work. The main idea of the groupings is to enhance the comparison/contrast aspect of the book.

Each grouping makes it possible for the reader to look at writers whose working methods are similar, yet unique. This gives the reader a chance to make some very particular comparisons within each grouping, and then wider comparisons among the three groups.

Readers will also draw their own conclusions about methods and choices beyond any links or connections I can draw. My hope is that the book is part of a chain reaction: playwrights reacting to a prompt in turn encourage readers to react creatively to the playwrights, and so on. Individual response and creativity is at the heart of this work. Readers may not like some of the plays or working methods presented—and that's good. What's crucial is coming to terms with why we react as we do: "I like this because—" or "I don't like this because—".

It's the "because" that's the true heart of creative work, as each person develops their own aesthetic and technique. This is the third major element of the book's intention: to provoke discussion, even argument. As the reader tracks the choices of a given writer, and agrees or disagrees with them, she furthers her own sense of values at all levels. The proof of these, of course, is in the next work the playwright undertakes, and whether this heightened awareness of one's own process is helpful or not. I believe it is, of course; others may feel differently.

Finally, in terms of content, the book concludes with brief biographies of the writers, and contact information. It is my great wish that these wonderful, giving writers will be sought out by theatres for commissions, hired to do panels, consultancies, etc. This is also an invitation for readers to try to reach the writers, and me (my e-mail address is included here, as well).

It is my hope that being able to reach any of us will help to continue the dialogue *Playwriting Master Class* initiates about process and choices in the art and craft of the playwright. People have sought me out because of my other books, largely through the Internet, with questions and observations provoked by these works. This has led to friendships and interchanges with individuals around the world. When I found myself in Townsville, Australia, at the World Interplay Festival in July '99, talking craft with writers and teachers from New Zealand, Africa, Italy, Australia, Poland, the Philippines, England, Scotland, Germany, and Hungary, among others, I suddenly felt plugged into the universal pulse that is theatre. The desire to create drama in a live context is alive and thriving around the globe; the need to examine and refine process is part of that energy. Out of understanding and sharing what each of us does, new voices emerge, new forms arrive, and the theatre continues to evolve. Facilitating communication is a major key to this evolution, and "World Theatre" is no longer just a phrase in a festival flyer.

In closing, I want to thank the writers for their work, for the gift of themselves. It is no light matter to be this vulnerable, and each writer deserves our gratitude for their contribution to our craft. They are masters from whom we have so much to learn, and we are their apprentices.

That brings us back to our starting image: picture yourself sitting at the feet of the wheelwright or the shipwright, learning by watching, emulating, questioning, then finding and refining your own methodology. *Playwriting Master Class* is our version of the time machine: a way of joining and deepening the continuum of the playwright's craft throughout history and into the future.

I

PART

Dreams

"Nothing happens unless first a dream."
—Carl Sandburg

"At least once a day, allow yourself the freedom to think and
dream for yourself."
—Albert Einstein

"We have these two ideas: the belief that dreams are part of
waking, and the other, the splendid one, the belief of the
poets: that all of waking is a dream. There is no difference
between the two."
—Jorge Luis Borges

THE TWO PLAYWRIGHTS IN THIS GROUPING ARE ELIZABETH Wong and David Crespy. Each worked on their contribution to this book through dreams and intuitive approaches. They are also linked in several other ways: both drew on a lullaby or children's song for a dramatic element for their play, and both cite Adrienne Kennedy as a major influence. This is a wonderful convergence of serendipitous elements from distinctly disparate playwrights.

As we know, there are constant tracks running in our brains—the subconscious and the unconscious. Day and night, these tracks are actively dramatizing our experiences, turning them into a complex poetry of visual and aural expression. Many writers—August Strindberg, Gertrude Stein, William Faulkner, Virginia Woolf, Richard Foreman, among many others—have tried to capture their stream-of-consciousness or dreamscapes in attempts to externalize this internal world.

I chose to begin with this grouping in order to emphasize the possibilities of a non-naturalistic approach to playwriting. I also wanted to stress that, regardless of form, all plays come from imagining and dreaming. Working through dreams and other non-conscious aspects of our lives has a long history and is a very exciting way of creating theatre, as we will see in the work of Elizabeth Wong and David Crespy.

1

CHAPTER

Elizabeth Wong:
Inside a Red Envelope

WORKING IN PUBLIC AND IN PRIVATE

ELIZABETH WONG IS A PROLIFIC WRITER WITH NUMEROUS television and stage credits. Prior to becoming a playwright, she worked in journalism. This may be a partial explanation for one of her many working methods—the aspect I refer to as "public."

More than any other writer for this book, Elizabeth talked about her project with other people before she worked on it. She refers to it in her journal as "canvassing for an idea," which is a unique method. In an e-mail, Elizabeth also described it this way: "It's like prepping the ground, and laying in seeds, and letting the ones that sprout faster and stronger come up." Elizabeth emphasized to me in further communication that this was only one way of working for her, underscoring the idea that process is particular to the individual and unique to the project.

Most other writers are very hesitant to discuss ongoing work with anyone, fearing an idea might get stolen, or that talking will water down their creative energy—they want to keep the emphasis on the writing process itself. Still, this method clearly worked for Elizabeth on this project, as her work toward creating Inside A Red Envelope will demonstrate, and may suggest similar ways of working for others. Her journal entries help give a sense of how this element of her process works. An observation she made in a letter to me dated April 19, 1999, gives an excellent general perspective:

> Overall, I noticed I tend to go on a 'fact gathering mission.' I talked very casually to lots of friends and acquaintances about the project, and while it never took up more than five minutes of any conversation, I found I needed to jar loose ideas by basically absorbing, and mainly rejecting, WHAT THE PLAY WAS NOT. Talking to people mainly helped me to determine WHAT THE PLAY WAS NOT (emphases Wong).

The private side of Elizabeth's process is also rather unique. As she notes in her journal, Elizabeth has an affinity for plugging into the subconscious through dreams and sleep in order to bring her writing from deep within herself. This aspect of Elizabeth's methodology meshes with what a number of writers have expressed, in various ways, as "letting the play think about me." This may seem facetious, but many writers, myself included, believe that the play has its own life in the same way that sculptors believe the stone already contains the form they plan to carve out. Elizabeth, in fact, refers to the play "writing itself," which is the sense that playwrights have sometimes. This only happens when the writer truly keeps in touch with her instincts and impulses, so that the conscious and subconscious become joined in a way that is like a wakeful trance. People experience this state all the time, without understanding it. Think of the times when you've arrived at a destination with no memory of how you got there. You clearly drove from home to the office because you're in your car, but your mind has gone so deep into its own concerns that it paid no attention to the mundane activities of driving. The ability to harness this kind of bi-level mental state is something that artists at all levels strive to accomplish.

Most writers carry around a mental assortment of ideas they're interested in, and usually one story pushes its way to the forefront. Once this main story/play has announced itself, the writer often enters into a kind of unconscious mindstream about her work. Daily life and dream life are collected by the stream, as with a flood, picking up stray elements as it courses through the landscape, and incorporating them. This stream can also be a conscious element—if the writer is willing to be aware of intentionally and actively connecting with the subconscious—and is therefore a vital tool. Here is what Elizabeth described to me in her letter of April 19:

> The other salient (and most important) characteristic of my process is I don't begin writing until I find myself waking up thinking about the play. Until I begin my day with only thoughts of the project and all the problems it raises, and the elements I'm juggling in it, I cannot seem to begin to write at all. Sometimes, I'd go to bed early, only to wake up and get myself to a pad/pencil or to the computer itself. Somehow, as I'm drifting off to sleep or waking from sleep, I seem to be "working" and solving my writerly problems. Unequivocally, this is an important part of my process no matter what the size or scope of the project. I have to tap into my subconscious in order to open the creative door. In my case, I really do have to 'sleep on it.' I think this dream state I try to achieve is part of this acknowledgement that my best creative impulses are the ones which arrive by instinct, and when I try to "think" too much, I merely clutter and botch the job.

Elizabeth's clear awareness of her process is an outstanding guideline for other writers. Even if a writer's way of working is radically different from what Elizabeth describes, the key is knowing what works best for oneself, and remaining faithful to one's natural impulses.

This is an excellent argument for keeping a journal. A journal, as this book helps to demonstrate, is a powerful way to connect with one's intuitive, instinctive side. The most effective journals combine discussions of one's work, snippets of dialogue, observations, annotations of interesting images (even those that may have nothing to do with the project at hand in an obvious way; anything that captures one's fancy should be recorded), clippings from newspapers or magazines, postcards, photographs, doodles, drawings, descriptions of dreams and/or fantasies, etc. I know writers who keep very meticulous dream/fantasy journals, in order to stay plugged into the non-rational track that occupies their minds for a large part of the day. The idea is to discover one's own levels of thought and ambition. What's crucial is being truthful to oneself.

To return to *Inside a Red Envelope*, Elizabeth's play combines elements of dreams and memories, and is clearly a very personal work that extends itself metaphorically into a piece that most audiences would find captivating and challenging. Her process, which begins outside herself, then spirals inward, has resulted in a play that captures her identity as a Chinese-American female, yet appeals to us because it touches on such universal themes as recurring dreams, fear of the unknown, and the ache of unresolved memories.

The drafts presented here represent a series of false starts that lead to the final draft. Elizabeth makes this observation about *Inside a Red Envelope*:

> I had trouble writing this play for you. Mainly I think it's because I wanted to force the play in one direction, but it stubbornly wanted to go elsewhere. When I found I was 'stuck,' it meant basically that the play and I were at loggerheads. I couldn't proceed. But when I finally abdicated to the 'desires' of the play, it wrote itself completely in about four hours on April 18. What surprises me is how personal this play is for me, a real surprise since I was trying mightily to make some structural ideas work using an 'impersonal' storyline. But by surrendering to a 'personal' take on the structure, the play moved into a more delightful direction. I find it ironic that by making it more personal, I was able to incorporate more readily most of my original thematic and structural ideas.

I have reproduced the majority of Elizabeth's journal because it provides such intriguing insights into her process. Following the journal, there are selections from initial drafts of the play, and the final draft as well.

JOURNAL & NOTES FOR KEY PLAY

(Note: some names are omitted for privacy purposes at Elizabeth's request)

March 13

Told A (producer/writer) over dinner at Mexi-catessen about the "key" project. He said he found a mysterious key recently in a drawer. He said he discovered that the key was to his own house, but from the previous tenant . . . he simply went about trying the key in different doors until he discovered it opened his back door. He ventured that "perhaps, the key wasn't as important, as the envelope . . . maybe something written on the envelope that makes all the difference." When I asked facetiously if I could steal his idea, he seemed very satisfied and said, "By all means, it's yours."

March 20

Told Alex about the project. He's nine years old. Mom was singing to Baby Steven, an old Chinese nursery rhyme, something I don't remember from my own childhood, but an effective song that delighted baby Steven. I'm canvassing for an idea, so I thought it might be nice to preserve the song, write it down . . . Alex started singing the song slowly, and helping me with the phonetic spelling, and in between singing and spelling, he suggested the following title: *Quiet Down Steven.*

Chinese Nursery Rhyme

Chinese (Phonetics)	English Translation
Aah jen doy.	Clap your hands
Wok duy doy.	Buy a banana
Duy doy hymn.	Bananas are very sweet
Wok woy lim.	Then buy a woy lim (field knife).
Woy lim lay,	The woy lim (knife) is sharp.
Qwat quoy bay.	And it cuts off your nose.
Woy lim saap,	The teeth of the knife are jagged,
Gwat qua naap	And it cuts your underarm.
Gwat ka sock.	And cuts your other underarm.
Woy lim hune	The knife is dull
Quat see hune.	It cuts your stinky butt.
Aah geck doy.	Clap your feet
Mun geck jang	Ask the heels of your feet.
Mun a Steven gay-see hong?	Ask Steven when he'll walk?
Hong houy nigh?	Where are you walking to?
Hong houy guy!	I'm going out to the street!
Hong houy guy, do mwat?	Going out to the street to do what?

Hong houy guy, my	
doong sigh!	Going out to the street to market!

March 30

Coffee with B (screenwriter). Told him about "key" . . . he recommended a book of plays to read by a Chinese playwright KUO PAO KUN. He also riffed on the idea, stuff about the key "talking" to the character. The key as a character for the piece. He thought it was a very "Asian" concept. He let me borrow the book of plays, *The Coffin Is Too Big for the Hole*. I read it, didn't really spark to writing, BUT this is a translation. There was a play in which the major character was a TREE, which interested me.

April 2

Boxing and hiphop dance class with Cousin Warren. He suggested that the key was a way to unlock dreams. He told me about his recurring dream of being in school and not being ready for the exam . . . an anxiety dream, he said, "I've been out of school for 20 years and I still have those dreams." I told him about my recurring dream, about being in mansions that are decorated with rich tapestries and long white staircases, I'm always descending down the stairs, chandeliers above, and below a banquet table festooned with ice sculptures and lots of delicious beautifully presented foods. A very restful, beautiful dream. ******THE KEY IS THE DREAM!!!!!!!!!!!!******

April 4

Lunch with C. Told her about the project. She suggested that the key was "the key to someone's heart." I told her I was thinking about my grandmother who lived on Meiling Way in Chinatown, and how she used to put a key into a Crown Royal bag and toss it down to us, as we shouted up at her from the street. There was no way to get into her apartment unless she tossed down the key from her third-story window. It occurs to me that two people thought the key was metaphorical, to unlock a dream or to unlock love. And two others thought it was a plot point, treated it like it was genre, a mystery but only a small element in a bigger mystery.

April 5

Talked with my brother Will. He liked the idea of the play being a dream. And he suggested that the dreamer misses their grandmother, so they dream about finding a key inside a red envelope left to her by her mother, and she uses the key to open a chest containing a picture of her grandmother . . . or maybe open the chest to find a piece of jewelry. His idea reminded me of Popo's (my grandmother) only material gift to me, a gold bracelet. I'm afraid to wear it because I may lose it and then by extension I would lose my grandmother . . . but when I put it on, I think of her, and it comforts me. Thank you, Will!!!!! The idea of a dream play made me think of Adrienne Kennedy's A Movie Star Has to Star in Black and White. I reread it. This play intrigues and baffles me, and wraps itself around me. I thought about an old play of mine, now stuck in ye old metaphorical drawer, The Warrior God in His Civil Aspect.

This title was used for Elizabeth's play before she decided on her final title. It was The Warrior God in His Civil Aspect, then The Warrior Goddess in Her Civil Aspect when the main character shifted gender, Dreams of Quan Yin, Dreams of the Goddess, and finally Inside A Red Envelope.

When I read the journal enough to be familiar with the flow of developing ideas, I found the next entry to be a huge leap. Quan Yin, or Kuan Yin, had not appeared in any way as a character or element of the play up to this point, then suddenly and powerfully emerged. I asked Elizabeth about this leap, and she replied in an e-mail:

> The conversation with my brother, thoughts of my grandmother's death, the pain of her passing . . . the idea of dreams, finding a cool title . . . moving jade Kuan Yin to a safer place out of baby nephew's reach . . . that day . . . all those preliminary conversations worked in concert to get me writing. But I never was interested in the details of Kuan Yin before. When my nephew Steven got to her, and I had to move the statue, I had my hands on her. I dusted her off, and I felt an impulse to investigate her. It was something really mundane, like saving her jade butt from an inquisitive baby. So that's the evening of April 5.
>
> So after I hopped on the net, and once I got more information on her, her "details" set in motion the actual writing. I saw the image of her standing atop a staircase. I liked this image. It reminded me of my own recurrent dream, where I'm descending a staircase into a fabulously-appointed room. So I think of her as the prime mover, the concrete thing, or physical key for me, that unlocked the floodgate of ideas about dreams, death, loss and pain, subconscious ideas that are always rolling around in my head. But Kuan Yin was the spark that propelled the writing and enabled me to access those ideas.

April 6

Went online, looked up information on the Chinese goddess Kuan Yin. Found a few references online. Kuan Yin is the Chinese Goddess of Compassion. Her name means "she who hears the sounds of the world." It is thought that she was about to enter heaven, but at the threshold, she stopped and turned back to heed the cries of the world. Her sacred number is 33. There was a princess who lived in 700 b.c., 12th Century, who lived on a sacred island, and she lived there for nine years healing and saving the shipwrecked sailors. It is also believed she can transform shape, into objects or animals, depending on who she is saving. I have always instinctively been drawn to Kuan Yin, even though I know only that she is the Goddess of Mercy. I have a jade Kuan Yin about four inches tall, and I have a Kuan Yin standing about 16 inch porcelain statuette of her. She reminds me of my favorite Shakespeare speech, "The quality of mercy is not strained . . ." Portia's speech was the first Shakespeare I ever memorized in high school.

April 7

Cannot seem to move forward on the play. Problem in figuring out the issue of the key . . . also to play around with the idea of Who is the dreamer? Whose dream is it? Which reality is it? Maybe reread Strindberg . . . *Ghost Sonata* or *A Dream Play*. Can't seem to write today . . . things seem overly complicated and dense. . . . Possible titles: *Cipher*, *Dreams Bisected by A Key*.

April 12

Can't sleep. Up late. It's about 3 A.M. Writing notes in a lined notebook, getting up from bed, writing, then going back to bed. The notes are the following: Might be better to have three characters, one of whom is a man. Like the way a dream reoccurs, have the dialogue repeat similarly. Maybe adjust the setting to include the staircase and three doorways with doors closed.

Possible dialogue:
"It's always the same. Like a door that opens, closes quickly."
"I find a red envelope in a drawer. I open it. There's a key inside, with a string looped in its eye. I get up and try to unlock all the doors of the house."

"I've never seen this key before, I don't know what it unlocks . . . "
*******REPEAT THIS PHRASE OVER AND OVER, "I found a key inside a red envelope," then add new information each time . . . or find phrases that can repeat and also shift TIME forward or backward!!!!!!!!!*********

GRANDMOTHER'S DEATH . . . need healing from . . .

Maybe Kuan Yin takes the key and gives it to the man, or the little girl . . . the Dream is the Key to the problem of the play and the key to the problem that the man and child need to solve. Also, could it be that they attempt to solve the problem (maybe the child weeps), first with sweets, then with the nursery rhyme, then with the key itself.

The key opens a chest containing the picture of her grandmother or mother . . .

April 13

Lay in bed, 8 a.m., thought of a possible title *Inside a Red Envelope*. It implies the key. Red envelopes are very Chinese and used for special occasions, birthdays, funerals, weddings, everything special is marked by a red envelope. Implies mystery.

Asked Will for details about the architectural project he is working on, also asked him what he hates about working with individual clients . . . looking to find "language" for the MAN, who is a busy overextended architect, who has no time for his own personal development, no time to examine his emotions . . . he pushes his pain down . . .

Possible Names for "Man": JAMES, KINGMAN, KING—all variations of my father's name. I like using family names in my plays, but this is the first time I've used my dad's.

April 14

Woke up with following ideas:

• Play is about an architect who had a recurring dream. Play is about three people who have the same recurring dream.********

• In order for the child to "open up" Kuan Yin has to say how they wish they could cry because they have learned as an adult to push down their feelings, to bury them deep, and now cannot tell what their feelings/desire are anymore . . . in fact they go through life as if they were in a dream, disconnected from any feeling of aliveness . . .

• Take out grandma references, let this come out at end when the child tells why he/she is crying. Monologue about dreaming about being buried alive. Explore ideas about recurring dreams.

April 15

Woke up with following ideas: ****Kingman is successful in the world, but he is split off from his emotions; culture values people who are rational, restrained, and self contained. He has buried his feelings and needs, therefore he looks good and is acceptable, but inside he's lost and hasn't dealt with grief.

April 18

Woke up with ideas about the play as a way of healing from a childhood dream. That the only way to heal as an adult was to accept and acknowledge pain from one's childhood. As a child, I could never grasp the death of my father. And maybe this is why it's been hard to trust people, they are always "abandoning" and cannot be relied upon to be there. Yikes, classic abandonment issues. All three feel buried alive. James who is the child Sparky who is also Kuan Yin. Dream: father buried alive. Feeling guilty that child didn't go get ice cream with father, prefers to build a fort out of pillows . . . me and Will and Dad. Our story and my nightmare. Change focus from grandma to dad. Completed first draft at 5:30 p.m.

The final two entries are of particular interest since they address the entirely different aspect of process/product: casting. It's a good reminder that playwrights don't think or exist in a vacuum. The point of writing is to see the work in production.

INSIDE A RED ENVELOPE DIARY—FINAL ENTRY

April 30

Woke up, thought of five new changes. Input them into computer, thought about how to send to Michael, and then decided to make no more changes after today since the deadline is May 1. Major consideration about casting . . . it's a dreamscape, so why not let the play be cast non Asian, see what happens. Also, take out some lines that would offend my brother re: architecture "fast food joints and template work" Change that!!! Also remembered a better image to help with the nursery rhyme, because it needs to be physical and to be childlike, the game of pattycake is exactly what it's like, thought of that out of the blue, really needs to be in the play to help clarify. This is my last entry.

INSIDE A RED ENVELOPE DIARY—FINAL FINAL
ENTRY—MAY 1999

May 3

Woke up, realized the casting requirements needed to be changed *again*. I thought it would enhance the play, to be cast with non Asians . . . the notion being that you take on any persona in a dream, and if I believe that line "you are me, and we are one," that would make everyone Asian American with an Asian American experience. But I think the play would not be served well with non-Asian actors . . . My brother Will read the play and he was pretty incensed, in fact angry and disappointed by the fact that I changed the casting requirements, citing that I was not being true to the play and that it would not achieve the ideas, but be so distracting from the central notion of the play, which is about healing, that the healing power would be overwhelmed by a mechanical device which doesn't advance the notion of healing. What is universal about the play is not that "we are one," but that whatever hurts us in our childhood might be healed. Will's argument convinced me, so I reinstituted the original casting directive.

Elizabeth Wong provided me with all her drafts, including early pages that simply had the "Warrior God" title, a brief stage direction, and nothing else. The most intriguing early drafts incorporate the memories of her grandmother, and feature a female primary character named Mimi. Each draft exploration that follows contains one or more key movements forward toward the final shape of the play. Note that Elizabeth wrote draft explorations on the same day in several instances and dated them, for instance, April 6, 6A, 6B, and so on.

The first draft exploration is the third attempt on April 6, labeled April 6B. It is the first to contain dialogue. It is a radical shift in title from the "Warrior God/Goddess" starting efforts, and the first time in which the Quan Yin (eventually Kuan Yin) character appears.

SELECTED DRAFTS OF THE PLAY

Draft Exploration dated April 6B, titled Dreams of Quan Yin

An elegant mansion. QUAN YIN, a beautiful Asian woman, dressed in Chinese robes with flowing sleeves, at the top of a magnificent red staircase.

QUAN YIN: At the threshold of heaven, at last! The flame of heaven is lavender. The clouds are the sweet faces of my mother and father, ancestors of their mother and father. World without end. I would step off this precipice, one golden foot in front of the other, to walk on air. But these voices rise up from the world. Anguished voices coming from a deep ocean of pain and suffering.

The following draft exploration moves into the personal realm, digging deeply into the playwright's memories of her grandmother. Much later, Elizabeth shifted the lost relationship from grandmother to father, but I find this a very powerful piece of writing. It also incorporates the character of Mimi, who changed several times before being bifurcated into the characters of James and Sparky.

Draft Exploration dated April 6D, titled Dreams of the Goddess

An elegant mansion. QUAN YIN, *a beautiful Asian woman with long flowing hair, dressed in white Chinese robes with floor-length sleeves, at the top of a sweeping and magnificent red staircase.*

QUAN YIN: My grandmother. Grandmother holds my hand tightly. She pushes back the creaky screen door. We enter a dark damp room. The butcher shop, a place of mystery. I am eight years old. I smell the feathers. I catch small snowflakes of them as they float from the wire cages onto my outstretched hand. I hear the squawking and clucking, the desperate flutter of frightened wings beating against the bodies of other birds, against the rusty wires of the rattling cages. I didn't know Death lived here, I didn't understand the eternal sleep of chickens. I loved going to the butcher shop, a live farm animal. I had dreams of horses, and red barns, and hay rides, and open pastures. I begged mother, buy me a horse, we could keep in it in the vacant lot across or in the alley behind my bedroom window. City girls don't keep horses. Grandmother points to a cage, she holds up five fingers. Senor Hernandez, says, "Si si."

Lights slowly reveal MIMI, *downstage, a pretty Asian woman dressed in flannel pajamas.*

MIMI: It always begins here. At the pause of a great white marbled staircase. I am in a mansion, a grand house of refinement and stillness. Threshold of heaven. Rich seductive tapestries hang on the walls to slow my upwards progress. My favorite is here—one hundred laughing babies, heads shaved, little dots of hair on the top, one hundred children with paper kites, bouncing balls, wooden tops spinning, little naked baby bottoms, peek-a-boo, through cleverly-slotted pantaloons. But this time, it no longer holds my interest. This is the threshold of Heaven. I am poised on the landing between this place and the next, ready for harmony, for peace, for serenity. All I have to do—is walk on air.

The next draft exploration changes the character of Mimi to a teenage girl who becomes the prototype for the eventual non-gender-specific character of Sparky. This draft also introduces some dialogue experiments, incorporating idiomatic language into the previously more formal speech of the characters.

Draft Exploration dated April 7, titled Dreams of the Goddess

An elegant mansion. QUAN YIN, a beautiful Asian woman with long flowing hair, dressed in white Chinese robes with floor-length sleeves, at the top of a sweeping and magnificent red staircase.

QUAN YIN: At the threshold of heaven, here I stand on the flat prayer stones which bear my name. These carved runes build the walls of the monastery, they line the roads of the villages of my sacred island mountain. I am ready.

Lights slowly reveal MIMI, downstage, an Asian-American teenaged girl in big clothes, with a baseball mitt, and tossing a baseball.

MIMI: It always begins, with me, like, on the landing of a really awesome staircase, all red carpet, fit for a princess. Now, if you look behind, the stairs just, you know . . . go up. It's like endless, which is cool, threshold of heaven, but you know, I'm not really ready to go in that *up* direction just yet. No way, the down staircase is bitchin'. I want to go down!

QUAN YIN: Cast no more lotus blossoms. Draw no more tiny circles on paper pagodas. Make no more endlessly fervent and noisy supplications. I'm sick of hearing the drone of suffering voices, Om Mani Padme Hum, Om Mani Padme Hum, Om Mani Padme Hum, Om Mani Padme Hum, oy vey, enough all ready! Forget about it! I quit!

MIMI: Going *down* the staircase, I guess it symbolizes like I'm going to H. E. double hockey sticks. Bad people go to hell, and I am a bad person. Everyone says, "Mimi, you have a crappy attitude." I say, "Hey, I'm in the middle of puberty!" (*Tosses and catches the ball for a while, then:*) My grandmother died three years ago today.

QUAN YIN: I do not want to hear the clamoring voices of endless human suffering. I do not want to be Bodhisattva. I do not want to be Quan Yin, goddess of mercy, she who hears the voices of the world rising up in pain. For centuries, I have quieted your swords and muffled your guns and smothered your atomic bombs. No more.

MIMI: Since my attitude is so crappy, when the family gets into the Honda to visit grandma at the cemetery on the anniversary of her death, I jack up everything, turn over the kitchen garbage cans, throw my little brother's basketball into the toilet. Stupid dumbass stuff. I grab my baseball bat, and I split.

QUAN YIN: I have left behind the scrolls of the sutra, the dharma of the great teacher. The great Buddha takes them from me. I have left behind the weeping willow branch, no longer will I sprinkle the divine nectar of Life into the moaning parched throats of wounded Humanity. The afflictions of humanity cannot be healed. (*Sighs*) Let me be a girl once again. (*Quan Yin begins to slowly descend the stairs*)　My favorite is here—one hundred laughing babies, heads shaved, little dots of hair on the top, one hundred children with paper kites, bouncing balls, wooden tops spinning, little naked baby bottoms, peek-a-boo, through cleverly-slotted pantaloons. A long time ago, I flew kites while standing on the head of a dragon, made little paper boats to sail and sink in my warm bath. I long for the innocence of my childhood, when I was sad, my mother would rock me and sing me a song.

MIMI: My grandmother taught me how to throw a baseball. She'd stand over there, and I'd stand here by this tree, and we'd toss the ball between us for hours. My nen nen, she loved baseball. She knew only, like, five words of English—she could say, "hello," "good," "bye bye," and "Home Run."

The next large step forward is in the April 11 draft, which is the first to incorporate the nursery rhyme recorded in Elizabeth's journal. The biggest leap is in the draft of April 12, in which the character of James appears for the first time, and where Elizabeth has settled on the title of *Inside a Red Envelope*. She has also selected the "Kuan" spelling for the goddess, explaining: "I got on the Internet and looked up Kuan Yin and noticed there were a number of spellings. I chose the most used one. Also, my mother's family name is Kwan, so that similarity probably had a subconscious effect."

The shift from the female character of Mimi to the male character of James is very interesting. Elizabeth comments on it in an e-mail:

You ask about my decision to change a female character Mimi to a male character James. I can tell you precisely why. I chose the name Mimi because it resonated, illustrated and underscored some ideas in my mind about dreams, about ego, id, anima, and animus. Mimi equals ego, a Copernican view, self-focus. Mimi also is a repetition, a deja vu, a name revisited. The play would have a repetitious structure, so I thought Mimi would be a good name to use in the play.

However, as I began to write, all my best laid rationale for having Mimi in the play went by the wayside. It was waylaid, and I cannot give you a decent reason, except James fit and Mimi didn't. James made sense, and the writing flowed. When it was Mimi, there was an 'inner' and inexplicable resistance. But when I abdicated and let James speak, then the play jelled for me, and just as inexplicably made sense.

I also believe James is less obvious, more subtle than Mimi. I remember thinking I liked Mimi and might go back to her as a character in some other play. Also, gender seemed to be important to the play, especially since the use of a non-gender- specific child was appealing to me. I wanted gender to meld, to suggest the anima and animus, explore some of Carl Jung's ideas in the play. If I wanted to use Kuan Yin, then for these gender questions to make sense to me, I needed Mimi to be a man. Again, notions of anima and animus, light and dark, yin and yang.

Draft Exploration dated April 12, titled Inside a Red Envelope

An elegant mansion. KUAN YIN, a beautiful Asian woman with long flowing hair, dressed in white Chinese robes with floor-length sleeves, at the top of a sweeping magnificent staircase.

KUAN YIN: I found a key inside a red envelope. It always starts that way. I find a key inside a red envelope in the drawer of a desk. I feel a wave of joy, of overwhelming sympathy. I tear the envelope across the top, and let tumble out onto the palm of my trembling hand, a key. Suddenly, I find myself inside a mansion lined with rich tapestries, wall to ceiling, a mansion bathed in an opaque, serene nourishing light like maternal milk. At the top of this sweeping, grand staircase, I drink the light.

JAMES, *a handsome Asian man in a business suit, appears at the top of the staircase. He doesn't acknowledge Kuan Yin.*

JAMES: I find this key inside a red envelope. It always starts that way. I find this envelope, the kind you get at New Years, and other "oh-casions." And this feeling hits me. (*He walks down the stairs, stops when he gets halfway*) Bam, a wave of . . . I don't know exactly what. I don't have time for emotions these days. I've got this pain-in-the-neck *client* making dumbass changes on site, *without* proper permits. The cheap bastard. Naturally, *the client* wants to cut corners.

    I say, if you want the best, you have got to use the best, use marble, invariably *the client* wants mud. That mentality ticks me off, but all right, fine, live in dreamland, okay, whatever *the client* wants.

KUAN YIN: I was standing at the threshold of Heaven, when I heard the Voices down below. In this hand, usually, I hold a sacred willow branch in my hand to sprinkle the nectar of renewed Life upon the heads of the wounded and heartsick.

JAMES: I tear the envelope across the top, there's this little key. Looks like the key to a door. Why do people like to keep old keys anyway, useless sentimentality. Throw those keys away. Throw out all the old keys, live in the present! Forget the past. Keep all those old doors closed.

KUAN YIN: In my other hand, usually, I hold the Sutra, the Dharma, words of the great teacher Buddha, words to heal light the way for the lost and to speak gentle words to the lonely. But I have no book. The branch, I cannot find. There is only this key.

JAMES: I'd throw it away, if it weren't for the fact, well, it was in a red envelope. A red envelope means something. There's uncommon significance here. Lost on me, but there it is. A minor mystery.

KUAN YIN: Yes, a mystery.

JAMES: I'm telling my dumbass client the steel beams won't support a dance floor, we'll have to retrofit a whole new structural system. I'm fiddling with the key, and suddenly I find myself inside a mansion of golden light. Standing in the middle of this classic antebellum staircase.

Lights slowly reveal MIMI, a young Asian girl, wearing a baseball cap.

KUAN YIN: And I see a child.

JAMES: And I see this young girl.

KUAN YIN: She's weeping.

JAMES: The poor thing is crying her eyes out.

The next set of drafts introduce the repetitions of key phrases and scenes. Elizabeth also introduces the sudden blackouts which bracket the repetitions. These drafts continue the incorporation of memories of the grandmother, which, as Elizabeth notes in her April 18th journal entry, abruptly change to memories of a father. The changes from draft to draft are very minor up to this point, with the shift to the memory of a father being the largest leap forward.

What follows here is the final draft of the play, which gathers in most of the elements of the preceding draft explorations. The "Playwright's Note" before the text of the play begins emphasizes Elizabeth Wong's casting preference.

Inside a Red Envelope

CAST LIST:
(1f, 1m, 1 child)
KUAN YIN, 20s, Goddess of Mercy
JAMES, 50s, architect
SPARKY, child about 10 years old

TIME:
The Present and The Past. Time has stopped.

PLACE:
An elegant mansion in a dreamscape.

PLAYWRIGHT'S NOTE:
Asian-American actors preferred. The gender of the child should be ambiguous.

An elegant mansion. KUAN YIN, a beautiful woman with long flowing hair, dressed in white Chinese robes with floor-length sleeves, at the top of a sweeping magnificent red staircase.

KUAN YIN: I was standing on the head of a dragon, riding the waves toward my destination, the threshold of Heaven. In my right hand, I held a sacred willow branch, I used it to sprinkle nectar upon the heads of the wounded and heartsick. But now I cannot find it, my hand—empty. In my left hand, I held the Sutra, the dharma spoken by the lips of the great teacher. But the book is lost; I cannot find it. There is only this—an old tarnished key.

JAMES, 50s, a handsome man in a business suit, center stage, reads several oversized blueprints spread on the floor.

JAMES: It always starts that way. I'm working late, big design review, big screw-up on the blueprints. No time for sleep, no time even to wipe my ass. The drawer of my desk pops open, out flies this envelope like it has little unseen wings. I'm watching it flutter to the floor, and here it is on top of all my blueprints, a red envelope, *laysee*. (*Picks up, examines a red envelope*) When I was a kid, I thought I could get rich off laysee. Happy Birthday, here's a red envelope, don't spend it all in one place. Nudge nudge, wink wink. Happy New Year, have some laysee. Happy Moon Cake Day, red envelope. Uncle Henry died, red envelope. "Hey hey, lucky money! Wink wink nudge nudge." Look inside. Suddenly, I'm inside a mansion of classic, unbelievable beauty. Textbook antebellum staircase, Ionic and Corinthian columns, gilt in gold. And the light . . . (*Sighs*) opaque, gentle, diaphanous, nourishing like maternal milk. I drank the light.

KUAN YIN: (*She walks down the stairs, approaches him*) Suddenly, I'm no longer riding the waves on the head of a dragon, I am inside a red envelope, tumbling out onto the palm of a hand belonging to a man, who is up to his . . .

JAMES: . . . ass.

KUAN YIN: . . . his ass in paperwork at the foot of a magnificent sweeping . . .

JAMES: . . . staircase. You, you, you spoke! I *must* be dreaming. You never speak. Usually, you just look at me. Usually, you stand at the top of that staircase, with quiet non judgmental regard. God, you're beautiful. Wink wink, nudge nudge. In a way, if you spoke, my vision of you would be ruined. Women drag a man into reality when they speak. Talking about unwashed dishes, unpaid bills, chores undone. But when they are silent, a man can dream. (*She turns away*) No, don't go. Beautiful women make me nervous. Please. No pressure. I come here hoping you'll speak to me. I feel like a teenager, like it's 50 years ago, still in high school, I'm a complete doofus. Goofball. A weenie, geek. Hi, I'm James, it's okay if you just want to stand there. Stay. Please.

KUAN YIN: I like this place, James. I feel safe here.

JAMES: Thank you for speaking to me. I'm honored. I'd like to impress you, tell you I designed and built it, but I just do hot-dog stands and two-car garages. So, can't take credit.

KUAN YIN: Yes you can. We built this place. Together, all three of us. All three of us built this fortress. James, do you know me?

JAMES: You are Kuan Yin. My grandmother told me about you, even had this small plastic figurine, she used to . . .

KUAN YIN: Plastic! Surely, you mean fine Burmese jade.

JAMES: Pardon me, a jade figurine of fine Burmese jade, fixed onto the dashboard of my old man's old station wagon. But you had a thousand arms and legs.

KUAN YIN: (*Laughing*) Oh yes, like a spider. All those arms and legs, looking in all directions simultaneously, sensing the afflictions of Humanity, offering expressions of Divine Mercy. That has been my job since I was 10 years old. I'd like to retire, but there's no end.

JAMES: When I was in the war, I thought I saw you in the sky. You put your robes around the bombs, you held out your hands and stayed the bullets. I didn't want to die then, I don't want to die now. I have clients, I have a wife, kids. I'm not ready.

KUAN YIN: You will be, someday. It will be as if you awoke from a catnap. You will yawn, stretch, remembering your true self. Waken to your true reality, and marvel you ever clung so tenaciously to this earthly Life, a silly funny recurring dream. Have you ever wondered why some dreams come to you again and again? They are urgent messages from your true self, beacons of remembrance, gentle elbows to nudge nudge wink wink you from your amnesia. James, I was on my way to heaven. I lost my book and my willow, instead I have this . . . I've been carrying it a long time, perhaps 40 years. But now it is Time to ask, "Will you take this from me?" (*Holds out an outstretched palm, on it rests—the key*)

JAMES: A key.

KUAN YIN: Yes, a key.

JAMES: I don't want it. Don't need it.

KUAN YIN: It belongs to you.

JAMES: No, no it doesn't. Useless sentimentality. Throw it away.

KUAN YIN: James.

JAMES: I don't want to remember. I don't want anything to do with true reality. I don't want this key, or any key. I don't want beacons of light, or answers to any questions. I'm not asking any questions. I don't want to wake up. It's taken me 50 years, but I've perfected the Art of Feeling Nothing. Not for my work, not for my wife, not even for my kids. Keep that thing away from me. Women! Always dragging men some place they don't want to be, suck us in with your silky voice, your long shiny hair, then BAM! Well not me. Stay away from me. Stay the hell away, do you hear? NO! Screw you! Go fuck yourself!

BLACKOUT! *Lights up. Kuan Yin at the top of the stairs.*

KUAN YIN: I was standing on the head of a dragon, riding the waves toward my destination, the threshold of Heaven. In my right hand, I held a sacred willow branch. In my left hand, I held the Sutra, the dharma spoken by the lips of the great teacher. But the book is lost; the branch, I cannot find it. There is only this—an old tarnished key.

James, center stage, reads several oversized blueprints spread on the floor.

JAMES: It always starts that way. I'm working late, big design review, big screw-up on the blueprints. See right here, the steel beams won't support a second-story dance floor, we'll have to retrofit a whole new structural system. Shit, no time for sleep, no time even to wipe my ass.

KUAN YIN: James.

JAMES: Actually, this is not my dream. This is your dream.

KUAN YIN: Does it matter?

JAMES: You are dreaming about a middle-aged man in a nice Versace suit, a conservative man, a man in a tie, a man who wears and minds his Rolex watch, a man who plays golf, badly. A man who happily builds you a mansion in the sky, who will take off your pure white robes, and kiss your soft smooth neck, and make a baby with you.

KUAN YIN: James.

Kuan Yin holds out her hand, palm up. SPARKY, a child, perhaps a boy, sits crumpled in a heap, in a special light. The child wears a little league uniform, baseball cap. The child's gender isn't clear, but the kid weeps, hugs his/her knees.

JAMES: No. That's not fair. I'm not ready. I'm NOT ready!

KUAN YIN: Tell the child then.

JAMES: I will. Hey, hey there, little buddy. Don't cry. Want some gum? (*No response*) Baseball huh? I used to play when I was your age, ten years old. No? Suit yourself, Sparky. Listen, listen . . . nothing personal, but this is a dream, that pretty lady there, she's a character in the dream, and so are you, I guess I am too. We're all dreaming the same dream. I'm going to wake up now, get back to work. Big design review in the morning. Stop crying, 'kay? Nudge nudge wink wink. Let's all wake up on the count of three, okay Sparky? Count to three. Come on, count with me. One.

ALL: One.

JAMES: Two.

ALL: Two.

JAMES: Three.

ALL: Three.

> BLACKOUT! *Lights up again. James stands at the top of the staircase. Kuan Yin, center stage, with the child huddled in a special light, half in shadow. Sparky sits in her lap; she takes Sparky's hands in hers for a game similar to "patty cake," sings in Chinese, a nursery rhyme:*

KUAN YIN:

(In Chinese)	(English translation)
Aah jen doy.	(Clap your hands)
Wok duy doy.	(Buy a banana)
Duy doy hymn.	(Bananas are very sweet)
Wok woy lim.	(Then buy a woy lim (field knife)).
Woy lim lay,	(The woy lim (knife) is sharp.)
Qwat quoy bay.	(And it cuts off your nose.)

JAMES: I know that rhyme. My mother sang it to me when I got frightened. At the end of the song, she'd tweak my nose and tug on my ear. (*Demonstrates*) A small gesture of comfort, but it worked. I wasn't afraid anymore. When I was a child, I had this recurring dream. I dreamt my father was alive, he was buried alive, and we had to go to the cemetery, get shovels and save him, dig him up, open the coffin, hurry hurry hurry before it's too late. Daddy is buried alive. He's buried alive. He's still alive.

KUAN YIN: It always starts this way. I find a key inside a red envelope.

THE CHILD: (*Overlapping*) I find a key inside a red envelope inside a drawer of my desk. I was riding on the head of a dragon. I hate vanilla ice cream.

JAMES: (*Overlapping*) And suddenly, I'm inside a beautiful mansion, filled with light.

KUAN YIN: (*Overlapping*) Suddenly, I'm inside a beautiful mansion, filled with gentle light.

JAMES: (*Overlapping*) Filled with soothing white light like mother's milk.

KUAN YIN: (*Overlapping*) I drink the light.

THE CHILD: (*Overlapping*) I drink the light.

JAMES: (*Overlapping*) I drink the light. (*James walks down the stairs*) I dreamt my Daddy asked me to go to the store with him, to buy some ice cream, but I was so busy playing with my friends. We were building a fort with pillows and blankets, my friends were sleeping over, it was fun making tunnels and secret hiding places with pillows and blankets, old cardboard boxes. He asked me what kind of ice cream?

THE CHILD: Get vanilla, Daddy. We want vanilla!

JAMES: But that night, Daddy fell off the bed, I heard the *thud* like it was thunder. Next thing I know, I see Daddy in a box and Mommy is crying. Vanilla ice cream makes me vomit.

KUAN YIN: When I was a child, I wanted to play and to laugh and run past the stones that lined the village, stones marked with my name. Speaking a prayer, *Om Mani Padme Um*, a prayer my ears did not want to hear. *Om Mani Padme Um*, a prayer so loud, so deafening, I wanted to scream. So much sorrow and sickness, so much grief and sadness. I stifled my childish desires. I had no right to be carefree.

JAMES: I stifled my childish desires, I did not deserve to be carefree.

KUAN YIN: No matter how much I missed my childhood, I buried these feelings deep.

JAMES: My father wanted me to go to the store with him.

THE CHILD: No, no thanks Pop, I want to build a fort with my friends.

JAMES: I ate his ice cream while he was dying. I built a fortress that night.

KUAN YIN: I gathered the shipwrecked to my sacred island, tended to their wounds. But in my dreams, I could see the future and the past all at once. This one last task. This one last burden. Then I can go home, then I can finally breathe. (*She holds out an outstretched palm*) James. (*Sparky gets up, approaches Kuan Yin, his/her hand outstretched*) Don't be afraid. I am with you. I am always with you. He is with you, always with you. We are one. But you must choose. You must decide. It's up to you.

Sparky takes the key, and puts it into a red envelope. Slowly, Sparky hands the envelope to James, who slowly takes it. They all freeze. Lights grow bright and intense, hot beacons of light shoot into the Audience, blinding white light. Then—

BLACKOUT!

END OF PLAY

Elizabeth Wong's process with her play is highly personal, as she herself has observed. It presents us with a picture of the playwright actively bidding the subconscious part of herself to take over the work, and guide it to a place where everything feels right for the author.

As mentioned in Chapter One, I extended an invitation to all the playwrights to write a further draft, if they so desired. Elizabeth's e-mail response completes the last fragment needed for our picture of this exceptionally intuitive artist:

> I'm at a stage of diminishing returns. I come to a sticking place
> in the genesis of a play, after it coalesces from my mind onto
> the page, when I feel I've preserved the intensity of my initial
> impulses and landed most of the ideas, so to tinker further
> may do more damage and flatten the play.
>
> When I feel this, I do not rewrite. I need to move to the next
> stage, which is to HEAR the play. As soon as I see the faces of
> actors working to understand this or that, as soon as I hear
> these breathing voices try to wrap around my words and ideas,
> then I can see my way through a rewrite. I rely on my immedi-
> ate gut visceral response to the text upon hearing it, I HEAR
> the clunkers, I HEAR the confusions, I HEAR the problems,
> and I trust I can slog my way, hacking and slashing, rebuilding
> and reconfiguring. As I reread this first draft, which is actually
> more like draft five, I find myself in need of HEARING the play.
> (Emphases Wong)

In the end, what began as a "public" process on this particular project for Elizabeth Wong went deeply into her private
psychological interior; it then must return to the public realm
in order to become complete for her. The play can only complete its journey by going from page to stage, and finishing
the circle.

2
CHAPTER

David Crespy:
Beshert

DREAMS AND THE REALM OF THE PERSONAL

DAVID CRESPY IS ASSISTANT PROFESSOR OF PLAYWRITING at the University of Missouri-Columbia, with a number of professional production credits and awards. He has also written scholarly articles, and served as associate editor for *Slavic and East European Performance*, and the *Journal of American Drama and Theatre*.

I invited David to join the group of playwrights for this book, based on an encounter we had at an Association for Theatre in Higher Education (ATHE) Conference in Toronto, in August of 1999. Prior to that time, I had known David largely through e-mail and telephone conversations (he contacted me initially about using my playwriting book as a text). At an ATHE workshop on alternate forms, David introduced the idea of working from dreams, a concept I found intriguing. I subsequently invited him to participate in this book with the proviso that he would develop a play through his use of techniques and theories involving dreams. The result is his play *Beshert*, along with a wealth of fascinating material on dreams.

As has been seen in the chapter on Elizabeth Wong, dreams can play a powerful role in the playwright's process. In David's case, this takes the form of playwriting that is often nonlinear, and incorporates a great deal of personal experience through symbols. In an e-mail, David elaborated on this aspect of his work:

I also wanted *Beshert* to flow more as a dream. I'm thinking of it as being a kind of dream story, like those described by Donald Braid in his article about the Scottish Travelers (the "gypsies" of Scotland) who tell dream stories that are nearly impossible to follow in a linear way, but have just enough narrative to be tantalizing. His article, in the October 1998 issue of *Text and Performance Quarterly*, is called ' "Did it Happen, or Did it Not?": Dream Stories, Worldview, and Narrative Knowing.' The sense one has from the stories, and that I'm hoping will become a part of *Beshert*, is the question: 'Did this really happen, or was it only a dream?'

I asked David to provide some background on his interest in this area, and he provided me with a wonderful narrative that I will quote almost in its entirety:

> I became interested in using dreams in my plays as a way to bring my training as an actor to use in my work as a playwright. My acting training at Rutgers had been Meisner-based, having worked with William Esper there. One of the things that I found very interesting is that Sanford Meisner wasn't able to use emotional memory as a way to evoke an emotional life within a character. He used a form of daydreaming to build on the concept of "What if" that is so central to Stanislavsky-based acting training.
>
> One of the things that this does for you as an actor is free your imagination. It also teaches you that if you allow your daydreams to roam freely, they have a very powerful effect on your emotional life. In addition, the things that trigger your emotional life can be rather odd and frankly bizarre—in other words, dreamlike. At the same time I was in the BFA acting program at Rutgers, I was studying poetry with Laurie Sheck, who advocated the use of dreams, paintings, and outside stimuli to stoke one's creative juices. However, my poetry was very abstract and nonlinear, while my acting training had been focused on a realistic technique. Somehow daydreaming and dreaming became a way of bringing the two together into a form of playwriting which was rooted in a visceral, personal reality but had a kind of magic wings that freed me from psychological realism.
>
> Marvin Carlson, one of my dissertation committee members at CUNY, knew of my interest in dreaming and drama, and suggested I study the work of Bert States, a phenomenologist

and performance theorist, whose three books on dreaming and fiction, *The Rhetoric of Dreams*, *Dreaming and Storytelling*, and *Seeing In the Dark*, had a powerful effect on my scholarship and on my playwriting technique.

What States has done, is look at the nature of dreaming, which he considers a kind of ur-fiction, and compare its qualities to fiction, which he considers a kind of voluntary dreaming. As a phenomen- ologist, he doesn't seek to interpret dreams using psychoanalytic technique or semiotic deconstruction, but simply to break down the phenomenon of dreaming and describe what it feels like, what the elements of dreams are like, and to classify these elements in a clear, evocative way— phenomenology works like art, it seeks a kind of personal essential metaphor for a particular phenomenon. His work on dreaming and fiction is very, very important, and offers a useful way to understand nonlinear fictional technique.

One of the biggest conflicts in my life has been finding a nonrealistic, nonlinear technique that has a strong base in reality and humanistic approach. Yet my writing has been moving beyond realism for a long time. Once you decide to break down the walls of a realistic style, you're left in a never-never land of a zillion nonrealistic techniques, i.e., absurdism, Dadaism, post-modernism, etc. At least when I use my dreams, I have a structure and a well of material available to me that comes from a very organic part of who I am.

However, I wasn't sure how to begin to use the nature of dreaming in my plays or how to teach this technique to other writers. I began to experiment, using Patricia L. Garfield's book *Creative Dreaming* (New York: Simon and Schuster, 1974). This book teaches you the techniques of the Senoi tribe of Africa to control your dream life and gather the gifts of creativity from your dreams. It also teaches 'lucid dreaming' techniques which help you become conscious during your dreams, yogi dreaming which allows you to develop focus and concentration within your dreams. Garfield's book also describes how to develop dream control in general by maintaining a dream diary, and developing the discipline to mine your dreams for creative material.

My ultimate goal is to pull all these exercises and information about dreaming and drama into a book of essays, exercises, and references to help dramatic writers make the best use of their dreams. As playwriting grows and changes, dropping some aspects of traditional dramatic structure, and embracing new playwriting techniques that challenge linear narrative, dreaming has been an organic way to develop an honest, intuitive, and disciplined stylistic approach to breaking realism's death grip, while avoiding throwing the baby out with the bath water. Using dreaming and dream structure in my plays allows me make the best use of theatricality by speaking in a shorthand everyone can understand, the language of dreams.

To clarify his application of this theoretical base, David discussed some approaches to writing from dreams in his journal. The following is an excerpt from an entry dated September 1, 1999, in which David outlines a series of exercises for working with dreams:

Excerpt from September 1

A) Collecting the dreams. There are many techniques here. A journal, a pad by the bed. The simple action of collecting dreams is a big start.

B) The next step is to start writing dreams. Imitating what happens in a dream.

1) Exercise #1: Single-mindedness. Allow a central action, or theme to plant itself in your dreamscape. You want or need something— it's simple, then allow yourself to go on an adventure to get it: and constantly shift the landscape as you move through the dream, transform the characters, the situations, but the need always stays the same or a variation of the same.

2) Exercise #2: Transformations. Create a simple two-person scene and allow one character to be yourself, and the other to be a friend. As the conversation progresses, keep shifting the friend's persona, at first be very specific about who that person is becoming, then allow bits and pieces of many personas to become a part of them.

3) Exercise #3: Journeys. Transform the situations and landscapes during a simple conversation. Allow the changes to continue even as the situation has an even keel.

4) Exercise #4: Allow time changes, slow the action, speed up the action of the scene. Keep it simple though, keep the conversation between yourself and your friend to have an almost boring quality to it.

5) Exercise #5: Write your character's dreams. Have your character tell us a dream they've had.

6) Exercise #6: Write out a dream from your childhood, then a recurring dream and recurring dream actions. Create a scene from these dreams.

7) Exercise #7: Dream language. Write out a monologue that allows a single important idea to flow through it, but write it in imagistic, descriptive language that makes no sense, but keep coming back to the original idea or need in the speech. There's something that you really need, that your character really wants, but is lost in the world of images flowing through the language. Don't give up on this need. Force the character to work through all the images coming through.

The beginning of this same entry from September 1 introduces some explorations David wrote to delve into the voice and personality of Nadya, Beshert's main character. (He uses the term "etudes" here, which is taken from my book, *Playwriting in Process*. I use the word etude to incorporate exploratory writing as well as writing for improving technique, among other applications.)

Excerpt from September 1
I'm working on etudes using a dream within a dream within a dream exercise, where Nadya is telling her dream and in the process her reality become a dream. She's with her friend Ann, and Ann herself becomes part of the new dream. It's really an exercise to see who Nadya really is, to get her to talk about herself.

The manner in which David is able to induce the "dream within a dream within a dream" reveals his process in a very clear-cut way. He primarily uses his own Exercise #2 described in the journal excerpt, but we can find traces of some of the other exercises as well.

These etudes are an excellent introduction to the excerpt and draft of Beshert we will examine shortly. The etudes are clearly linked, though not in a linear fashion that would tell a coherent story, which is an ideal use of etude work. The linkage is Nadya, and her dreams, which is all that David needed in order to get a sense of her mind and language.

This kind of exploration is critical to a playwright's craft. It represents a willingness to go outside the confines of plot in order to discover possibilities in the characters that may not be rational or even applicable. The point is to push the boundaries to see what else might be there, or to see if the boundaries even need to be heeded. Sometimes a basic idea has far more complexity than one might suspect. There is no way to know this unless explorations are undertaken.

This is work that is risky—it's easy to introduce ideas that may complicate the initial concept, or to wander off course in other ways—but there are no real gains without taking some chances. The hope is that one will discover elements that had not been previously considered. These elements often add extraordinary texture to a work, or "free up" a playwright's perspective to see new angles in the original work. Ultimately, explorations feed back into the play, even if indirectly, because they help broaden and strengthen the writer's sense of character and situation.

In the etudes that follow, we are able to see David blur the lines between dreams and reality, once again raising his key concern: "Did this really happen, or was it only a dream?" You will also notice elements here and there that will appear in *Beshert*, often in altered form (such as the reference to a mumu in Etude #1, and the glasses in Etude #2).

Beshert - Etude #1 *Dream exercise*

NADYA *sits at a table across from her friend* ANN, *who is a feisty, petite Asian woman of about twenty-four. They're at a student union at the University where* NADYA *teaches.*

ANN: No, go ahead and tell me. I love dreams.

NADYA: It's a flying dream and a tunneling one. I'm inside the roof of a cave, maybe it's my own mouth because it has a kind of softness to it.

ANN: Gross, but I'm with you.

NADYA : And there is Jerry with me. At least I think it's Jerry, because he's wearing a dress like my mother used to wear. A mumu kind of thing.

ANN: (*Guffaws*) Jerry in a dress. That's even more gross.

NADYA: It's a dream, okay. Are you okay?

ANN: I'm fine. Why are you asking?

NADYA: Just that you seem to be getting a little green around the gills.

ANN: Well, I need my gills. And green is normal for gills.

NADYA: That's a weird response.

ANN: It's a weird day. Go ahead, I need to get to my class. I want to hear this dream.

NADYA: So Jerry and I fly out of this cavern place and we race over the trees. There's this bomb blast and I'm being taken far away from my sons. They're way over on the other side of the planet. And I'm crying.

ANN: Uhhhhhhh.

NADYA: What's wrong?

ANN: I'm fine. Really. It's okay.

NADYA: And it's then we're at a party, and all my great aunts are there.

ANN: Oh, yeah, you've told me about them. (ANN *suddenly becomes* ROSE WISE, *shifting her clothing, her face, her glasses*). Go on, tell me about your grandmother.

NADYA: You should know everything, you're her.

ANN: Don't be stupid, I'm Ann. You're telling me your dream.

NADYA: Bubby, don't sit there and tell me you're Ann. You're Bubby.

ANN: Nadya, you need to change your medications or something.

NADYA: The party is a funeral at times, and at other times is some kind of dance event. I'm performing some kind of postmodern balletic something. I'm watching it, and I'm in it all at the same time.

ANN: So darling, how long have you had these dreams?

NADYA: You just called me darling the way my grandmother used to call me darling.

ANN: Do you want to crawl under the table with me? It'll be safer there. We'll be safe from the fall out.

NADYA: Why does this feel wrong to me?

ANN: Look at your hands. Look at your hands. (*They crawl under the table*)

NADYA: I'm trying to tell you this dream. It's heartbreaking. I'm so alone in the world. I'm just so alone. And I'm afraid.

ANN: Don't be afraid darling. But hurry up, I've got to teach my freshman comp course, and they're little animals if I don't get there in time.

NADYA: I can't tell you my dream, Ann. You look like my Bubby, and we're under a table.

ANN: Eat this.

NADYA: What is it?

ANN: It's a little kugel. You need to eat a little kugel.

NADYA: This is getting harder and harder to understand.

ANN: Put some soy sauce on it. And some guacamole. It'll taste better that way.

NADYA: This is a dream isn't it?

ANN: Look at your hands.

NADYA: It's a dream.

ANN: Yes, and you knew that. But what happened in that other dream?

NADYA: I'm not telling you. I'm leaving this dream now.

ANN: Then leave the dream. I'm going to get very large now and become an amoeba and engulf you. My brains are going to spill out of the top of my head and and ooze you. . . .

ANN's brains begin to ooze out of the top of her head. NADYA gets up, screaming silently, running away in slo-mo. Blackout.

Beshert - Etude #2 Nadya's Dream Vision

NADYA: I was taken to a place near some water, like the Nile, and I was abandoned there. Near some buildings that looked both old and huge and powerful, but also abandoned and creaking. I knew if I looked up at them the bricks of the building would topple down on me, because the buildings were so frail. My Bubby was there.

ESTHER WISE enters, she is a plump woman with short hawk-like nose, looking a little like Al Lewis in drag.

ESTHER: Darling, it's the Nile and inside that tower is a devil creature.

NADYA: We flew to the top of the tower, hovering near evil.

ESTHER: I love flying, I wonder what kind of flight this is? Do we get a lunch or what?

NADYA: Bubby, we're flying in a dream, we're not on an airplane.

ESTHER: So smart, my granddaughter is so smart. Sweetheart, why don't you get those things to put in the eyes. I see them on television all the time.

NADYA: Even in my dreams, my bubby wants me to get rid of my glasses. I love my glasses.

ESTHER: What's that large man laying on his side on the ledge over there?

NADYA: We flew over to, and hovered near a gigantic man who was slowly gaining mass by absorbing the marble of the building he was lying near.

ESTHER: His veins are coming out of his skin and growing into the building. He's getting bigger, darling.

NADYA: It was the evil growing, the building itself started to develop hair, and muscles and nails, and we were sinking down to the feet of the growing marble giant.

ESTHER: I'm not here anymore darling, I'm your brother Elliot.

ESTHER *turns into* ELLIOT, *a dark-haired young guy with curly hair and a somewhat dim-witted expression.*

NADYA: Elliot?

ELLIOT: Cool! We're like flying around. Hey, Noddy! Whoa, that guy over there is like ten stories high or something. He looks like somebody we know. Maybe he found out about my bar mitzvah or something.

NADYA: My brother Elliot had the largest most obscene bar mitzvah in the town of Freehold, NJ.

ELLIOT: YES! It was righteous.

NADYA: Actually it was anything but righteous. It was gross, with three hundred people, Animals, circus acts, just about anything you could think of—two rock bands. My parents hated it, but my rich Uncle Bruce had made a lot of money with Disney in Hollywood and he loved Elliot. Uncle Bruce couldn't have kids and he and Elliot were like brothers.

ELLIOT: Oh, man. That marble monster guy is like reaching for us. Shit! He looks like . . .

NADYA: The monster kept reaching for us, trying to get me to kiss his huge feet. He was lightning fast for a huge marble giant. He started to talk to us and sounded like John, my ex-husband, or my like almost ex-husband.

JOHN: (*His voice huge, deep, and echoey*) Kiss them. Kiss them. Kiss my feet.

NADYA: He was still forming, his veins still growing into the ground moving over the soil of the desert, absorbing the earth and becoming part of it.

JOHN: (*His huge voice ripe with pleasure*) Oh, feels so good to get bigger.

ELLIOT: Gross, man. He's getting like enormous. We've got to get off the planet.

NADYA: (*Being blown backwards*) Suddenly Elliot and I were forcing ourselves into outer space. We were moving faster and faster backwards away from the earth which was rippling and changing as huge veins smashed through land masses and oceans and the entire earth started to turn into John.

JOHN: Bigger, I'm bigger, God I'm so fucked, I'm getting bigger.

NADYA: He was as big as a planet and I was hovering in outer space, when all of a sudden I saw one of those huge veins shooting across space toward Elliot and I.

ELLIOT: It's coming, man, it's bad. It's really moving toward us, I'm like afraid or some such shit.

NADYA: As I watched in horror, the huge vein hit Elliot and
   punched right through him, then all these little veins startled
   rippling through him, and he was absorbed. A smaller vein shot
   out at me, even though I was getting away, and it started to get
   smaller, but reached out to me and it just glanced my toe, but it
   bit into my toe and started to spread into me, and I start to feel
   really funny, like I was about to orgasm or something, it was
   getting better and better, even as I saw the veins rippling
   through me. I was really getting higher and higher into the
   orgasm of it, when I saw John's massive face looming over me,
   and I was horrified as I was being absorbed into him. I started
   to fight the pleasure, I started to rip away from John, and I felt
   horrible pain as I saw my own leg and lower body tearing away
   from my upper body, with blood shooting out everywhere, and I
   was exploding with pain, but I knew that I had to get away, and I
   started to get very hard, super hard and egg-like, but I could
   hear John's voice even as I turned into this shooting egg.
JOHN: Nadya, come into me! Don't do this, don't cut off from me.
   Eat some granola or try these vegetables.
NADYA: Granola and vegetables shot all over the place as I
   became a rocket egg and shot far, far away from John, who was
   bleeding horribly from the wound I left. I was just a shooting
   egg now, and I had no feelings, but it felt better than being
   absorbed into John.

These explorations give us a firm foundation in the theatri-
cal/dream world David is exploring. We need to examine his
journal entries now to move on to the next level, which is that
of the personal. Commenting in an e-mail, David said:

My plays are usually very autobiographical; my biggest
influence as a writer is Adrienne Kennedy, whose plays speak
to the deepest part of my consciousness. The autobiographical aspect of them can be very difficult at times, as I tend to
write about material I am still living. This was the case with my
play Men Dancing and it is my best play to date (or at least it's
the play that has garnered me the most awards). I've been
wrestling with Beshert over this issue, although as I get closer
to finalizing my divorce, I'm beginning to get some distance
on this material for revision purposes.

It is my contention that all plays are personal in that the
subject matter must be something that deeply affects the

playwright or the work will be one-dimensional. However, the playwright often hides that which is personal in order to create a work of art, and not autobiography. This is also true in David's work. If one encountered Beshert (or Men Dancing) without any introduction or inside knowledge, it would be very difficult to discern what is personal or not, yet the stories would be as strong. We, however, have the rare luxury of knowing something about the inside situation and comparing that to the dramatized story.

This is precisely what Playwriting Master Class is for: pulling aside the curtains so one can see not only the person operating the special effects, as it were, but how they're using these effects. David Crespy, like many of the other playwrights in this book, is incredibly brave and open. He shares his life with us, then shows us how he turns parts of his life into a work of artistic power—playwriting alchemy.

The journal also records several dreams that have a clear impact on Beshert. One of the most fun elements of David's work is to look at the etudes and the journal, then see how David has combined portions from each into the play as it evolves. You will also see, particularly in the entry of September 7, how David spends time exploring the back story, or past history, of the characters.

JOURNAL

August 20

I've just started the playlet, Beshert, which is Yiddish for one's intended love. It's about a young woman, Nadya, who is plagued by her dead grandmother and great aunts, whose souls have been trapped into Nadya's grandmother's furniture. This play is typical for me; it's close to home and it plays with humor and magic in ways that I find entertaining (although not always easy to stage or make sense of). I've just come to this play after thinking about it for about a week. Its coming at a time when my mother is dying in NYC of pancreatic cancer, even as I pen these words. It's also coming at a time when I'm recently separated from my wife.

Plays come to me in a picture and a title. I often just pop out the title as I'm working. I have to walk around with a play for a while. For this play, I've had to reestablish my relationship with my grand-mother who died this past March. I've gotten all her furniture from her apartment and it's been strange to live in the space that's been created by these large, looming pieces of furniture.

August 25

A dream (whether it works in the play or not—we'll see). I'm below the earth, in some demilitarized zone, someplace that hasn't seen the light of day since the 1940s during World War II, dead bodies sealed within are decomposing, and continue to decompose as I move in and over the passages. The passages take me up to a party where there's some kind of dance event, which I'm suddenly partic-ipating in. The dance is a sort of yogic ritual and it seems like it is huge. Then I'm back down in the passages, which somehow lead to a large van. I'm following my friend Russ, who is much larger than I, he's up into the van when a woman (is it a woman) shoots at the van rapidly. The gun shots seem to be tiny, rapid-fire bursts, and the bullets seem to home in directly at a small hole in my chest over my heart. I'm hit, but I just feel a little woozy. I want to get all those tiny bullets out of my heart. Russ is hit much worse than I, and we're both whisked away in emergency vehicles, while a crowd circles the woman, watching her patiently as she struggles to reload her rifle.

We're whisked away to the party, and somehow we are healed and are able to fly, we fly back to the mansion (Russ flies higher and faster than I can) with the underground passages, and the continu-ous party, with all kinds of tasty foods, and the decomposing corpses in the passages below. I know they are there, but I'm not concerned. There is a production of one of my plays going on, and I'm told it's wonderful (by whom? I'm not sure). I'm left with a vague sense of well-being; I'm having a production soon by my alma mater, Rutgers, that will move to New York. Go figure. END OF DREAM.

I'm again wrestling with this play. The title seems too flip and glib and silly for what this play is about. A husband to the young woman begins to flesh out in my head. A waspy sort of guy, very holistically oriented, a hiker and outdoorsman, overpowering, but oddly sex-less, and cold. He's Nadya's estranged husband. It's my way of work-ing through my recent separation from my wife. I'm Nadya, of course, and my wife is this guy. What's his name? Something short and powerful, but maybe a bit odd and WASP-y, like Clint or Doug, or Walt (are these odd and WASP-y names?). He's there in the room, in the wardrobe.

Also I need to start exploring the great-aunts who are based on my grandmother and her sisters. In real life there was Rose, the eldest, then Rae, who is still alive now, though she's in a dementia, and the two twins, Gloria and my grandmother Nora. My grandmother I adored. She was always loving, crotchety, warm-hearted, a mouth like a sailor (son-of-a-bitch bastard was her favorite croak) and loved a joke. She remarried at age 70, to a Jewish delicatessen-owner, Max, from NYC. He was a good-natured old fellow, also a bit crotchety, but kind. My real grandfather was a bit of a pill, from all my memories of him, and from the descriptions of my mother's cousins.

But somehow these aunts, Nadya's aunts, are much more kvetchy, more agitated than my aunts. They're not getting along at all. And Nadya is in the middle of a crisis; her job as a young professor is falling apart, she's doing too much, her husband has left her for another man, her mother's dying, and her grandmother, the one she loved so much, has already died. She's feeling all alone in the world and wondering why she should go on. Her two kids are with her husband tonight, and it's so lonely without them.

September 5

A dream. My mother's bed is by a window in an oppressive apartment. I hear her shushing and clucking to call me to her. She wants to look at my eyebrows. She says to me, "your eyebrows. They're tufted." I say, "yes, they're tufted. I've always had tufted eyebrows." She laughs and I laugh. It is a nice moment. Then I'm moving around the apartment—which is where? I don't know but it has a colorful quality to it, though where my mother is leaf-strewn and wet. She's just inside from a patio.

Then I've come from some dank playwriting workshop center, where the artistic director is recalling how he had to help me because I was so friendly and bought him his lunch. He's very young and boyish but I've broken the rules by taking a script that had a certain numbering system without signing it out. Oddly enough the literary manager points out to me the blackboard where the scripts are kept noted and shows me how it lights up when it's being used. The chalk actually lights up.

And we all start talking—about these scripts—and then we're walking out onto the dock of this nice lake, it's so blue, where everyone is in the water except me. I'm wearing a suit and I don't want to get it wet—but everyone is trying to duck me. I get a little wet around my pant legs, but I'm able to skirt over the water, Jesus-like, to avoid really wetting my outfit; though one big black guy—my dramaturg?—is trying to get me to dance into the water off of the dock. I don't want to, but he's big and powerful and he has a winning smile. I find myself skipping over the water as he sort of ballroom dances me over the edge of the dock over the water, and then back onto the dock. At one point my feet leave the ground, and he's throwing me, after having built up momentum, to a spot over the trees. I'm flying up over the trees and there is a huge mushroom cloud forming behind me, with a rush of killing vapors, radiation, and heat zooming over the landscape just at my feet. I'm zooming faster and faster toward a kind of paradise of light, but behind me the darkness is rising up higher and closer, and I feel it singeing my shoes which are turning into webbed feet . . .

September 7

I've just awakened from a dream that ended with me feeling my mother's kiss on my neck. It's such an evocative feeling; my mother's breath and lips on the little hairs on the back of my neck. It brings back my childhood in Freehold, NJ, instantly. In the dream it happens as we are standing in front of an avant-garde art gallery near a large body of water, admiring a banner that has been put out by the mother of the artist who is also a woman. We've wandered out from the gallery opening party and the artist's mother wants us to admire her handiwork. And then as we stand there I feel my mother wrap her arms around me from behind and kiss my neck.

I've been thinking more and more about Nadya and her husband John. Again, I'm playing with my own relationship with my wife (or soon to be ex-wife, former wife, what nonnegative term can we give our former spouses?) and I'm making her this character John. I see John as this red-headed, no-nonsense, outdoors type. He's been the one who looks after the kids, has an organic cooperative garden, and needs someone to support him. He doesn't make enough money to live. He's cold, tanned, loves to cook and cooks vegetarian food very well. He doesn't know how to love Nadya, who is overwhelming, crazy, pushy, highly intelligent, questioning, not entirely subversive, but definitely liberal, who loves to eat out, to live life.

What happened is Nadya wants John to replace her father who was never there for her. Her dad was an absentee workaholic, a good guy, but one who seemed to be so engrossed in his work that he had no interest in her. Nadya dated and lived with John, who's five years older than her, after meeting him in Austin, TX, at an organic cooperative food store (which was a bit of a pick-up joint). She was about twenty-three, he was about twenty-eight. He was a revelation to her, after growing up in New Jersey. When she came to Austin, she learned how to be more open in her lifestyle, more laid back. She had an artsy apartment that her parents disapproved of, and found her style. She was writing poetry then, and was beginning to find an interest in scholarship, though she didn't want to admit this to the rest of her MFA classmates. She let her hair grow long, wore wild and woolly dresses and a leather jacket, and just let herself become herself.

She met John and went on cool trips; she went hiking and stuff and went into the desert with him and camped. She found him distant, yet vital and exciting. She weighed less than she had ever weighed in her life, and was looking fantastic. She wrote wild poetry, sang in a rock band, and just had a ball. At the same time, she was getting more and more interested in literature and scholarship and started thinking about an academic life.

She and John both finished up their degrees at the same time. John finished his undergraduate which he had taken up after many years of being separated from his father, who had divorced his mother in a very bitter split-up. John had reconciled with his father, though he had cut himself off from his mother who was an alcoholic. His dad liked having him around.

September 15

I've been in mediation for several months now following my separation from my wife. And I've been to New York to see my mother who is like a skeleton. Each of these women are so foreboding in my life. My mother has always been a source of terror for me; and yet, also, of delight. My mother's father, Phil (my Pop-Pop), is coming out of her now. Pop-Pop always seemed to be an unhappy man, with all his illnesses and opinions. He spent the last few years of his life as a security guard for a perfume factory. But he had been a banquet manager, store-owner, hotel manager, bartender, etc. He was the banquet manager at the Americana Hotel in Palm Beach, Florida, and was an elegant, southern-born Jew.

I've seen my grandfather in my dreams quite frequently. He had a Mark Twain look to him, with his dashing white moustache and his slim severity. He had a very handsome face that became very distinguished as he grew older, and unlike many people who settle in the New York metropolitan region, he never lost his southern accent. It always lingered in his voice, though he hadn't returned to the south (except for stints in Miami as a bartender/banquet manager). He's very much a part of who I am; a dark part, and a part that loves telling stories.

October 2

The one thought that has come down to me from this experience is the meaning of the word "Beshert," which means, in Yiddish, one's intended love. What does it mean to be one's beloved, that something is decreed in the most ancient of documents that this young man and this young woman are intended for each other. What it means is that the whole of the Universe waits upon their connection, their private magic, that the archangels and lesser angels, and other beings of the heavenly host wait upon their meeting. That when they make love a shaft of light will fly up from their bed and in perfect synchronization with the spinning of the planets and the movement of the galaxies, one true love will be born and consummated, and of that love there will be a child, and that child will be the light of the world.

Isn't that what is meant by Beshert? Don't each of us want this connection? Not necessarily with another human being, but with the world, with an animal, with every lonely being on this planet. To heal the lies, the pain of existence, to find a way to get away from the darkness of existence and the knowledge that this may all end, very, very soon.

As we will see with the drafts of *Beshert*, David constantly moves forward into the realm of the personal with the play, while expanding the power of the dream-images. There are three drafts of the play to examine for their progression into this realm. I have included only a portion of the first and second drafts, because of space concerns, and the entire third draft. Note that the cast list is included only in the first draft because the characters don't change in their descriptions throughout the play.

DRAFT EXPLORATIONS OF THE PLAY

Excerpt from First Draft

Cast :

NADYA FINKLESTEIN: A bright, dark-haired woman of thirty-five, recently separated from her husband. She's a young academic in English who also has a career as a writer of short stories. She sports thick black glasses and somewhat eccentric clothing.

ESTHER WISE: NADYA's maternal grandmother, now deceased. In NADYA's dream world she has become a heavy old dresser. In life, she was a warm, heavy, but scolding, kibitzer. She loves a good laugh at her own expense, but she's not without opinions of her own. Spent most of her adult life on her feet as a store owner with her husband.

ROSE WISE: NADYA's maternal great-aunt, ESTHER's oldest sister. Born in Russia, ROSE shares much of ESTHER's warmth and humor, though of the Wises, she's the wisest and always the sister in charge. She was much older than the three younger sisters, and the unofficial mother of the twins, ESTHER and SARAH.

SARAH (SALLY) WISE: NADYA's maternal great-aunt, ESTHER's twin (fraternal) sister. SALLY is the sharp-tongued, pretty sister, married (unhappy) into wealth.

JOHN MORGAN: NADYA's estranged husband. He is a back-to-nature, vegetarian, subsistence farmer. Big, handsome, red-headed, and utterly demanding.

A large ornate bed surrounded on either side by two large dressers; a short fat one to the left, a tall elegant one to the right, and a large wardrobe at the foot of the bed. Night tables with tall old-fashioned lamps on either side of the bed. In the bed is NADYA Finklestein, a young woman of thirty-five, dark-haired, pretty in an odd, fetching way, and at present, soundly asleep. She snores with gusto. Her coke-bottle-thick glasses sit on a pile of books on one side of her. There are books piled everywhere. Nothing is heard but snoring, suddenly punctuated by the sound of a dresser drawer, on the right, suddenly flying open.

NADYA: (*Suddenly swallows a snore, and wakens*) Huh?! What?! (*Another drawer opens*) What was that? What? (*She flips on the light, slips on her glasses, sits up. She wears an old-fashioned nightgown*) Is someone there? John? No! (*Bops herself in the head*) Stupid. Can't be him! God, am I stupid. Did I leave my clock radio . . .

NADYA fiddles with her alarm clock. Another drawer slams open loudly: NADYA screams, and suddenly from the short fat dresser drawer, an elderly woman's voice springs out. This is NADYA's BUBBY, her maternal grandmother, ESTHER WISE.

ESTHER: You've got to make sure the cards are wrapped in plastic, you understand. They get mildewed.

NADYA: (*Deeply weirded out*) Bubby? Bubby, is that you?

The wardrobe flings open, dresses fly out, along with another woman's voice, older, more cherubic, kooky. This is ROSE WISE, BUBBY's sister.

ROSE: What mildew? There's no water in the cards! I can't find anything in here! I can't find anything. The hell with playing cards.

ESTHER: They go in plastic! It keeps them . . .

NADYA: THIS ISN'T HAPPENING!

ROSE: You put *everything* in plastic. I was afraid to sleep over your house because I was afraid you'd put me in plastic.

ESTHER: I should have! It would have shut your mouth.

ROSE: Kish myn tuchis.

NADYA: Aunt Rose?

ESTHER: Look at her.

ROSE: Don't tell me about it. I see her. What is that schmatta she has on?

ESTHER: She sleeps in it. Don't ask me. It's from her father's side. The Finklesteins.

ROSE: All of them crazy.

NADYA: Aunt Rose, can you hear me?

Another drawer slams open and shut from the tall dresser, the voice of SARAH WISE bursts out. She's ESTHER's twin sister, very elegant, educated.

SARAH: Could the two of you pipe down? How's a girl supposed to get her beauty rest?

ESTHER: Kvetch, kvetch, kvetch. My back drawers are killing me and Pirella needs her beauty rest.

SARAH: If you didn't eat like a pig, you wouldn't have gotten so fat.

NADYA: Aunt Sarah? Is that you?

ROSE: She must be dense, is all I can say.

SARAH: Rose, is that any way to speak about your great niece? She's all we've got.

ESTHER: My granddaughter; look at her with those glasses. A man she'll never find looking like an owl with a crew cut.

ROSE: It's what you get letting your daughter marry a Finklestein. Junk men, all of them. And out-of-their-minds communists.

ESTHER: He ran a very successful salvage business, if you want to know.

SARAH: Rose is right, not our kind of people.

NADYA: Look! Don't talk about my Dad that way!

ROSE: Is she talking to us?

NADYA: Well, yes. I am.

ESTHER: What are you reading there, darling?

NADYA: Oh, uh, nothing great, just a little Butler, some Showalter. Old stuff.

ROSE: What is she talking about?

NADYA: Feminist theory. It's really neat; very carefully written.

ESTHER: Take it from me, darling, that won't get you a Jewish husband.

ROSE: The Finklesteins were all like that. Book worms with glasses.

SARAH: Oi, and her uncle, Sam's brother, Harry, dressed in black at every cousin's club.

ESTHER: Smoking those long women's cigarettes.

ROSE: A fagala!

ESTHER: Worse! A reform Jew!

SARAH: Horrible. Nobody in our family is reform. Finklesteins were all left-wing communists.

ROSE: Like there would be right-wing communists.

ESTHER: They say Frank Sinatra was one of those.

NADYA: Shut up! Why don't you all shut up?!! Just shut up! (*Pauses a moment*) I can't believe this. I can't believe I'm talking to my dead Bubby's furniture.

This excerpt provides us with a solid foundation in the tone and style of *Beshert*. As the first draft continues, we get more background on Nadya and her grand-aunts and grandmother. Her grandfather's spirit emerges through her, wanting Nadya to have a Jewish child so he can occupy the child's body. Then her husband, John, arrives, planning to take control of her life again. To protect herself, Nadya throws on layer after layer of her dead female relatives' clothing. Evoking a reversed *Medea*, John is dressed in battle gear and has brought Nadya the cooked remains of their children. Nadya is able to use the "power" of the "clothes of the matriarchs" to defeat John. At the end, the phone rings, waking her from the dream, and it's Joel, a man Nadya's met at her synagogue and who will be her future Beshert love.

Many of the elements of the plot get changed in the second draft, then return in the third draft. I asked David to articulate the reasons for the changes. He responded in an e-mail:

> The first version of the play really focuses on the incident of the grand-aunts speaking to Nadya through her grandmother's furniture. There's a lot of interplay between Nadya, her grandmother and her grand-aunts. I loved the funny interchanges between them, and I didn't try to make sense out of any of it. I put that draft aside, not really looking at it much, and worked on the second version of *Beshert*. This one came out as a kind of monologue at first, answering questions I had about Nadya, who she was, who her siblings were, etc. I tried to give her more of a voice. In the first version, she seemed reactive rather than proactive, so I wanted her to take control of the play a bit more.

Not only does Nadya take control of the play more—direct address to the audience is a big leap forward—but in the second draft David includes some of the persona-shifts we witnessed in the etudes, as Nadya morphs into various characters.

Some additional elements add more theatricality and fun to the second draft, such as the furniture making an entrance. There is also greater compression, which did not exist in the first draft.

Excerpt from Second Draft

An empty stage. A shaft of light. Into this light walks NADYA FINKLESTEIN. *She is thirty-two, dark brown hair cut severely short, large framed glasses that make her seem both owlish and pixie-ish. She is small, but well-endowed and womanly. She has an engaging smile and a self-deprecating manner. She doesn't realize it, but she is beautiful and desirable, though that is the farthest thing from her mind right now. She moves toward us and speaks.*

NADYA: My problems began with the arrival of my grandmother's furniture to my duplex in West Minster, Missouri. (NADYA *watches a large heavy dresser and mirror make its way across the stage*) My grandmother had died in April of lung cancer, at the age of 87. She had the illness for about a year or more, but it had been in remission. Her lungs had finally given way, and in the middle of kibbitzing with one of the nurses, she had died. She had been very ill and my brother and two sisters had gone to see her, but no one was there when she died. (A *taller, but also massive, dresser makes it way across the stage.*) My brother, Elliot, who is a lawyer in Manhattan, sent along my grandmother's belongings to help me out in my situation. Here he is:

She becomes her brother by putting on a few costume pieces: some Gap-y clothing, different glasses. She makes him handsome, big-shouldered, and menschy. He's also deeply ironic and a smart-ass lawyer.

ELLIOT: My sister's basically an idiot. What can I tell you? (He *smirks helplessly and disappears*)

NADYA: (*Discarding the outfit*) When he's not a jerk, and a typical lawyer, my brother is really very sweet. My younger twin sisters, Rebecca and Rachel, otherwise known as R & R.

NADYA *becomes both of them, exchanging a bow between them. They're very feminine and pretty in a way that* NADYA *is not. They wear party clothes and work in advertising; both are very bright, but shallow.*

NADYA as RACHEL: (*Who has a lateral lisp*) You know it's not that you're stupid, Nadya. You're just kinda witchy-looking.

NADYA as REBECCA: (*Rebecca is a post-modern retro-valley girl*) You

could be really pretty if you wanted. Hey, I just sold a big
account today, guys! Let's party!

RACHEL: Kewl! I love advertising.

NADYA: They lived in small apartments in the upper 90s, had cute
boyfriends with party houses on Fire Island and my brother had
a houseful of gorgeous Norwegian furniture in Westchester (and
no wife, so ladies, he's available), he didn't need any of Bubby's
stuff. I don't really get along with my family really. We don't
have much in common. Except that we grew up together and I
miss them. And I got all of my Bubby's furniture. (*An enormous
wardrobe moves across the forestage.* NADYA *is surrounded on three sides
by the furniture*) My situation was this: after fifteen years of co-
habitation, my husband John no longer wanted me as his wife.
Why? I'm not really sure, except that it had to do with my
inability to live within his lifestyle. John was a vegetarian environmentalist, who had worked as a librarian at Yale. He didn't
believe in vaccinating our children, insisted that all of our food
be organically grown, our children be home-schooled, and we
build a log cabin in the woods, put in a crop and subsistence
farm. (*A large full-size bed also of an antique, ornate style rolls on of its
own accord.* NADYA *sits at the foot of the bed*). As a cultural materialist feminist scholar of obscure pop cultural folk texts, I was
clearly not the right person to build a log cabin and make a garden grow. I was much more interested in applying feminist theory to texts created by nearly invisible folk art writers who
exemplified the otherness typified by those who had, not of any
of their own accord, become victim to the hegemony of the
white, male, European gaze and who were thus marginalized in
odd and poignant ways. (NADYA *crawls up into her bed*)
Unfortunately we had two small children, Dylan, six, and
Benjamin, three, who John, my ex-husband, wanted to continue
to home-school and basically keep to himself. Though I was
buried in my work as a young scholar and had tended to allow
John to have the majority say in the raising of our children, I
was terrified of losing them. There was of course my mother
who was dying of pancreatic cancer in New York and my budding relationship with my own brother Elliot and my two sisters, Rebecca and Rachel, who had stopped speaking to me
when I had married John who wasn't Jewish. Our father is dead.
Of AIDS. Several years ago. His name was Victor. I think my
father was the savior of the world. And now the world will not
be saved. (*Pause*) If you hadn't guessed, I'm Jewish. I have these
biblical moments. Not that that means anything, but I am and

that's all there is to it. I've been known to attend the Friday night services and I enjoy praying in Hebrew but the whole patriarchal God thing really gripes me. Yet having been raised within the conserva-dox Jewish netherworld of conservative and orthodox Judaism I couldn't handle the bongo, tambourine and guitar that our local rabbi at our local Hillel enjoyed using to spice up our services. Still there was this guy there who has recently asked me out for coffee. He's very quiet, handsome . . . but this is all too soon and I'm still legally married so I couldn't possibly . . . his name is Avi for Avigdor. Anyway the services at this temple are very liberal and inclusive and all that, but I'm uncomfortable there with all this loosey-goosey, warm feeling Judaism. (*pause*) Call me reactionary, but I'd rather listen to chanting than bongos. (NADYA *lies back in bed. A shaft of moonlight splashes across the bed and there is sound of birds and crickets. Night sounds*) It was one night after Friday night services that I was laying in bed after a weekend without the boys and me not being able to see them for another two days. I stared up at the ceiling and tried to name off major feminist scholars and their essays to see if that would help me drop off to sleep, but then I realized things would work much faster if I focused on a single essay by a white male European author of some renown who's work utterly bored me. I tried Kant at first, but then found that Marshall McCluhan was much more boring and suitable to the task. I fell asleep.

NADYA *gently snores. A soft breeze blows across the room. Night sounds. Then a distant sound of a crash. Glass. One of drawers on the large squat dresser slowly pushes open. It slides out and then back in again. Another drawer slides out. A bit more suddenly. Then another; this time with an audible slam out and in. NADYA squints open one eye. A drawer violently slams open and then closed, then another, and another. Clothing shoots out of the drawers onto the bed. Both of NADYA's eyes open, she slowly sits up. Then comes a long woman's moan. It is unearthly. This is ESTHER WISE, NADYA's maternal grandmother.*

ESTHER: Augghhhhhh!

The doors of the wardrobe fling open and clothing shoots out onto the bed. Another groan is heard from the wardrobe. This is ROSE, ESTHER's sister and NADYA's great aunt.

At this point, the script becomes relatively similar to material we've already seen in the first draft excerpt, though there are some intriguing changes. Once the female relatives are established, the character of John enters as before. But John is dressed differently now, as David describes: "John is dressed in a very outdoorsy, but folk-granola fashion. He has short red hair, is very muscular and brawny in a compact way. He looks like a warm human being, but when he opens his mouth he becomes like a soviet apparatchik." However, he still brings his grisly food offering with him, and attempts to reclaim his control over Nadya. David's choice to soften and humanize John's look has served to make the character's actions even stronger.

Other changes in the draft are powerful emotional shifts that incorporate more of David's personal life. These are the addition of the lullaby, "Oifen Pripichuck," sung by Nadya's unseen mother, who is dying, and the insertion of Nadya's grandfather, Nathan, into the mix differently than the first draft.

Excerpt from Second Draft

SARAH: She's certainly not her Nathan's granddaughter. He wouldn't have put up with this.

ESTHER: Nathan, how would you have handled this?

NADYA: (*Talks to us as she becomes* NATHAN. *Adds white hair and a mustache. Picks up a glass of scotch*) My grandfather was a southern Jew, from Jacksonville, Florida. He grew up there, with his mother Minnie. She was from Austria. She had a southern accent with an Austrian curl to it. She beat the hell out of him. And he died at sixty-five after many years of colitis and diabetes. (As NATHAN, *with a slight southern accent*) I'd kick that son-of-a-bitch's ass from here to North Carolina. He's put a spell on her. Son of a bitch. When I was a boy we'd take kids like him and throw them up behind the barns and beat the shit out of them until they'd cry for their mamas. Probably would have cut him too. A couple times. Shit. (As NADYA) My grandfather was regularly beat up by the local kids. There weren't too many Jews in Jacksonville, and he didn't get along with anybody. And when he grew up and had my mom, he was very tough on her.

Sound of a woman singing in Yiddish. It is "Oifen Pripichuck" a Yiddish lullaby. NADYA *pulls off the moustache and listens.*

NADYA: Tante Rose, is Mom going to live?

ROSE: No, my darling. Not for very much longer.

Nathan's appearance here is very brief compared to what we will see in the third draft, but getting some perspective on him is an important step into deepening the script. At the end of the second draft, "Oifen Pripichuck" is sung in its entirety. The other change in draft two is the on-stage presence of Nadya's future love, now named Avi, who is played by the same actor playing John. This addition is also incorporated into the third draft.

In an e-mail, David describes some of his choices going into the third draft:

> I read the two versions of *Beshert* to my students in my Theatre 211 Intermediate Playwriting course. The students, being thoroughly Midwestern, found the Jewish cultural material of the first version utterly mystifying. They liked the second version because it explained some of these cultural symbols and language, although they felt that the first version was more active. So my immediate goal was to combine the two scripts into one, keeping the best and losing the worst—assuming, of course, that I knew which was which.
>
> I liked the opening monologue, but tried to pare it down a bit; I lost Nadya's Yuppie sisters, and trimmed some of the other biographical stuff, focusing on Nadya's eccentric scholar's voice. I think of Nadya as being passionate and eccentric, seriously misguided perhaps, but bright and ambitious. I tried to keep the constant kibbitzing and kvetching of grandmother and her sisters, but tried to focus it, and clarify what these spirits wanted of Nadya. I also wanted to take the magic dressing scene of the first *Beshert* and the battle between John and Nadya, while keeping some of the grandfather material from *Beshert* II. I also wanted to tighten the ending of the play, keeping some of the lyrics of "Oifen Pripichuck" which is a lovely Yiddish melody (despite it's somewhat ungainly title), while not forcing the director to do the entire song (except, perhaps, as a curtain piece).

The complete third draft of *Beshert* follows here. It brings together elements of the first and second draft, while introducing still more theatrical qualities to the piece.

The complete third draft of Beshert
An empty stage. A shaft of light. Into this light walks NADYA
FINKLESTEIN. *She is thirty-two, dark brown hair cut severely short,
large framed glasses that make her seem both owlish and pixie-like. She*

doesn't realize it, but she is pretty and desirable. She moves toward us and speaks.

NADYA: My problems began with the arrival of my grandmother's furniture to my duplex in Westminster, Missouri. (NADYA *watches a large heavy dresser and mirror make its way across the stage*) She had died in Lakewood, New Jersey of cancer, at the age of 87. Her lungs had finally given way, and in the middle of joking with one of the nurses, her heart stopped. My brother and two sisters had seen her a week before, but no one was there when she died. She basically kibitzed herself to death. (A *taller, but also massive, dresser makes it way across the stage*) My brother, Elliot, who is a lawyer in Manhattan, sent my grandmother's belongings to help me out in my situation. Here he is: (*She becomes her brother by putting on a few costume pieces: some Gap-y clothing, different glasses*)

NADYA as ELLIOT: My sister's basically an idiot. What can I tell you? She graduated valedictorian from our high school in New Jersey, wrote this phenomenal essay, and got a scholarship to NYU. When she came out of their performance studies program she was basically a freak. So, she's like doomed to this sad weird academic existence. And she got dumped by her husband. It's like pretty rough. (*He smirks helplessly and disappears*)

NADYA: (*Discarding the outfit*) When he's not a jerk and a typical lawyer, my brother is really very sweet. And recently, because of our Mom's bout with pancreatic cancer, we've become very close. (*An enormous wardrobe moves across the forestage. NADYA is surrounded on three sides by the furniture*) My situation was this: after fifteen years of co-habitation, my husband John no longer wanted me as his wife. John was a vegetarian environmentalist, who had worked as a librarian at Yale. He didn't believe in vaccinating our children, insisted that all of our food be organically grown, our children be home-schooled, and we build a log cabin in the woods, put in a crop and subsistence farm. (A *full-size bed also of an antique, ornate style rolls on of its own accord. NADYA sits at the foot of the bed*) As a cultural materialist feminist performance semiotician of obscure pop cultural folk texts, I was interested in applying feminist theory to narrative phenomena created by nearly illiterate folk art writers who exemplified the otherness typified by those who had, not of any of their own accord, become victim to the hegemony of the white, male, European gaze and who were thus marginalized in odd and poignant ways. Clearly I was not the right person to make a garden grow. (NADYA *crawls up into her bed*) Though I was buried in my work as a young scholar and had allowed John to raise our children, I was terrified of losing them. I was utterly alone in Missouri. My father was . . . is dead. Of AIDS. To me, he was the savior of the world. And now the world will not be saved. (*Pause*) I'm sorry, I have these biblical moments. I've been known to attend the Friday night services and I enjoy praying in Hebrew but the whole patriarchal God thing really gripes me. Still there was this guy there who asked me out for coffee. He's very quiet, handsome . . . but this is all too soon and I'm still legally married so I couldn't possibly . . . his name is Avi for Avigdor. Anyway I'm pretty left-wing, and feminist and all that, but having been raised in conservative Judaism I'm uncomfortable at the Hillel with all its loosey-goosey, warm feeling Judaism. (*Pause*) Call me reactionary, but I'd rather listen to mournful chanting than bopping bongos. (NADYA *lies back in bed. A shaft of moonlight splashes across the bed and there is sound of birds and crickets. Night sounds*) It was one night after Friday night services that I was laying in bed after a weekend without the boys and me not being able to see them for another two days. I stared up at the ceiling, and as a soporific, tried to name off major feminist scholars and their essays, but then realized it would be much faster if I focused on a single essay by a white male author of some renown. I tried Kant at first, but then found that Marshall McCluhan was much more suitable to the task.

NADYA *gently snores. A soft breeze blows across the room. Night sounds. Then a distant sound of a crash. Glass. One of drawers on the large squat dresser slowly pushes open. It slides out and then back in again. Another drawer slides out. Then another; this time with an audible slam out and in. NADYA squints open one eye. A drawer violently slams open and then closed, then another, and another. Clothing shoots out of the drawers onto the bed. Both of NADYA's eyes open, she slowly sits up. Then comes a long woman's moan. It is unearthly. This is ESTHER WISE, NADYA's maternal grandmother.*

ESTHER: Augghhhhhhh!

The doors of the wardrobe fling open and clothing shoots out onto the bed. Another groan is heard from the Wardrobe. This is ROSE, ESTHER's sister and NADYA's great aunt.

ROSE: Oiiiiiiii! Oiiiiiii Vey Is Meir.
ESTHER & ROSE: Auggggggh!!
NADYA: (*Deeply weirded out*) Bubby? Bubby, is that you?

The wardrobe flings open, dresses fly out, along with another woman's voice, older, more cherubic, kooky. This is ROSE WISE, BUBBY's sister.

NADYA: Aunt Rose?

ROSE: Esther! I'm stuck!

ESTHER: So how do you think I'm doing!

NADYA: This is . . .

ESTHER: I've never been so uncomfortable.

ROSE: Wait a second. (*There is a pause. Suddenly the doors of the wardrobe flutter open a bit*) Ah . . .

ESTHER: What?

ROSE: Wiggle a little. You'll feel better.

ESTHER: Oh! (*The drawers of the dresser open and shut a bit*) Ah . . . yes. . . .

NADYA: (*Walking closer, book in hand*) Bubby! Aunt Rose. Are you in there?

ESTHER: Look at her.

ROSE: Don't tell me about it. What is that schmatta she has on?

ESTHER: She sleeps in it. Don't ask me. It's from her father's side. The Finklesteins.

ROSE: All of them crazy.

NADYA: Aunt Rose, can you hear me?

ESTHER: My granddaughter; look at those glasses. A man she'll never find looking like an owl with a crew cut.

ROSE: It's what you get letting your daughter marry a Finklestein. Junk men, all of them.

ESTHER: He ran a very successful salvage business, if you want to know. What are you reading there, darling?

NADYA: Oh, uh, nothing great, just a little Butler, some Showalter. Old stuff.

ROSE: What is she talking about?

NADYA: Feminist theory. It's really neat; very carefully written.

ESTHER: Take it from me, darling, that won't get you a Jewish husband.

The tall dresser suddenly begins to shake and shimmy. Its top drawer bursts open.

SARAH: Auggggh! Ooof! Where am I?

ESTHER: Oi. It's Pirella.

ROSE: Sally.

SARAH: I can't move. Something's wrong.

ESTHER: Little miss perfect.

ROSE: You're a dybbuk.

SARAH: A what?

ESTHER: A dybbuk! Don't you know what that is?! You were the one married to the Rabbi!

ROSE: Sally, you're a ghost. You've possessed that dresser.

SARAH: I can't move. Help!

ESTHER: Just flutter the drawers a little, you'll feel better.

ROSE: Like this. C'mon Esther, we'll show her. (ESTHER AND
ROSE *flutter their drawers*)

SARAH: Oh . . . wait, let me try. (SARAH's *drawers flutter a bit.
Delicately. Ladylike*)

ESTHER: That's it. Kind of.

ROSE: Can't you put a little more life into it?

SARAH: I'm a lady. Not big galumping zaftig cows like the two of
you. Esther, couldn't you have chosen a dresser that was a little
less dumpy?

ESTHER: Pirella! Listen to the way she talks to me!

ROSE: Don't let her get your goat! That's exactly what she wants!

SARAH: If I didn't say anything she'd dress up in any schmatta.
Like that meshugah grand-daughter of yours. Look at her. (*All
three pieces of furniture turn toward* NADYA) She's like every
Finklestein I ever met. A lefty. Hangs out with people who don't
want to work. Her father was a garbage collector.

ESTHER: He wasn't a garbage collector, he was a sanitation engi-
neer. A nice boy.

ROSE: Sally's right, Esther. Sam was a garbage man.

ESTHER: He wrote beautiful stories, that one.

NADYA: (*To the audience*) My father was a writer. He had been an
engineering student in college and designed a recycling plant
on the outskirts of town. He wrote children's books.

SALLY: A loser. I'm sorry, my dear, but your father was a loser. A
nice man, but no spine and no future. Worse! A reform Jew!

NADYA: Aunt Sally, why don't you mind your own business for a
change?

SARAH: Horrible. Nobody in our family is reform. Finklesteins
were all left-wing communists.

ROSE: Like they would be right-wing communists?

ESTHER: They say Frank Sinatra was one of those.

NADYA: Shut up! Why don't you all shut up?!! Just shut up! (*Pauses
a moment*) I can't believe this. I can't believe I'm talking to my
dead Bubby's furniture.

ESTHER: Nobody's criticizing you, darling. Just relax.

SARAH: She could use some criticism. Married a goy.

NADYA: Aunt Sally, we talked about that word! It's demeaning.
He's a non-Jew.

ESTHER: The man looked like a Nazi with the red hair and blue
eyes. Cold.

ROSE: Did your mother ask you to get married so young?

SARAH: I went to college and I got married after two years.

ROSE: (*Imitating her*) I went to college and I married a Rabbi and I'm thin and I'm perfect. Pirella!

SARAH: Maybe you should've stopped eating twenty-four hours a day and you'd have been a little thinner.

ROSE: At least my husband loved me. And didn't run around with ladies from the congregation. Pirella! Boss!

SARAH: You take that back!

NADYA: I'm not going to listen to this. This is a dream. You're all just a dream.

ESTHER: Look, we're upsetting her.

NADYA: No! NO! I'm having another publication anxiety dream. I'm going to get published any day now. And then I won't have these dreams anymore. And my furniture won't talk to me.

SARAH: Don't kid yourself. Life is pain! Trust me! Especially for women.

NADYA: I'm feeling better already.

ROSE: I'm glad you can feel better about yourself with your kids staying with that goyishe John, and you only having them part time. And him asking you for child support.

NADYA: Well, I moved out. I moved out and John doesn't have a job.

ROSE: And you supported him. Oi. With three degrees, you'd think this one would have a little brains.

Suddenly a song is heard in the air. It is a wistful sound of a woman singing in Yiddish.

NADYA: That's . . .

ROSE: It's her again.

ESTHER: Such a pity. So young. Not even sixty-five. Even I lived to my eighties. My poor daughter.

ROSE: (*Sighs*) Cancer.

ESTHER: Cancer.

SARAH: It breaks my heart. I remember, Esther, she had those braids. As thick as your fist. Beautiful auburn hair. And such a good natured child.

The voice becomes louder, clearer, the woman is singing "Oifen Pripichuck," a sweet Yiddish lullaby.

NADYA: Mom?

SARAH: Cancer. Such a terrible disease and so heart-breaking.

ESTHER: I died of cancer and it wasn't so bad.

SARAH: You were so busy talking you didn't notice. The nurse probably had to say, "you have to stop joking now, darling, you're dead!"

NADYA: My Bubby and Tante Sally were twins. Tante Sally was slim, blonde, and beautiful. My Bubby was short and round and a kibitzer. She loved to eat, to drink, to tell jokes and stories. She worked in retail with my grandfather.

ESTHER: Your grandfather was a very good man.

ROSE: Now let's not go too far, Esther.

ESTHER: What could he do? Nathan had colitis and diabetes his whole life.

SARAH: That man was a walking irritable bowel.

ESTHER: He loved me. He didn't care that I was heavy. He treated me like gold.

ROSE: Esther, come back to reality.

NADYA: Bubby, they're telling you the truth! Pop-pop was not good to you. Uh. Uh. (NADYA *is flung forward in the bed, with a scream. She rises slowly; her voice is male, elderly*) Esther!

ROSE: Who was that?

ESTHER: I don't know. There's someone else here, I think.

NADYA: Esther, I like a three-minute egg. Not a two minute egg. Not a four minute egg. Three minutes. Is that too much to ask?

ESTHER: (*Suddenly a mouse*) Yes, darling. Three minutes. I know. (*Pause*) You're right. It's him.

NADYA: I'm a sick man. I've got a moustache and a wound. A wound in my intestines.

ESTHER: I know it hurts.

NADYA: It hurts all the goddamn time. It's like a knife. (A *roaring reverberating moan*) All my pain, and my years in retail. In management. I ran a hotel like clockwork; I ran it like a castle.

SARAH: Here we go.

NADYA: And there you were, at my side.

ESTHER: Yes, my darling.

NADYA: Leading our grandchildren around the Hotel. Like a little hen with her chicks.

ESTHER: The hotel Walt Whitman, in Camden, New Jersey.

NADYA: What a shit hole. That town. But the hotel.

ESTHER: The last bit of class in Camden. And you were the manager. I was so proud.

NADYA: I get no relief from the pain, Esther. Even now.

ESTHER: I'm sorry, Darling.

ROSE: Why don't you let it go, Nathan.

SARAH: Yossi always said the unhappy Dead hang onto life because they are so afraid.

NADYA: Yossi was an smug, Israeli, spoiled boy schmuck.

SARAH: He was class, which you weren't. Who ever heard of a Jew from Jacksonville, Florida. What kind of Jew were you?

ESTHER: Leave him alone, the man has two ulcers.

ROSE: What do you want, Nathan?

NADYA: For my granddaughter to save me. To have a great grand-child that I can enter.

ESTHER: We have two great grandchildren. Dylan and Benjamin.

NADYA: Little goyishe nothings! I'll bite off their foreskins with my teeth. I'll cut their blonde throats!

ROSE: Nadya! Stop it! You're their mother! Nathan, leave that girl's body!

NADYA: (Screams as she wrestles her grandfather's soul out of her body) Aauughhhhhhh!

ESTHER: This is what happens when girls study too much the books.

NADYA *flips forward on the bed, writhing. She stops. She is herself. She sits back up. The sound of a man moaning gently is heard. It is JOHN, NADYA's ex-husband. The moaning increases, his breathing is heard. NADYA becomes agitated.*

NADYA: Bubby? (*She is answered by silence*) Bubby, answer me! Aunt Rose? Aunt Sarah? Where are you?

ESTHER: (*A whisper now*) The key.

NADYA: What?

ESTHER: The key is in an envelope in the top drawer in my dresser. Use it. Open everything. Take what you want.

The breathing and moaning offstage becomes almost ecstatic. The wardrobe begins to shake back and forth. NADYA, in a kind of trance, falls forward again, grunts, pops back up, jumps out of bed, pulls the key out of an envelope in the top drawer, opens all the drawers, and then rifles through the drawers of the dressers, she begins to put things on: old panties, mumus, sweaters, old lady berets, scarves, hundreds of scarves, she adds layer upon layer, raising around the room, until she is huge with clothing. Her breathing and moaning becomes amplified, matching that of the male voice offstage. She moves through the room, elephant like, and then mounts the bed, swaying and moving in the mounds of clothes. She and the voice off-stage reach an orgasmic yell, and she collapses.

JOHN: (*Off-stage, a whisper that echoes like wind*) Nadya.

NADYA: John?

JOHN: Nadya.

NADYA: Stop it. Leave me alone.

JOHN: Nadya, I'm coming to you. (*The wardrobe shakes more, becomes more and more violent*)

NADYA: What am I wearing? Oh shit, oh shit, I gotta stop with the Haagen Daz after ten o'clock.

JOHN: (A *huge monstrous whisper*) NADYA!

The wardrobe bursts open, and JOHN *enters in combat gear. His hair is bright red, and his face is covered with grime and blood.*

NADYA: (*Backs up to the top of the bed*) What do you want?

JOHN: To help you end it all.

NADYA: I'm not going to end it all. I'm going to get tenure.

JOHN: Careerist shit. Hungry?

NADYA: I'm not. Why are you asking?

JOHN: Here's something. I can't eat it. It's meat.

NADYA: Meat?

JOHN: (*Pulls a small hand and arm out of his bag*) I thought you'd like it since you like meat.

NADYA: No.

JOHN: It's Benjamin. He's been getting on my nerves.

NADYA: (*In tears*) John, you love Benjamin! How could you have hurt him?

JOHN: You had to have meat.

NADYA: I didn't want this! YOU'RE THE ONE WHO WANTED OUT!

JOHN: Oh, and here, a little brains fried in butter. Isn't that what meat-eaters find delicious? (*He pulls out a mass of blackened flesh and flings it at her*)

NADYA: No!!!

JOHN: A mother who doesn't love her sons, who cares more about tenure than her children.

NADYA: This is a dream! And I can fight you.

JOHN: Fight me, but you love me. You've always loved me. (JOHN *circles* NADYA, *pulls a lasso from his pocket. Swings it over his head*) You don't understand, Nadya, I'm going to put you back in your closet.

NADYA: I didn't do anything to you! I just tried to be all the things you wanted me to be and I couldn't be in that prison anymore.

JOHN: You really wanted it all didn't you? There! You're nicely bundled now. Now for the slicing and dicing. Let's just talk to our studio audience, shall we? (*Roar of applause*) Ladies in the audience, when preparing your average young Jewish wife for slaughter, do you know the basic steps? Clean her, dress her properly, a little seasoning and tenderizing and then . . . (*Pulls out an enormous, shining knife*)

NADYA: John, don't hurt me.

JOHN *plays the knife across* NADYA's *body,* NADYA *screams. Suddenly a slam from one of the drawers of the dresser.* JOHN *looks up. Then another slam, and another*

NADYA: Bubby, don't let him do this to me!

ESTHER: We're dead, darling, we can't help you. But you can help yourself.

SARAH: You're wearing the clothes of the matriarchs, sweetheart.

ROSE: The mumu's of our darkest desires.

ESTHER: Panty hose that lined the house of Sarah, Rivka, and Leah.

NADYA: Yes!

SARAH: Our power lies within the garments that we acquired.

JOHN: (*Visibly weakening*) Don't listen to them!

ROSE: Rise up against your granola-headed oppressor, Nadya!

ESTHER: You have our berets, our aprons, our brassieres, our schmattas.

NADYA: Yes, your high heels, your muffs, your blouses and skirts,

JOHN: You don't believe any of them. It's all a lie! (*Sinks down to one knee,* NADYA *pulls off her robe*)

SARAH: Our costume jewelry, our purses and handbags,

ROSE: Our compacts, our eye liners, our hidden plastic bags of medications and makeup.

NADYA: The tiny mirrors attached to lipstick containers which flash secret codes when we open and close them.

JOHN: Shut up! Stop listening to them. All that materialistic crap! What about our walks in the woods? The nature centers and cooperative organic farms?

NADYA: (*Rises, circles* JOHN *who has now collapsed on the bed*) The secret karmic qualities of chochkas that line the shelves of our homes like footsoldiers in the war of culture.

ESTHER: Trumpeting our Jewishness, our kvetchiness, our endless kibitzing!

ROSE: We'll always triumph over evil, it's in our scarves, our girdles, our pant suits and our leotards.

JOHN: Nadya, Nadya . . .

SARAH: Our mauve lipstick, Chanel #5, Jean Naté moisturizer and Camay, the beauty cleanser.

ESTHER: Our hair conditioner, shampoo, and plastic shower caps . . .

JOHN *moans and writhes in pain*

NADYA: Wait! Stop! You're killing him!

ROSE: Our sisterhood meetings, the little yarmulkes we knit, my deviled eggs.

ESTHER: My gefilte fish and my roast chicken.

SARAH: My kugel and kasha varnishkes.

ESTHER: My pot roast and browned potatoes.

JOHN *lets out a horrible scream and expires.*

NADYA: Oh, Bubby. Oh, Aunt Rose. Aunt Sally.

JOHN *sinks into the bed, disappearing.*

He's leaving me. I'll be all alone.

ROSE: Let him go. The Goyisha prick! And red hair! What kind of woman marries a man with bright red hair!

NADYA: I loved him.

SARAH: You're forgetting everything darling, everything we told you.

ROSE: The new one is coming. This marriage to the goyishe granolahead; it was doomed from the start.

NADYA: So why didn't anyone ever tell me?

ESTHER: Darling, who can talk to a woman who reads Julie Kristeva? You have all the answers? We're just poor inner voices that spread guilt and self-censorship.

ROSE: We just worm our way into your thoughts and sow doubt and fear.

SARAH: What is family for, after all?

NADYA: Where's my mother? I want my mother. (*Soft moan is heard. A woman singing "Oifen Pripichuck"*) Mom? Can you hear me?

ESTHER: She's nearly gone, Nadya. She'll be with us soon. But right now she's making her move to eternity. It takes a lot of concentration.

NADYA: (*Sobs*) Mom! It's too soon. Too soon. I'm not ready to be an orphan. (*Can't catch her breath*) I can't breathe. I'm so alone. (*She desperately takes off the clothing*)

ESTHER: She had the thickest braids, your mother. And she wouldn't date any man who didn't reach the window on our front door. She was peculiar that way.

SARAH: That's because any man who didn't reach the window on the front door was a midget. She didn't want to marry a midget.

ROSE: Solomon Feingold was not a midget. He was compact. He would have provided for her instead of that Finklestein. Pinko!

NADYA: Tantes! Tell me what I did so wrong? I married the man I loved? I don't understand why he left me. Can anyone out there in the audience tell me? Was is something I did? I know I'm not beautiful, but he loved me once. Why did he stop loving me? Was it because I worked too hard on my PhD? Was it because I was not attentive to him? I gave him two sons and nursed them for three years. Why didn't he love me anymore?

SARAH: We can't tell you, darling.

ROSE: You've got to figure that one out yourself.

ESTHER: It was not to be. That's all. But this one who took you out for coffee.

ROSE: Oh yes. Beshert.

NADYA: He's a student. I can't get serious with a student. He's much older than me too. He's like ten years older than me. And he's still a student.

ESTHER: He's Jewish. He's handsome. He's bright. He asked you out. So go out with him. Give him a chance.

NADYA: Jewish men are whiny. They're materialistic. They want mothers not wives.

ROSE: All lies. Spread by anti-semites. Like yourself.

NADYA: I'm not.

SARAH: Then go to your crazy Hillel with the bongos and go out with him.

NADYA: It's too soon. It's only a few months that we're separated.

SARAH: So we're not saying have sex with him.

ROSE: Don't do that, please.

ESTHER: Just have coffee and cake and chat. Like we old-fashioned folks did.

SARAH: And then, invite him over to meet your boys. Take them all to the park and play with them. If he likes the boys, then go to a show with him.

ROSE: But don't touch him, and don't you let him touch you. Just gaze into each other's eyes. Let him see how sweet and giving you are. And you look into his eyes and fall in love with the sound of his voice, the shape of his ears, the nape of his neck.

ESTHER: And if you can get close to him, see if you can't smell him a little. His cologne. And you wear something nice too. Let him smell you. And always dress carefully, conservatively, except for some little something that's . . .

ROSE: Sexy. A little sexy. Not too much. You don't want him to go insane or anything.

SARAH: And do this for a year and don't touch. And then you'll have built up a nice tension.

ROSE: He'll beg you to marry him. And after he marries you.

ESTHER: The sex will be so good it'll curl your toenails. Four times a night I bet.

NADYA: Bubby!

ROSE: Well, look, that's the fun of it. You keep your hands to yourselves until you marry him. Don't even kiss him.

NADYA: Not one kiss.

ROSE: Beshert, my dear. You're beshert. You'll be kissing soon enough. Just remember those two little boys and how they'll have to adjust to him. Take it slow. So slow.

ESTHER: Romance is in the waiting. You two will build up like pressure cookers.

SARAH: It's the late twentieth century, after all. People are so free with themselves, with sex. If you show a little restraint.

ROSE: A lot of restraint.

ESTHER: After the chuppah, four times a night. Your toenails will curl and fall off, you'll see angels . . .

SARAH: and you'll levitate. Like a yogi. Trust us. He's waiting for you. Over there.

NADYA turns to look. JOHN is now AVI; dark-haired, shy, intellectual, a little nerdy, but nicely put together and very Jewish.

AVI: I don't like the bongos either.

ROSE: (*Whispers*) Beshert.

NADYA walks to him. AVI walks to her.

AVI: I've always wanted to keep a kosher home. My mother's home was kosher. Would you do that?

NADYA: Kosher. I don't know. Maybe. Is it hard?

SARAH: (*Whispers*) Beshert!

AVI: Let's have coffee sometime. Do you like Gramsci? Or Raymond Williams?

NADYA: Yes, I'm . . . Marxist.

AVI: Really? Me too!

ESTHER: (*Whispers*) Beshert!

SARAH: Really, Esther, did your daughter have to marry a Finklestein. They're all pinkos!

ROSE: Pirella! Shhhhhhhhh.

Offstage the voice of NADYA's mother sings "Oifen Pripichuck." NADYA and AVI walk closer to each other. They begin to join the mother off stage, singing "Oifen Pripichuck."

NADYA & AVI:
Oifen pripichuck brent a fayerl,
un in shtub is heys.
Un der rebe lernt kleyne kinderlekh
Dem alef-beyz . . .

(English translation)
At the fireplace a little fire burns
And in the room it's warm,
And the Rabbi teaches little children
The aleph-bet . . .

AVI *whips out a handkerchief and holds it out to* NADYA *who grasps hold of it. They circle each other.* ROSE, ESTHER, *and* SARAH *audibly sigh, their drawers quivering. The lights fade slowly with a final spot on* AVI *and* NADYA, *slowly smiling, circling each other in peace.*

END OF THE PLAY

In *Beshert*, David has explored dreams from a number of angles. He used dreams as a way of entering the world of the character, and dreams inform the style of the play throughout. The other interesting element is that Nadya dreams her own past, present, and future, so that the play seems like a self-willed fantasy about what Nadya wants to happen but can't get to until she's worked through some of her needs and fears through dreaming.

This is a powerful use of an unusual process. David Crespy combines the deeply intuitive parts of himself with the intellectual parts to create a nonlinear work that has great resonance for most of us. Returning to an earlier quote from David is the best summary: "Using dreaming and dream structure in my plays allows me make the best use of theatricality by speaking in a shorthand everyone can understand, the language of dreams."

II

PART

Journeys

"One doesn't discover new lands without consenting to lose sight of the shore for a very long time."
—Andre Gide

"The real voyage of discovery consists not in seeking new landscapes but in having new eyes."
—Marcel Proust

THE PLAYWRIGHTS REPRESENTED IN THIS GROUPING are Elena Carrillo, Gary Garrison, and Velina Hasu Houston. Each began with one play in response to the prompt, and ended up with an altogether different play.

As the quotes above imply, there is considerable risk in this kind of process—and considerable payoff. The "personality of process" in this group of playwrights is a willingness to pursue a path to completion even though it may lead to a destination that is not quite right. As we will see, each playwright in Part II fashions a first play that works, but does not entirely satisfy their own taste and theatrical perspective. To reject what others might have found sufficient reveals a spirit that is committed to search for its best levels of expression, even if it means throwing out or letting go of an initial effort. Writing "to order"—by which I mean to satisfy the prompt requirement of this book—is no easy task.

This is not to suggest that the playwrights in Parts I and III are any less courageous or self-demanding. The chief distinction is that the playwrights of Part II wrote one play first, then finished with an entirely new play. This may not reflect accurately their normal process, but it turned out this way for the book, which affords us an opportunity to observe some intriguing struggles, as well as bold uses of process and rewriting.

3

CHAPTER

Elena Carrillo:
One Wasp

"THE JOY OF TAKING THE JOURNEY"

ELENA CARRILLO MAY BE THE MOST ECLECTIC OF THE playwrights. She has published fiction and poetry, and won awards for her plays and fiction. She served as editor of the *Rio Grande Review* for two years, and co-edited *The Student's Guide to Playwriting Opportunities.* Elena is also very knowledgeable about computers, has published numerous articles in the field, and works as a technical writer. Lastly, she is a history buff, with particular interests in the Civil War (with a novel-in-progress about the post-war era), and Victorian England. This eclectic quality may be the root of her restless search for the right play for this book.

Elena's work resulted in not one but three plays as she struggled to find a response to the "key" prompt that felt natural to her. Her efforts to write a play that really worked for her is the essence of what *Playwriting Master Class* intends to convey: Writing is not just the act of recording or laying out a story, but a search as well through one's own values and life experiences to connect meaningfully with the inner and outer worlds. Elena's journal will provide us with a variety of views on this search.

We will examine a portion of her first play, *The Poodle Play*, several drafts of *Three Strings*, the elusive second play, and a full draft of *One Wasp*, the final play.

The Poodle Play was never completed, but Elena's thoughts

about the piece provide us with an excellent introduction to her process. To get a bit of grounding, here are the opening moments of *The Poodle Play*:

Excerpt from **The Poodle Play**

> At Rise: LEO and TENCHA *lean across from one another over a desk in an office. They are breathing hard as if they've been chasing each other around. They both look angry. Between their huffing, we hear the faint sounds of a dog barking. The sound seems to be coming from inside a large file-cabinet. LEO finally leans back and relaxes a little.*

LEO: All right. That's enough.

TENCHA: I agree. (*Beat*) Well?

LEO: Well?

TENCHA: Are you going to give me the key or not?

> LEO *holds up the key as if he might, then puts it into the desk drawer and closes it pointedly.*

LEO: No.

TENCHA: Leo . . .

LEO: Give me one good reason why I should!

TENCHA: Leo!

LEO: One!

TENCHA: If you don't give me that key right now, I'm calling the SPCA.

LEO: (*Laughs*) My god you're being dramatic.

TENCHA: That little dog is going to die.

LEO: He's fine. He's barking isn't he?

TENCHA: Leo, that's not funny. He'll run out of air and you know it.

LEO: It's a file cabinet, not a fireproof safe, Tencha. He's fine!

TENCHA: This is pointless. If anything happens to that dog we'll be the first ones they suspect.

LEO: What do you mean *we*?

TENCHA: You wouldn't!

LEO: You're the one who made the big fuss at the reading. You're the one who bolted right out of her chair and shouted for all the world to hear: "The *dog*? Was she insane?"

TENCHA: We were all shocked. I saw your reaction too.

LEO: Well I wasn't the one announcing it to the press.

TENCHA: You won't get a dime if you kill that little mutt and try to pin it on me, Mister. Your hand prints are all over the murder weapon.

LEO: What weapon?

TENCHA: (*Points to the file cabinet*) That!

From inside we hear a very pitiful whine.

Elena's journal entries are very helpful in letting us into her process with the first play of her journey. Her journal, as you will see, is wonderfully detailed and provides us with many insights on her thinking from start to finish.

March 17—Draft 1—The Poodle Play

I begin with my first image for the "key play": A little yappy dog is locked in a file cabinet. The key to the cabinet is locked in a desk drawer. A man and woman are fighting over the key. The woman wants to save the dog, but in truth, they both want the dog dead.

I already question this image before it's even out of the gate. The scenario is rather obvious, after all, I think, but it's my self-appointed task to try to work through the exercise without a whole lot of intellectual intervention here, so I will plow forward and see what comes of this initial spark.

The truth of this is that I have in the back of my head an image that was born out of a play reading I just attended. The reading was of a monologue in which a character goes through psychological layers of exposition using a single prop and metaphor (a circle) to become many different things—a steering wheel, a tire swing, a plate, etc. The monologue was about this character's inability to resolve a conflict between his father and the woman he married, and how the relationship with the father has worn on the marriage.

In a later clarification, Elena explains more about the image from the play reading, which ultimately led to her final play and true destination: *One Wasp.*

> At one point in the reading, the character talks about splitting up with the wife and there is a digression concerning martini glasses that hung on a rack in the kitchen. This was where the image of the "glass bat" came to mind. I wanted to write a play called "Glass Bats," but wanted to keep the props simple and couldn't wrap my brain around how to juggle a martini glass and a key, so I didn't immediately see this idea as a candidate for writing at this time.

It's interesting to see that Elena had the "key," in effect, to the last play all along, yet needed to take such a complex route to get there. This is an ideal reminder to all of us who write plays that we work very hard to arrive at our final destinations. Some plays come easily, of course, but the vast majority do not. Even seemingly "easy" pieces, such as ten-minute plays, often resist our grasp.

What's evident in Elena's process (and those of our other playwrights) is the willingness to learn by reaching farther and digging deeper on each try, and being willing to fail. Those of us who teach remind our students constantly that there is always more to learn from failure than success, though only half believe us. Elena's struggle to find the play that best worked for her at the time she worked on this project, *and* to incorporate the prompt is an excellent yardstick for those disbelievers.

Her journal continues the commentary on *The Poodle Play*:

March 19—Draft 1—The Poodle Play
Still not happy with the basic premise of this play. Not only do I feel like it's too "naturalistic" in its approach, but it's also neither a fresh take nor a particularly clever take on an old theme: bloodsucking relatives vie for an inheritance and have to wrestle it from the family cat/dog/gerbil/laundry man/whatever. The dialogue comes easily enough because the premise is rather simple and the argument itself is already destined to go in X way—it's a pretty simple, straightforward argument, after all.

The identity of the man and the woman is also very nebulous to me. I thought at first that they might be husband and wife, but that creates a dynamic that doesn't make sense—if that were the case (they being married) then they would be working together, not at odds. If they were siblings, however, they might start out working together and then become competitive. This, however, strikes me as predictable as everything else in the premise.

March 20—Draft 1—The Poodle Play
Slogging through to a draft, I think that having a whole shape of the play established will help me better visualize what can be done with it, but I'm not seeing much room for major overhauling. It's simply a short play about two people arguing over a dog in a file cabinet. It has no layers, no real intrigue, and no honest dramatic tension for me. In order to improve on this run-of-the-mill scene, I feel like I would have to start completely from scratch.

At this point, Elena shifts gears, moving toward *Three Strings*, which appears to be a radical departure from *The Poodle*

Play, but is actually connected, as we shall see. Leaving behind one play to begin another is a bold step, and one that paid off well.

Writers often get hung up on their first idea, trying to *make* it work by sheer force of will, which can be a disastrous choice. The idea may be a weak one, or it may be one that needs more time to mature in the writer's mind. In either case, it probably needs to go in the proverbial drawer for a while, which can be scary. Some writers tend to worry that they'll never have another idea, or if they let go of their initial concept it will vanish. It's important to be as honest with one-self as possible about a given work in order to see how you really feel about it. If the play is no longer flowing, if it is no fun to write, perhaps it's time to move on, and see what's next. It's a risk, but in artistic efforts nothing comes of playing it safe. (Of course, there are writers who leap from project to project, never completing most of them, but that is a different kettle of fish.)

Elena's articulation of her decision to shift from *The Poodle Play* to *Three Strings* is both insightful and funny. Maintaining a sense of humor about our work may be one of the most important tools playwrights have.

March 27—Draft 1—*Three Strings*

Starting from scratch is sometimes the best thing you can do when an idea has gone gaflooey on you. I could spend a great deal of time turning that dog in the cabinet idea upside down and backwards and inside out, but I don't think I could make it fly no matter what I do to it—it simply isn't working, isn't giving me the kind of expression I was hoping for.

What I did then, was just divest myself of all the "rules" of the assignment (not that there were any real rules to begin with). Sometimes the brain creates blocks when there is nothing standing in your way simply because it feels it needs to work against something or else: if the writing comes too easily, then it wasn't really "work," and therefore not valid. So I just let some images waft into my head, specifically not thinking about keys or drawers, but thinking about faces, images, actions—asking myself the question that often helps me get started: if I were in a theatre right now, what is it that I would like to be seeing on the stage?

In this case, it truly wasn't a little dog locked in a cabinet while two people fought, it was something a little darker, and much less grounded in reality.

New Image: Three women, three generations. A church. The somber tone of a funeral. The only hold-over from the first idea is the idea that these characters are dressed for a funeral (as I had imagined the first characters dressed in mourning attire for the reading of the will which made the dog the sole beneficiary).

Elena elaborated in a later e-mail about her decision to move on from *The Poodle Play*:

> I knew that *The Poodle Play* was a dead duck from the start, but I also knew I had to write it—perhaps to prove to myself that it was a dead duck. It was the scene which was most immediate in my brain when I first sat down to write, and was most imme- diately active, which I wanted—I liked the idea of opening a scene with two people chasing each other around a desk, but never had any clue as to how I could sustain it. In moving on to *Three Strings*, I wanted to make amends for having plunged into the project in what I thought was a frivolous manner. I don't know how to be non-self-critical in this step. I never took *The Poodle Play* seriously, and the decision to start a new draft was based on my preparedness to write something less silly.

The move toward *Three Strings* came a bit closer to her own background. Elena is second generation Mexican-American (with a little German thrown in for good measure). Some of her work reflects life on the border, and issues related to the contemporary Hispanic family. *Three Strings* reflects the latter, and incorporates some elements of Elena's Catholic upbring- ing as well.

Three Strings also includes elements which are, as Elena mentions in the previous journal entry, "less grounded in real- ity." In other words, we can find our work lacking because it doesn't suit the mode of expression we want to use at a given point. In fact, *Three Strings* is more a Gregorian chant than a play, as Elena herself observes below. As such, it uses sound in ways that are innovative: the voices speak inner thoughts— and not always such charitable thoughts—in outward, rhyth- mic patterns, creating a theatrical expression of prayer and chanting. Elena comments on this quality of sound in her next journal entry:

April 1—Three Strings
Before I began writing, I thought for a while what I wanted the play to "sound" like. I am not a great fan of musical theatre, but I do think that language is, at heart, musical and lyrical and its own kind of music.

I had previously toyed with this idea in a full-length play, with some degree of success, I thought, though finding a way for the play to be accessible on the page for evaluators instead of a "need to hear it" sort of thing, made it difficult to judge the real success of the experiment.

In this play, I have the opportunity to work more intimately with what I may have been trying to tackle on too large a scale: creating text that could then translate easily to a kind of rhythm or musicality based on the acting choices and direction given. In this way, the play can be layered with sound even beyond the text provided.

The following is the second draft of *Three Strings* . The cast description included here will not differ in the subsequent drafts, and therefore won't be repeated.

Second Draft of Three Strings
At Rise: Three women stand side by side facing out. They are dressed for a funeral. The first woman, NANA, is very old, wears black clothes, and a black veil which covers her hair, but not her face. The second woman is her daughter, MAMA, who is also in black, looking very chic, with too much make-up and a fancy hat. The third woman is her daughter, ANNA, younger than twenty, dressed fashionably in muted colors. All three women hold rosaries in their hands. Instead of crosses at the end of their rosaries, each string of beads ends with a large gold key. They make the sign of the "cross" but draw a different shape—a circle and an "L" perhaps—something which suggests a key. They begin. During the first part of the rosary, the actors should establish the mood, manners, and attitudes of each character.

ALL: Our Father, locked away in heaven, hallowed be thy name. Thy kingdom come, thy will be done, on earth as it is in heaven. Give us this day, the key to understanding, and forgive us our trespasses as we forgive those who trespass against us. Lead us not into temptation, but deliver us from evil, Amen. Hail Mary full of grace, the Lord is with thee. Blessed art thou among women and blessed is the key to thy heart always. Holy Mary, mother of God, pray for us sinners, now and at the hour of our death.

MAMA *and* ANNA *continue the rosary quietly.*

NANA: Oh holy God in your infinite mercy, look kindly on my brother Fructoso. I know he was not always a good religious man, but he was a hard worker and loved his family deeply.

NANA *and* ANNA *continue to pray the rosary quietly.*

MAMA: Ay Dios (*Not a supplication*), what was it Gina said? Uncle Fructoso—a womanizing lout? I can't believe she would say something like that. *Today* of all days! At his funeral you would think the poor man would deserve some respect. How would Aunt Carmen feel if she heard Gina talk like that?

MAMA *and* NANA *continue to pray. These alternating rounds continue throughout the duration of the play so that the constant sound of the rosary being recited underscores the voices.*

ANNA: (*Impatiently*) This sucks.

NANA: And forgive him, oh Lord, for all of his trespasses, for I know there were many. He was a loving father to his two boys and a good husband in spite of his failings. He was a good man, Lord. But he was a man, after all.

MAMA: And what was that she said about him and Marta Velasquez? My god, could it be true? Right there in the parking lot of the Piggly Wiggly? I shouldn't think about that. No, I shouldn't even *think* about it. I mean—that man's dead for god's sake. Oh. I shouldn't think "for god's sake," should I? Not in the church. Sorry God. Sorry.

ANNA: God this sucks.

NANA: I loved my brother, Lord. And I know that my love alone cannot be enough to save him, but please take it under consideration when you judge him. He was loved after all, and gave much love—maybe too much in the wrong way, but his intentions were always good.

MAMA: Gina probably only said that because she always hated Fructoso. She never said anything good about him. Probably because she was in love with him, the poor thing.

ANNA: This really really sucks.

NANA: I know, I know, the road to hell is paved with good intentions, but please, Lord—it's not as if he did not work hard and support his family in spite of his restless spirit.

MAMA: He was such a handsome man so many years ago. And he did marry Maria DeLaTorre and she and Gina were friends in high school. Maybe not so good friends. Maybe she made the whole thing up. But so cruel after all these years? And today of all days?

ANNA: This sucks, like big time.

NANA: And, in your name, remember how he took in Beto's sister Velia when her fiance was killed in Korea—Bless those who suffer, Lord—out of only kindness he took her into his home and gave her a room to call her own.

MAMA: I wonder if he and Velia Fuentes . . . no. Not in the house. Not with Carmen right there in the house! Gina was jealous—that's why she said what she said . . . that's all.

ANNA: (*Sing-songy*) Suh-ucks.

NANA: It was these charitable acts, Lord. He gave to everybody. And so it was no wonder he never had money. He was a generous man.

MAMA: Then again, it would explain why he and Carmen never had any money—even when the boys were grown, they were always flat broke. Carmen never bought a new refrigerator in the twenty-five years that they were married.

ANNA: I'm not going to say sucks anymore.

NANA: That man worked forty years of his life with his hands. Worked hard. And never asked anybody for anything.

MAMA: He was always asking my Enrique for money. Always always always.

ANNA: You shouldn't say "sucks" in church.

NANA: He had the heart of a good man, Lord.

MAMA: He was an embarrassment to poor Carmen

ANNA: But this *does* suck.

NANA: A good, good man.

MAMA: And there was his drinking, I know, but that doesn't mean that he was unfaithful. Does it?

ANNA: I feel bad because I didn't even know him. Last time I saw him he was drunk and ringing the doorbell at 6 A.M. to ask for a cigarette.

NANA: A good good heart.

MAMA: He was just really pathetic.

ANNA: I thought he was a bum or something.

NANA: He bore no malice toward anyone.

MAMA: I always hated it when he was around.

ANNA: I was only a kid then. Mama shooed me away from the door.

NANA: He only wanted to live a good life, Lord.

MAMA: Always coming over to ask for cigarettes.

ANNA: She was yelling at him like he was some kind of pervert or something.

NANA: Take all these things into consideration.

MAMA: I know he was family, but what a disgrace!
ANNA: He walked away sort of limping the way drunk people do—
   one foot steadier than the other.
NANA: And I know you will find room to forgive him.
MAMA: And I just couldn't even look Carmen in the eyes.
ANNA: I felt sorry for him.
NANA: You will take pity on his soul.
MAMA: Can hardly look at her now.
ANNA: Well I'm sorry you died, Uncle Fructoso.
NANA: Rest in everlasting Peace, Fructoso.
MAMA: May God have mercy on your soul.
ALL: Amen.

> Simultaneously, the women put away their rosaries. ANNA wraps hers
> around her wrist and nods approvingly at this new fashion accessory.
> MAMA tosses her rosary irreverently into her purse and shakes it to the
> bottom with all the loose change. NANA places hers carefully into a drawer
> in the podium. Blackout. End of Play.

The next series of journal entries are very helpful in understanding the evolution of *Three Strings*.

April 26—Draft 3—*Three Strings*

I am letting the play sit a long long while after the third draft in
order to let it soak in, to let it "think about me" as someone once
said. Working too closely with the material and under the self-
imposed pressures of deadlines and that devil named "quality,"
it's sometimes best for me to pull waaaay back and away from
the project in order to salvage some perspective (or, rather,
regain it).

On a very basic level, I am interested in what I've done up to this
point—not crazy about it, but certainly intrigued by the possibilities
for further drafting. Right now I feel that there is no real story, but I
am not one-hundred percent sure that this is about "story" for me.
If I think of this piece as music, then for me "story" is something
which should be implied or suggested, rather than actualized. I
think often of the pervasiveness of music television and video
music—there must be a bridge between the stage and that medium
and many people have dabbled in all sorts of hybrids, but what
would a fusion which maintains the most essential integrities of
both mediums actually look like? From here I want to try different
things "musically" with the draft, particularly the idea of the characters speaking in "rounds" and trying to find a rhythm where it could
be sung if there was actual music.

April 27—Draft 4—Three Strings

In the 4th draft, the first thing I realized is that I had to let go of the notion of these characters speaking in rounds—it finally did not make sense to me, since in an orchestra, a viola does not wait until the violin has played its note, while the cello waits for the viola, but they all play together and as counterpoint in harmony (or intentional disharmony depending on the music you prefer). Not only is the turn-taking structure that I built into the play confining, but it also creates predictable rhythms.

I am also feeling that the indication of the background rosary may not be enough to integrate the prayer into the music of the dialogue. Scripting the prayer (and liberally editing and choosing particular repetitions) may prove far more effective.

May 2—Draft 5—Three Strings

I had been thinking a long time about how it was important to me that the key really play a more integral part in the action of the play, and when I began to work at breaking down the text into a more disjointed "score," I was struck with the idea that however much I wanted this piece to be sort of a waving sea frond without a particular Aristotelian drive, it was lacking something—one of the characters needed to be struggling against an obstacle regardless of however much I wanted to fight the urge to give the play an "arc." The key was easily the solution to the problem. If the question was: what should happen to the key, and if the characters all had a stake in the outcome of the key's final disposition, then there would be a stronger tie to the overall "event."

Although I am only halfway through incorporating this idea (draft 5), I think it is helping to shape the play nicely. It has also brought focus to what should and should not be said about Uncle Fructoso as a character. Much of what I had written in earlier drafts is being eliminated in order to focus down on this issue of the key and Fructoso's secrets.

May 3—Draft 5—Three Strings

It's interesting to me how even though I changed the circumstances of the play I had initially begun with, I still ended up with the same theme—the end results of someone's death impacting on a set of characters who then must grapple (or in Anna's case not grapple) with the aftermath.

I'm stopping at draft 5 for the time being because although I feel like the play needs work, I am also having a hard time staying focused on the individual character's throughlines—and this is where a reading would be most useful. I do not think the play is finished in any way at this point, but I do need to step back from it and get some perspective on whether the basic ideas are working—and whether there is clearly something to track through it—that it starts and finishes in a satisfying way. Right now I'm still feeling like it's missing an element, but I have to give it some breathing room to see if it might not answer some of its own questions here.

I feel like I'm forcing the story. It's not my usual process to "make up" the story. I usually let the story dictate itself to me. In this case, I am twisting its arm and it's resisting, of course.

In the fifth draft, Elena makes a huge leap forward into the language of the piece—creating a "score" for it, as mentioned in the journal. She maintains the alternating sentence structure, but breaks it up into much smaller units and incorporates overlapping dialogue as well, so that we have solo voices mixed in with trios ("ALL") and duets ("NANA/MAMA"). This shift, combined with her efforts to integrate the key element more, creates a rather different play from the second draft, though the essential plot has not changed. One can certainly hear the music more clearly, and the issue of the dead man's secrets have a different, more urgent quality now.

Another major change is the relationship of the characters to Uncle Fructoso, who has now become Nana's son, Mama's brother, and Anna's uncle.

(Note: the opening description of the characters and their actions remains the same.)

Fifth Draft of Three Strings

NANA: Our Father . . .

ALL: . . . locked away in heaven . . .

MAMA: . . . hallowed be thy name.

ALL: Thy kingdom come, thy will be done, on earth as it is in heaven.

NANA: Give us this day . . .

ALL: . . . the key to understanding . . .

MAMA: . . . and forgive us our trespasses as we forgive those who trespass against us.

ALL: Lead us not into temptation, but deliver us from evil, Amen.

The women continue to pray in alternating rounds. This continues throughout the duration of the play so that the constant recitation of the rosary underscores the voices.

ALL: (*Quietly underscoring each other*) Hail Mary full of grace, the Lord is with thee. Blessed art thou among women and blessed is the key to thy heart always. Holy Mary, mother of God, pray for us sinners, now and at the hour of our death.

NANA: Oh holy God in your infinite mercy, look kindly on my son Fructoso.

ANNA: Oh Lord (*Not a supplication*), I didn't know Uncle Fructoso very well.

NANA/MAMA: He was a man of many secrets.

MAMA: Though, now that he is dead, I am sure there will be answers.

NANA: He was a quiet man. Reserved in his confidences.

MAMA: I have to admit I am just burning with curiosity.

NANA: His life was a curiosity.

NANA/MAMA: But his private letters could/will no doubt reveal him.

MAMA: And might say at last if what Gina said is true.

NANA: Gina spoke so badly of him.

MAMA: Fructoso—a womanizing lout. . . . She was pretty hard on him.

NANA/MAMA: Unfairly.

MAMA: But we will know now.

NANA: I have the key to his letters, Lord. He entrusted it to my safe-keeping.

MAMA: Nana has the key.

NANA: I know he was not always a good religious man.

MAMA: I shouldn't think about these things.

NANA: But he was a hard worker and loved his family deeply.

MAMA: *Today* of all days—at his funeral—the poor man deserves some respect.

ANNA: (*Impatiently*) This sucks.

NANA: And forgive us.

ALL: And forgive us our trespasses.

NANA: And forgive him, oh Lord, for all of his trespasses, for I know there were many.

MAMA: And even if what Gina said is true . . .

NANA: He was a loving father to his two boys and a good husband in spite of his failings.

MAMA: And it could be . . .

NANA: He was a good man, Lord, but . . .

MAMA/NANA: . . . he was a man, after all.

MAMA: Could it have been true . . .

NANA: Even if it was true . . .

MAMA/NANA: . . . about him and Marta Velasquez . . . .

MAMA: My god, could it have been true?

NANA: I shouldn't think about that.

MAMA/NANA: No, I shouldn't even *think* about it.

MAMA: I mean—for god's sake—oh, I shouldn't think that. Not in the church. Sorry God. Sorry God. Sorry . . .

ANNA: . . . God this sucks.

NANA/MAMA: I loved him, Lord.

NANA: And I know that my love alone cannot be enough to save him, but please take it under consideration when you judge him.

MAMA: However he may be judged.

NANA: He was loved after all, and gave much love—maybe too much in the wrong way, but . . .

MAMA/NANA: . . . I know his intentions were always good.

MAMA: Gina always hated Fructoso. That's why she never said anything good about him.

NANA: And Lord help Gina to heal the anger in her heart.

MAMA/NANA: She was in love with him.

MAMA: Poor thing.

ANNA: This really really sucks.

NANA: The road to hell . . .

MAMA/NANA: . . . is paved with good intentions.

NANA: But he is gone now, Lord.

MAMA: And now he is gone.

NANA: And are questions better than answers?

MAMA: And questions can be answered now.

NANA/MAMA: Answers can be deadly.

ANNA: This sucks, like big time.

NANA: Bless those who suffer, Lord.

MAMA: How poor Carmen has suffered already.

NANA: Bless those who suffer.

MAMA: Being married to a drunk, a womanizer . . . .

ANNA: (*Sing-songy*) Suh-ucks.

NANA: He gave to everybody. He was a generous man.

MAMA: He and Carmen never had any money—even when the boys were grown, they were always flat broke.

ANNA: I'm not going to say sucks anymore.

NANA: He worked forty years with his hands. Worked hard.

MAMA: He never worked.

NANA: And never asked anybody for anything.

MAMA: He was always asking for money.

NANA: Never asked for anything. Always was giving.

MAMA/NANA: Always always always.

ANNA: You shouldn't say "sucks" in church.
NANA: He had the heart of a good man, Lord.
MAMA: He was an embarrassment to poor Carmen
ANNA: But this *does* suck.
NANA: A good, good man.
ANNA: I didn't even know him. Last time I saw him he was drunk—ringing the doorbell at 6 A.M. to ask for a cigarette.
NANA: A good good heart.
MAMA: Pathetic.
ANNA: I thought he was a bum or something.
NANA: He bore no malice toward anyone.
MAMA: As his letters will prove, I'm sure.
ANNA: I was only a kid then.
NANA: He only wanted to live a good life, Lord.
MAMA: Poor Carmen, the disgrace of it all.
NANA: Lord, take all these things into consideration.
MAMA: I know he was family, but what a disgrace!
ANNA: He walked away sort of limping the way drunk people do—one foot steadier than the other.
NANA: And I know you will find room to forgive him.
MAMA: I just couldn't even look Carmen in the eyes.
ANNA: I felt sorry for him.
NANA: Take pity.
MAMA: Can hardly look at her now.
NANA: Pity, Lord.
MAMA: And poor Nana. He was her golden child.
NANA: Fructoso, my golden child.
MAMA/NANA: Golden.
MAMA: Everyone will know now.
ANNA: I wish I had known him.
NANA: Nobody knew you.

The women stop praying. NANA *holds up the key contemplatively.*

ALL: What should/would/could I do?
ANNA: Sorry you died, Uncle F.
ALL: Rest in everlasting peace.
NANA: Rest in everlasting peace, Fructoso.
MAMA: (*Vindictively*) May God have mercy on your soul.
ALL: Mercy on your soul.
NANA: Amen.
MAMA: Amen.
ALL: Amen.
ANNA: Amen.

> *Simultaneously, the women put away their rosaries. ANNA wraps hers around her wrist and nods approvingly at this new fashion accessory. MAMA tosses her rosary irreverently into her purse and shakes it to the bottom with all the loose change. NANA takes hers off, thinks about it, and then finally places hers carefully into the casket. She closes the lid slowly and makes a final sign of the cross. Blackout. End of Play.*

Following this draft, Elena makes a decision to try an exploration intended to go deeper into the characters:

May 4—Monologues—Three Strings

I broke the play down into three playlettes (essentially three monologues—one from each character). This helped me to see the path each character takes throughout the short duration of the play. I think it was most helpful because it helped isolate the throughlines for each character so that I could address their particular needs one at a time, rather than worry so much about the structure or the rhythm for the time being.

Mama's character feels the least accurately developed, so I'm taking more time with recreating her character and her drives. I'm much clearer about Nana, though I feel she needs to be expressed more clearly as well—if the largest decision to make in the course of this event is Nana's, then she needs to have the boldest arc, and right now she's sort of meandering toward her resolution without any real struggle.

Anna's character is the least developed, but I think that's appropriate for her since she is basically indifferent to the funeral proceedings and sort of a counterpoint to the busy heads of her progenitors. I like that she doesn't have much to say and that her comments are limited to a very narrow knowledge of the deceased.

I am also toying with the idea of taking away the power of the secret that Fructoso is hiding. (and changing his name for God's sake). I wonder, if we don't know what it is that Fructoso did (and imply several things through the character's comments), then maybe we'll have a more powerful dynamic. He's gone from being brother to son—now I'm also thinking that maybe he should be husband—then the implication can be that he was unfaithful or a child molester, or what?

I feel like the sorcerer's apprentice now because now I don't have just one story to wrestle with, I have FOUR! While breaking out the characters is very helpful to me usually (to be able to look at throughlines, etc.), it's overwhelming at this stage. It magnifies the problems I see in the script: that the story is unfocused and that the rhythm and action are dictated too much by the structure.

The monologue exploration of *Three Strings* follows. Since the essence of what each character says from the fifth draft to this exploration doesn't change that much, only the first monologue is excerpted. It's important to note, however, that Elena is still working at the rhythmic integration. The basic etude she's using is where the writer separates all of one character's lines from the script to see what that character says without reference to any other lines. This is a very useful etude because it can show you immediately if a character is passive or repetitious. It is also an etude born of the computer age, since retyping all this would be a lot of frustrating work.

What Elena does here is somewhat different from the essential etude. She refers to these as "playlettes," because each piece is not simply one character's lines pulled out. Instead, each playlette is a focus on one character while the other characters remain involved, but away from the forefront; the story is still told.

Notice as well that Fructoso has returned to being Nana's brother now, and not her son.

Excerpt from *Three Strings*: Nana's Monologue

At Rise: Three women dressed for a funeral etc. They make the sign of the "cross" etc., and begin the rosary.

NANA: Our Father . . . etc.

The women continue to pray throughout the duration of the play so that the constant recitation of the rosary underscores the voices.

ALL: Hail Mary full of grace, etc.

NANA: Oh holy God in your infinite mercy, look kindly on my brother Fructoso.

MAMA/NANA: He was a man of many secrets.

NANA: He was a quiet man. Reserved in his confidences. His life was a curiosity.

MAMA/NANA: But his private letters could/will no doubt reveal him.

NANA: Gina spoke so badly of him.

MAMA/NANA: Unfairly.

NANA: I have the key to his letters, Lord. He entrusted it to my safe-keeping. I know he was not always a good religious man. But he was a hard worker and loved his family deeply. And forgive us.

ALL: And forgive us our trespasses.

NANA: And forgive him, oh Lord, for all of his trespasses, for I know there were many. He was a loving father to his two boys and a good husband in spite of his failings. He was a good man, Lord, but . . .

MAMA/NANA: . . . he was a man, after all.

NANA: Even if it was true . . .

MAMA/NANA: . . . about him and Marta Velasquez . . .

NANA: I shouldn't think about that.

MAMA/NANA: No, I shouldn't even *think* about it. I loved him, Lord.

NANA: And I know that my love alone cannot be enough to save him, but please take it under consideration when you judge him. He was loved after all, and gave much love—maybe too much in the wrong way, but . . .

MAMA/NANA: . . . I know his intentions were always good.

NANA: And Lord help Gina to heal the anger in her heart.

MAMA/NANA: She was in love with him.

NANA: The road to hell . . .

MAMA/NANA: . . . is paved with good intentions.

NANA: But he is gone now, Lord. And are questions better than answers?

MAMA/NANA: Answers can be deadly.

NANA: Bless those who suffer, Lord. Bless those who suffer. He gave to everybody. He was a generous man. He worked forty years with his hands. Worked hard. And never asked anybody for anything. Never asked for anything. Always was giving.

MAMA/NANA: Always always always.

NANA: He had the heart of a good man, Lord. A good, good man. A good good heart. He bore no malice toward anyone. He only wanted to live a good life, Lord. Lord, take all these things into consideration. And I know you will find room to forgive him. Take pity. Pity, Lord Fructoso, my golden son.

MAMA/NANA: Golden.

NANA: Nobody knew you.

The women stop praying. NANA *holds up the key contemplatively.*

ALL: What should/would/could I do?

NANA: Rest in everlasting peace. Rest in everlasting peace, Fructoso.

ALL: Mercy on your soul.

NANA: Amen.

ALL: Amen.

End of Play

As we can see from the following journal entries, Elena's struggle with *Three Strings* continued.

May 5—Draft 6—*Three* Strings

Changed Fructoso's name to Tomás—that's a lot better. I'm going to print the latest draft and live with it for the evening before I decide whether to change my angle on the "secret". I have already decided also that the characters need to be speaking more particularly to somebody—Nana to God, Mama to Tomás, and Anna to . . . well I'm not sure about her just yet.

May 18—Draft 7—*Three* Strings

Going through another major rewrite to implement the changes I have been considering for the last few days. I'm going to print out the three separate monologues again in order to make the changes and compare the threads. The most significant thing that will happen in doing this is that Anna's role in the flow will become significantly more important. My intention is to leave a big ol' question mark lingering over Anna's head—what does she know or understand about her uncle? I am also eliminating the Gina thing. It creates confusion because the characters are talking about someone who isn't on stage, and there's no easy exposition to explain her relationship to the family, to the uncle, etc.

May 19—*Handwritten draft*—*Three* Strings

Removing the play from the realm of the computer is, for me, a last-ditch effort to save the dying whale. Although I have not yet given up on the piece going somewhere at this point, I think that any time I return to writing pen-to-paper, it's a clear indication that there is an innate desire to connect back to something more "real." I think, at this point in the draft, I'm trying to accept that I am not writing for myself, but writing for what I assume about the audience's expectations of me—a Hispanic woman writer should write about Hispanic women. This has always played false for me, no matter how many different ways I've approached it, and frankly, this play is no different

Having settled into the final intention of the piece, I hand-wrote the three monologues on a single set of pages—using one color for each character and writing the continuous thought/voice of each character (leaving room between each beat to fill in the other voices). What came out of this was a stronger sense of each character's wholeness without consideration for the other voices (and therefore without concern of conflicting thoughts/ideas, etc.). It was also helpful in seeing where the draft was repetitious without the repetition serving (and so a great deal was cut). All of these cuts and re-focusing on a more oblique character of Son/Brother/Uncle Tomás allows the play more room for more purposeful repetition, echoes, etc. Now that the characters are built around a more central idea or mystery, weaving them together and creating an atmosphere of sound will be much easier.

May 20—Draft 8—Three Strings
Still feel like there's something missing. It's hard to know how much to put and what to omit, but there seems to be an element—perhaps what, more precisely, is in the lockbox—that's needed to make the whole piece work better. Ultimately, I'm not convinced that the project is successful. It seems to do what I intend for it to do on some levels—in terms of the "sound" of it, but I'm not sure that it's a good, satisfying piece of theatre as opposed to a more random sound sampling. I don't know at this point whether it tells a whole story or relates a specific experience with any actual clarity.

Five days later, Elena returns to her journal to record another leap forward in her process.

May 25—Draft 1—One Wasp
I'm fed up with the unnecessary complexity of what I've created with Three Strings. I want to connect back to something simple. The idea of a single voice, a single prop, a single "event." I love layers, I love mysteries, I love the Chinese puzzle box, but I remind myself that some of the most technically and metaphorically complex creations are also the most simple. I'm listening to my instincts telling me to return to the source, and I know that I cannot do that through Three Strings because it was not born out of the source to begin with. The source was that first monologue, the glass bat, and the idea of a lost relationship.

There's nothing like being able to cut loose from a project that seems to be fighting you all the way. The instant I was able to drop the Three Strings, I found a more focused, centered way of putting words on the page which felt natural. Sometimes, I put a lot of energy into feeling like I "must" finish something for a specified venue rather than enjoying the thralls of knowing I just "want" to finish something for the sheer joy of doing so.

So my Key Play had to go through three incarnations to get to the place where it's at now. I had to write three different stories altogether to find the one which was most likely to be a play. Working on *One Wasp* was less strenuous than the others. I wrote only three drafts and the changes from draft two to three were not significant, I don't think. I don't believe the play is absolutely complete, but I do feel that it is a strong start—much stronger than, say, the seventh draft I had done of *Three Strings*. So I am pleased with the work, regardless of—or perhaps because of—the struggle which brought me to find it.

One Wasp was built out of an image which, actually, doesn't even appear in the play: a martini glass. Initially, the story revolved around the woman's resignation about her lost love as embodied in a wedding gift of martini glasses which hung in the kitchen rack like "glass bats." I liked the idea very much, but the emblem of the bat proved problematic—I couldn't resolve the metaphor with the event of the play. I struggled with this for half a draft, and then, one afternoon, in the midst of packing for a move of my own, a wasp actually *did* come into the house. I pursued it as the character Eva does, and was dismayed when I heard it buzzing in the trash can. I was sitting at the dining room table, trying to write, while the buzzing persisted. I was half-caught between pity for the wasp and fear that it would recover fully enough from the blows I had dealt it and emerge from the can to sting me. A thought went through my head—this is why it's nice to have a male roommate around. If he had been here, he would have killed it properly the first time around.

And it was from there that I realized that it wasn't a bat I wanted to write about (that will be another play), but a wasp. A dying wasp in a garbage can.

The rest of the draft just flew from there. The structure seemed to fall in naturally—it needed three parts and a framework (or in this case, an epilogue). It needed a key. The key was set from the start. I knew I was tired of struggling with the idea of a key in the practical, obvious sense. I wanted a key that was different. A key to a puzzle, a key to a map, something less than (or more, pending perspective) an actual literal key. The sardine can was evocative for me because I remembered as a child, opening cans of sardines for my father, who loved to eat them with crackers and onions and tomatoes. One of the great joys of my childhood was having the honor of preparing this special plate.

Eva's original name was Elise, but I changed it when I realized that wasp could be seen as an acronym. I don't necessarily object to people reading it that way, but I did want to dissuade them of that idea somewhat by making sure the main character had a somewhat ethnic name.

The draft of *One Wasp* that follows is the third, and final, draft. It is not for any of us to say whether it's a better play than *The Poodle Play* or *Three Strings*. The most important fact is that it satisfied Elena as the playwright in the ways which were important to her in the time of writing—especially in regard to finding her way back to an original, if elusive, image.

The subtitle of this book refers to the "personality" of process, which is such a critical component of all our work. Ultimately, we must let go of our plays and see them into the collaborative nurturing (one hopes) of development and production. Until that time, however, the play is the playwright's alone; it is only the playwright who must be pleased with his or her work.

Third draft of One Wasp

At Rise: A woman wearing a shirt with pockets standing in light, a can of bug repellent, a flashlight, a tall kitchen trash can, and an unopened can of sardines. The woman, EVA, takes a deep breath to compose herself before she speaks.

PART ONE:

EVA: The Things That Bug You. (*Beat*) A wasp got into the house somehow. I just finished cleaning, throwing stuff out. It wasn't a yellow jacket. It was one of those big black ones . . . buzzing loudly against the glass, making the pane resonate. I should have left it alone, but I was afraid of being stung. The buzzing was absolutely maddening. I didn't think. I just picked up the still-rolled newspaper, and thwacked the wasp right against the glass. I guess I was expecting it to smush up. I was surprised— even annoyed—when it didn't. It fell onto the sofa beneath the window and buzzed in circles furiously, wildly stinging the cushion and the empty air. And it wouldn't die. Its hard insect armor and the softness of the couch cushion meant that every blow I dealt just pissed the thing off even more. I hit it harder and harder . . . will you *just* die? Will you *please* just die? (*Pause*) One of its little back legs broke off. Its wings were all crumpled. Finally it grew still.

Blackout. Crickets chirp. The high-pitched whine of a mosquito can be heard. Then a sharp slap.

EVA: Ow!

AS HIM: (*Waking*) Wha? Huh?

EVA: Mosquito.

AS HIM: Oh.

EVA: I'm getting eaten alive. There must be a hole in the tent.

AS HIM: Did you close the flap?

EVA: Yes I closed the flap. The little buggers are squeezing through somehow.

There is the sound of loud snoring, another slap.

AS HIM: (*Surprised*) Huh? Wha?

EVA: I'm getting eaten! How can you sleep?

AS HIM: Put some repellent on.

EVA: I did.

AS HIM: Put some more.

EVA: I put a lot. I think they like it.

AS HIM: Well put more.

EVA: Great advice, thank you.

There's the sound of rustling.

AS HIM: What are you doing?

EVA: Looking for the repellent. (EVA *finds the flashlight. She turns it on, we see her face*) Here it is. (*She shines the flashlight on the repellent*)

AS HIM: Good. Good night.

EVA *picks up the repellent. Lights out. We hear a long jet of spray— comedically long, with a few punctuating last spritzes.*

EVA: (*Coughing*) That ought to do it.

AS HIM: (*Coughing*) Trying to drown them? Or us?

EVA: Just shut up. Why don't they ever bite you?

AS HIM: You're such a bug magnet.

EVA: I would stay up the whole night, breathing the garden-scent freshness of the repellent while he snored. Szzzzxxxxxx. Szzzzzzzzzzxxxxxxxx. (*Lights up. She is holding the aerosol can*) "Bug magnet!" I'd spray half a gallon of this stuff all over my body until I reeked and still by the end of the summer I would be covered with red and purple splotches all over my body that were so swollen that I looked like I had some heinous flesh-eating disease. He never got bit once. "Bad Blood," I'd say. "Lucky," he'd say. Lucky. (*Beat*) It's different when you, say, lose your Aunt Bertha to cancer. There's a diagnosis, a long wait to see the outcome of various treatments, slow resignation toward the inevitable, and then death. And even death is not final because there's grief. And grief lingers. (*She sprays the aerosol. Inhales the mist*) Lingers poisonously. When a person dies after a long illness, the grief is expected, prepared for, orga-nized carefully to lessen the blow. But when a person is suddenly gone—like in a freak accident, it's just that—freakish. You cannot prepare for it and the grief sweeps over so suddenly that you don't even know what to do with it at first. You dash around frantically trying to rub it off onto something else, stash it away in boxes, close your eyes and hope that it's just passing. It's just passing. Just passing. It *is* just passing, but it's not like a parade where you can watch it go by and afterwards return home at the end of the day, kick off your shoes and lose yourself in the evening's TV programming. It's not just something you can toss out. Toss out.

Beat. There is a buzzing sound.

PART TWO:

EVA: The Things That Remind You. (*The buzzing persists. She looks warily into the trash can.*) It's still alive. God. The wasp. I thought I killed it, but it's still alive and now lost somewhere in the trash can where I tossed it, newspaper and all. I can't very well dump out the trash looking for it.

She shakes the bag in the can a little and listens as the wasp vibrates against the plastic. She looks frantic, then sprays into the can with the mosquito repellent, which only makes the wasp angry. The buzzing grows louder, more painful.

EVA: Die, die, you miserable thing! Die! (*Beat*) I'm not angry with the wasp for living. I'm angry because of the absence of him. This would have been his job—to handle whatever creepy-crawly was trapped and dying in our trash can. Our trash can. (*She suddenly throws the aerosol into the trash can, looks satisfied*) Anything you don't want can be discarded.

Beat.

PART THREE:

EVA: The Things That You Love. (*Beat*) Truth is, our marriage was a freak accident. There were signs, but we ignored them. You're supposed to have doubts, right? If you don't have doubts, then something must be wrong. You must not be seeing things clearly. You're deluding yourself. (*She picks up the can of sardines*) There were the sardines. Sardines. Who the hell eats sardines? It's a canned meat, first of all, which should tell you right away that it's bound to be disgusting. Like that canned ham that makes those sticky-kissy noises as it schlooops out onto the plate. It's like dog food, okay? And all right, I eat tuna, yes, it's true. But tuna is the end result of a lot of processing and when it gets to you, it just looks like a bunch of meat—you can't tell where the head and tail once were. Tuna also smells infinitely less fishy. (*She studies the can, finally concedes*) Okay, so it was a petty gripe, but stinking up the house with sardine plates and sardine cans was only part of it . . . . See, he would come home, drunk—which is fine; I never had a problem with him going out once in a while and having a good time. He liked to go out and play pool. He and his buddies would lay bets on every play of the game. Stupid bets. He'll make the shot, he won't make the shot, if he makes the shot, you have to tell the male waiter that you think he has a nice ass—that sort of thing, you know? And there was plenty of drinking involved. Always tequila shooters and choice beers for the winners, watered tap specials for the losers. I never knew whether he was winning or losing, he got trashed pretty much the same. Then he'd come home, stagger into the kitchen, grind open a can of sardines and bring them to *bed*. To *bed*, okay? I mean, it was bad enough when he ate them with crackers and onions at the kitchen tables, but to *bed*? And there's me, roused out of my sweet slumber by an odor you can't *even* begin to imagine. I flip on the light, and there he is! He's sitting up in bed—fully dressed because he's too smashed to get his shoes off—and he's eating sardines out of the can *with his fingers!*

Lights out. Flashlight comes on as if a nightstand lamp. We see EVA's face, just horrified beyond consolation.

EVA: What. Are. You. Doing!

She shines the light on the can of sardines and then back to her terrified expression through the course of the dialogue.

AS HIM: (*Drunken murmur*) Hungry.

EVA: My. God.

AS HIM: Want some?

EVA: The stink! What on earth. . . . What're you . . . . god, you're drunk, you are!

AS HIM: Mmmm. Good.

EVA: That's disgusting! You're disgusting!

AS HIM: Ah, honey, but I love *you*.

EVA: Don't *even* touch me with those fishy fingers. (*The light holds on the lonely sardine can for a long, long fade.*) I would lay there in the half-dark, listening to him slurp down the sardines, one after the next. Sluuurp, chew chew. Sluuuuurp, chew chew. Gulp. Ugh! My skin crawled. I clutched my laundry-fresh pillowcase under my nose. Smell the garden-fresh scent, I'd tell myself. Smell the clean freshness. But all I smelled was sardines. He'd pitch the can into the garbage can. Kerplunk, went the tinny emptiness. And then he'd snore. And I would lay there in the dark, trying to smell through all that stinky fishy smell while he snored 'til morning. Szzzzzzxxxxxxx. Szzzzxxxxxxxxxxx. 'Til the alarm went off.

Blackout. Sound of a weak alarm. Bzzzz. Bzzzz. Bzzzz. Lights up suddenly on EVA looking into the garbage can. The buzzing is the wasp. It grows weaker and weaker until finally it stops.

EVA: Epilogue: The Things You Miss. (*Beat*) I could not believe he was gone. For a long time. Went 'round and 'round in my head in perfect denial. Then the bed grew cold and the dishes went unwashed and the newspaper . . . the newspaper went unread. So I used it to kill a wasp. (*She looks in the trash can sadly*) It's dead now. I haven't heard from it, so I think it's safe to say I killed it. (*Beat*) I killed it. It's just one measly wasp. But that's a hard thing to say.

She takes up the sardine can and almost starts to speak, then changes her mind. She moves to throw the can away. She finds that she can't. She is very emotional as she grinds the can.

EVA: The real denial was not seeing . . . all the time we'd been married . . . had been a fugue of some sort. Not mine or his, just a shared hysteria. And it only *seemed* to have been suddenly all gone in an instant when actually it had been fading out for years. (*She finally gets the can open. She takes a deep inhale. She reels back from the smell*) Whoa! Yeah, that's it all right. That's the smell.

She laughs and goes to throw the can of sardines in the trash, still finds it difficult, pulls the key off, tosses the can, and looks at the key, resigned.

EVA: I won't miss the sardines.

She ties the plastic bag at the top and then breathes deep, enjoying the fresh emptiness of the space. The light pulls in tight as she pockets the tin key, smiling sadly.

EVA: But I will miss the snoring.

She starts to exit with the trash. Blackout. End of Play.

Elena added a final, retrospective journal entry, which speaks to her work far more eloquently than I could.

January 3—Retrospective—One Wasp

With the advantage of many months of perspective, it is much easier now to go back to the work I did this past year on the ten-minute piece, and look at it more critically in terms of process. As with most of the work I do, I seized the key image and was off and running from the instant the gates were opened. This resulted in the enthusiastic, though blithering draft of *The Poodle Play*, which I abandoned shortly after I began it simply because I knew that its origin lay in the excitement of the moment and that it had no real fuel to sustain it. When I then began working on *Three Strings*, I fell into the secondary process mode that I have come to recognize as typical of myself as a writer—in short, it was a play about an idea and (structure) architecture. I have a tendency, like all writers, to nurse my neuroses by returning to the same themes, which for me revolve around choices, the responsibility for those choices, and how various people cope with that responsibility. In *Three Strings*, three generations of family women struggle to made decisions about the death of a man who had a particular relationship with each of them. That was essentially the idea. The character of Tomás went from being the youngest girl's great uncle to uncle, and I even considered making him her father. In the various drafts he was a drunk, he was a philanderer, he was a pedophile. I just never could land, ultimately. I discovered that I was more in love with playing with the structure of the piece, playing conductor with the music of the voices and overlaps and repetitions and choruses and refrains, than I was in solving the essential story problems. I realized, in other words, that the piece was less a play than just an exercise in exploring a "tercet" as it could be reproduced on stage without actual music.

Having then gotten the flush of total unhinged excitement and then too-controlled intellectualism out of my system, I was able to move on, and within a few drafts, managed to connect to a play that had been sort of waiting in the wings for these first two acts to play themselves out. *One Wasp* tumbled out onto the page from a jumble of actual and subconscious realities. The wasp itself was real, as I described before, and the woman's failed relationship was a metaphor for the sudden onset of an unpredicted sense of loss that leaving my life-long hometown had left in me. Eva's (Eve, first woman) seeking closure through cleaning out the last vestments of her lover's things echoed the bittersweet (ooh, I hate that word) refreshment I had experienced knowing I was on the cusp of a new life.

One Wasp was, then, a channeling of the hyperactive energy that drove my first false start with *The Poodle Play*—it was written in one sitting—and the intellectualizing and thematicizing (both in the conceit of the single flashlight and the motif of regret) of *Three Strings*. These two energies synthesized to create a play with what I felt was a much better, more even, temperament. So for me writing,

4

CHAPTER

Gary Garrison:
Cherry Reds

"LONNIE IS UNHAPPY . . ."

GARY GARRISON IS A MEMBER OF THE FULL-TIME faculty of the Dramatic Writing Program at NYU's Tisch School of the Arts. His plays have been produced by a host of theatres, including the Open Door Theatre, Expanded Arts, Brooklyn Playworks, Circle Rep Lab, Manhattan Punchline, Alice's Fourth Floor, and The Miranda Theatre, among others. In 1999, Heinemann published a collection of his essays on playwriting: A *Playwright's Guide to Survival: Keeping the Drama in Your Work and Out of Your Life.* Gary's book is an excellent companion to Heinemann's other books on playwriting, including this one.

As I contacted playwrights for this project, my concern was to have a broad representation of styles, backgrounds, and perspectives. I have known Gary for a number of years through projects with the Kennedy Center/American College Theatre Festival (KC/ACTF) and the Association for Theatre in Higher Education (ATHE). I knew that he was a brilliant, sometimes outrageous teacher (once, he actually dropped his pants standing on a desk top to reveal his boxer shorts with red hearts all over them to make a point with students), and a tremendous advocate for student playwriting. I also knew that he was very active in the Gay and Lesbian Theatre Focus Group with ATHE, and concerned about gay issues in the arts. We had served on many panels and workshops together, but I realized I did not know very much about Gary's writing. The logical correction to this was to invite Gary to contribute to this book.

When Gary and I initially spoke, I mentioned the diversity I hoped for in the book. I told him how valuable it would be to have a play with a gay perspective included. I was surprised when he told me he'd never written a play with gay subject matter. I told him it wasn't a requirement for his participation, of course, but since this was an issue for him, perhaps the book presented a timely opportunity. Gary encapsulated his response in his journal in a way that captures that initial conversation, and in Gary's inimitable style:

6/15

So I'm going to do something that I've never done before—write a gay play. Have I avoided it? Was I afraid of it? Was I afraid of me? Thinking back on all of my work, I don't know that I've even written a gay character. My own homophobia? I think, if I'm not kidding myself, that I thought that writing something gay was too easy, too accessible. Until *We Make A Wall*, I wasn't really comfortable writing men, let alone gay men. Who's to say that I have to write gay men? Why not lesbians?

It's not that I'm afraid of being "out." Puuuuhhhlease. I've never been in (except to my family), so being out in my writing is no biggie. So what is it? What's kept me from writing about being gay, gay men, gay relationships? Am I too close to it? Does it interest me? Do I understand it?

In the past I've written women. Straight women. Straight, eccentric women with an edge. I like women. I love women. Women are complex, fascinating, facile creatures. Does that mean that I don't perceive men that way? Hmmmmmmm.

Do I even like men? Hmmmmmmm.

Can I sexualize a man but think of him with no deeper connection than that? Hmmmmmmm.

Interesting questions. What has Michael Wright gotten me into? (Yeah, wouldn't I just love to play the victim! No way.)

Gary's struggle to write his play is another fine example of the complex variables in the playwright's process. His excellent insights into the issues of creation and identity reflect on the universal experience of writers. Self-doubt and uncertainty are part of any playwright's daily efforts. The question is how one copes with these problems. Gary's ability to articulate his feelings openly and push on to write one play and then another provides us with an important glimpse into one writer's approach. Certainly, his willingness to actively confront the problems he was having is a useful paradigm for writers at all levels.

The work journal entries that follow are a virtual workshop in process.

6/16

Confused about what to write about. Can't seem to focus my thoughts. Something that fascinates me: how men, in my case, have to dance around each other to figure out if there's a MUTUAL attraction between each other. In other words, I like you, but do you like me? And I don't want to let you know that I like you, because what if you don't like me and reject me? And though I've been rejected by the best of them, and rejected at least a hundred times in the last year, it's still painful to me. So I'll drop little clues and hints and hope you'll drop little clues and hints, and maybe our clues and hints will reveal ourselves and we'll find out that we're both attracted to each other. Of course, if that happens, the real trouble begins.—What do I mean by that? . . . Hmmmmmmm.

6/18

Michel (my companion) and I went to a carpet store today to look for carpets for the house in Rhinebeck. And I got this idea: one guy—a salesman in the carpet store, new on his job, eager to please, eager to prove his value, needs the job, needs to belong somewhere, is helping a customer who is a man—we're unclear of this man's sexuality. And through the course of the scene, the customer is discreetly trying to discern if the salesman is 1) gay, and 2) potentially attracted to him. So the customer baits the salesman by interpreting images in the carpets they're looking at as male erotic images and prods the salesman into acknowledging that he sees the same images. Because the salesman is closeted and can "pass," but doesn't want to lose the customer . . .

I'm rambling. Clearly I haven't thought this through. Maybe I'll just try writing it.

6/19

Tried writing it. It was shit. Didn't listen to my own advice: don't start writing until you know something about what you're writing about, or at least more—than less—what you're writing about. It was a muddled mess. I hate when I do that. Blech! I'm trying to write about that dance people do with each other when, from a place of vulnerability, they're trying to figure out if they're attractive to the other person without giving themselves away—giving their power away.

6/20

Saw an A&E special on Cleopatra. She wrapped herself up in a carpet and unrolled herself to Marc Anthony as part of her seduction. I like that image. I'm going to use that somehow in my play.

6/21

Michel gave me the title of my play: *Rug Store Cowboy*, because I was talking to him about it, and I made the customer a cowboy from Texas. I want to play with the importance of visual body images in the gay community. I want to explore how we encode our seductions with cues for the objects of our attractions, using clothes, a butch walk, a deep voice, all things masculine to project masculinity. We have to appear masculine. Have to. Non-negotiable.

So maybe it's a much simpler story: two guys, one a customer, one a salesman. The customer is from Texas, cowboy, used to be married, butch, tough, rugged, manly, visits New York each year. Used to go with his wife, but now that they're divorced, he comes by himself. He finds himself in a rug store he used to visit with his wife. He meets the salesman who's new on the job and has to make a sale because he's working on commission and desperately needs the money. But he's closeted. And what we watch is this very subtle dance between these two men who are exploring their interests in one another.

But what's the conflict? Ahhhhh, there's the rub.

Let me just get in my head what I'm trying to write about.

1.

I've gone blank. Isn't that interesting?

6/23

Opening: the cowboy rolls himself up in the carpet. Lights up. The stage is empty, except a rolled up carpet. The salesman comes on stage, calls out the customer's name, at which point the cowboy unrolls himself at the salesman's feet. The salesman is speechless. The cowboy smiles.

Yeah, but what the hell does that mean? And what kind of guy would roll, then unroll himself in the carpet? I like the idea, but it's not plausible, is it?

Maybe I'm thinking too naturalistically. Maybe I should push out against that confinement. Most of what I write is naturalistic, so what the hell do I know about other forms? Hmmmmmmm.

6/24

Okay, let me try this one more time. Random thoughts. What am I writing about:

1. Two gay men who meet each other and are attracted to each other, but neither one can tell if the other is gay. So the first "dance" is the "is he gay or not" dance; the second "dance" is "is he attracted to me" dance.

I'm going about this all wrong. What's the goddamn conflict? Let me start there. Gay or not, men or not, what's the conflict?

The following is an excerpt from *Rug Store Cowboy*. I have included about half of the script to give the flavor of what Gary was attempting. As Gary points out in a later journal entry, the play was not working for him—did not "hook" him—and there was only one complete draft attempted.

The excerpt provides us with a useful contrast between its language, style, and ideas versus those of the play *Cherry Reds*. One of the things I find fascinating about any playwright's work is the evocation of voice from work to work. By having *Rug Store Cowboy* and *Cherry Reds* to look at we can recognize the essence of Gary's voice in certain uses of vernacular in both plays, and yet each play has a distinctive "over" voice as well. The "over" voice is the narrator's tone we can sense in the play, rather than see directly. This sense comes to us through various elements: perspective on the characters, choice of structure, choice of style, and even in the tone of the stage directions. The "over" voice sets the terms for the entire play, and helps convey the contract made between the play, its interpreters, and the audience. One contract might say, for instance, we are in a dark comic world where character is more important than plot. Another contract would say that we are in a realistic world in which the story is well-balanced with the characters, and so on.

The story of *Rug Store Cowboy's* requires a more naturalistic voice, and this shows up in virtually every aspect of the piece, beginning with the setting and character descriptions. *Cherry Reds*, by the very nature of its main character and structure, demands a far more expansive voice, which we recognize instantly in its highly theatrical setting. In both cases, Gary intends to convey a sense of empathy. In *Rug Store Cowboy*, the empathy is achieved in a fairly direct line through the character who is on the spot, Bradley, in whom we witness a complex struggle. In *Cherry Reds*, the empathy is generated by things outside the character—a world Lonnie D seeks to live with and understand but often cannot—and so the line is rather indirect.

Draft Excerpt from Rug Store Cowboy

The stage is empty save one large rolled-up Persian carpet off to stage right. BRADLEY, 35, tall, lean, wearing his version of "dress for success" enters with a slip of paper in his hand. He looks around the empty space, looks off to both sides of the stage, and then timidly calls:

BRADLEY: Mr. Fisher? (*He walks towards the carpet. Louder*) MR. FISHER?

Slowly the carpet begins unrolling without Bradley noticing. When it hits Bradley's feet, he yelps and steps over it incredulously. NOLAN FISHER, 35, smiling from ear to ear, rolls out the end of the carpet.

NOLAN: Mercy! Oh, my God, it was hot in there! Thought I was gonna puke or die! And what a helluva way to go. You came just in the nick of time, Mr. Bradley. What took you s'damn long, boy?

BRADLEY: These are new rugs. They just came off the truck, so there's no . . .

NOLAN: I thought I was gonna expire. Honest to God, slap your pappy if I'm lyin', I thought I was about to take my last breath.

BRADLEY: You could have just unrolled yourself, Mr. Fisher.

NOLAN: I coulda done a lot of things, like not roll myself up in that goddamn rug in the first place, but I was bettin' that's somethin' you've never seen. Right? Am I right? Tell the truth, Mr. Bradley . . .

BRADLEY: . . . It's just "Bradley." That's my first name . . .

NOLAN: . . . I don't care how long you've worked here, has anybody ever rolled themselves up, top to toe, in a carpet to your memory?

BRADLEY: (*Flustered*) This is only my third day, Mr. Fisher.

NOLAN: No shit? Well, then I've just given you a helluva story to tell someone tonight over supper, huh? Now, how bad is that? Third day on the job and some wild, Southern lunatic rolls himself up in a carpet while you're doin' your price check thang, and then unrolls himself and lays at your feet like an old hound dog. And the whole time you're a-thankin', "what the hell is he doing?" Is that what you're a-thankin', Bradley—what in God's name is he doin'?

BRADLEY: (*More nervous now*) Well . . . truthfully . . . it's, it's a little unusual.

NOLAN: A little?! Oh, now you're just being polite.

BRADLEY: Alright, well, I admit, I thought it was strange. I didn't know what you were doing.

NOLAN: Well, ease up there, pal, 'cause even I don't know what the hell I'm doin'. I'm just doin' it. I'm just, you know, livin' it. Moment to moment, carpet to carpet. It's the way of the world, baby.

A long awkward pause. Nolan stretches out on the carpet. Bradley looks over his shoulder, then off to the other side. Finally:

BRADLEY: Mr. Fisher . . .

NOLAN: Nolan.

BRADLEY: Nolan—this is a little awkward for me—but, uhm, are you going to stay down there long?

NOLAN: You mean right here? On the floor?

BRADLEY: Exactly.

NOLAN Well, I could stand . . .

BRADLEY: (*Quickly*) . . . That'd be good . . .

NOLAN: . . . but I'd rather just lay here like a big, fat mama sow.

BRADLEY: I think I'd rather you stand.

NOLAN: And I think I'm buying a carpet from you—an expensive carpet if I know my Persians, Bradley, and in my house, I lay around a lot . . . especially on the carpet. Can't stand a stiff carpet. Give me something soft, baby, 'cause that's what I'm looking for. Sometimes a carpet's the only goddamn comfortable thing in someone's whole house—you ever notice? So we're just gonna think on all of this as a little test drive. S'that good for you?

BRADLEY: Sure. Of course. Absolutely. It's just, you know, my third day and I don't really know the people here, and they don't know me and if they look over here and see you, you know, on the ground, laying down . . .

NOLAN: (*Smiling wider*) . . . like a big, sloppy hog . . .

BRADLEY: . . . I'm not sure what they'll do.

NOLAN: Do? Oh, now look, puppy, that's an easy one. They ain't gonna do nothin', 'cause no one does nothin' round here. Haven't you noticed? The people that work here hardly take a breath 'cause it takes an effort. Love that. S'why I come here when I'm visitin'. Hate pushy sales people. Hate those little tail-gaters that follow you round and round and round 'till you just want to slap 'em out of the universe. No one bothers you here.

BRADLEY: Except me.

NOLAN Only because it's your third day. Hell, you got to make an impression. Nothing wrong with that. (*Rolling on his side*) So what's the damage gonna be for the carpet? And don't dick me, Bradley. Tom's an old friend of mine, so I usually get the "I'm A Friend of Tom's" discount.

BRADLEY: Right, right. He told me about that. So with the list figure and then Tom's discount . . .

NOLAN: Bradley, why don't you come down here?

BRADLEY: (*Alarmed*) Why?

NOLAN: 'Cause I'm down here.

BRADLEY: I don't think that's a good idea.

NOLAN: Why not? We're just gonna sit on the Persian and talk the serious talk. Why would anybody object to that? We're making a deal here. We're gettin' down to the bottom line figures. I'm thinking, "should I pay cash or use a credit card," and you're thinking, "Shit! This is my first big sale."

BRADLEY: Don't you think we could both think that standing up?

NOLAN: Well, hell ya'. But I prefer thinkin' about it sittin' down.

A *long moment. Nolan smiles at Bradley. Bradley finally realizes something.*

BRADLEY: Oh. Oh, wait. Alright. Alright, I get it. Is this, like, a power thing for you, or something?

NOLAN: Naw, it's a "my ass is tired" thing. I've been walking all over your cement city for three damn days and I'm just tuckered out.

BRADLEY: (*Not buying it*) I don't know.

NOLAN: Bradley, you thankin' way too hard, pal. It's this simple: there are verticals, and there are horizontals. You're a vertical. I'm a horizontal . . . every chance I get. Makes gettin' vertical worthwhile.

BRADLEY: (*Defensive*) I'm not just a vertical. I get horizontal. Plenty of times. Just not in a rug store, thank you. And certainly not in my place of business. And quite frankly, I can't believe I'm hav-ing this conversation with a stranger, so if you want to buy the rug, it's fifteen thousand, less Tom's discount, which would bring it to thirteen thousand . . .

NOLAN: . . . and with tax, that'll bring it back up around fifteen thousand. (*Standing up*) No, thanks, Bradley. But thank you, sir, for your time. (*Nolan begins to walk away*)

BRADLEY: Wait! Nolan, I'm sorry. I got a little . . . you know, whatever . . . and I shouldn't have, so if you'll . . .

NOLAN You spoke your mind, baby, that's all you did. Don't apologize for that. It's good for you. Look, it's no big deal. But I still don't want the rug because Tom's being a cheap son-of-a-bitch and he knows it.

BRADLEY (*Afraid of losing the sale*) Well, maybe you could talk to him.

NOLAN: Naw, I can't talk to Tom. That never quite works out.

BRADLEY: How come?

NOLAN: Well, it all starts with Ricardo—that guy over there with the black hair. See, Ricardo's got a big boner for me. When I get up to the cash register to pay for this thing, he's gonna wink at me and stare at the hair on my chest. Jonquel, the girl standin' right beside him, will get mad at Ricardo for looking at me 'cause she's always had a crush on Ricardo, and pines for him no matter how many times everyone tells her the boy is way gay. When she sees me walking to the counter, jealousy's gonna eat her up, and she'll grab a Newport out of her crumpled package and take a cigarette break, slamming the front door when she goes out. David will step out of his office and ask who just slammed the door, then he'll see that Jonquel's gone, that Ricardo's still looking at the hair on my chest and put two and two together. He'll come and shake my hand, ask me how long I'm in the city for, and say something about how I look better and better every time he sees me. Then he'll hike his pants up so they snug his butt cheeks, then find an excuse to come around the counter so he can give me a clear eye shot of what he thinks is his best feature. And while he's standing there, he'll need a pencil—the boy always needs a pencil—and he'll cross to the counter to reach for one and will brush my arm in the process. He'll let it linger, waiting to see if I'll move it, and when I do move it, he'll think it's all okay 'cause it was an accident anyway that we were touching in the first place while he reached for his pencil. Then my friend Tom—who ordinarily would give me a BIG discount—will walk out of the office, see David playing the same old games that sent them to couples therapy five years ago, then walk back into his office to look at his insurance policy to see if he's met his deductible, so he can go to back to his personal therapy to vent the anger that didn't come out in his couples therapy. So that leaves you. And I'm just waiting to see where you fit in to all of that.

BRADLEY: I'm not sure I do.

NOLAN: I'm not sure you do either.

A stare-off. What next? Both men are incredibly self-conscious. Slowly, Bradley lowers himself to the ground, and sits on the carpet.

As the play continues, Bradley eventually admits that he's attracted to Nolan, but has been put off by Nolan's manner of speaking and his Wild West clothing. The two agree to have dinner, and the foundation of a relationship is established. As the journal entries that follow will show, Gary left this play very quickly for a new play that felt much more natural to him as a writer. *Rug Store Cowboy* establishes, however, a critical theme that will lead directly to *Cherry Reds*: the issue of identity.

In *Rug Store Cowboy*, the major dramatic question is not whether Bradley will succumb to Nolan's seduction, but whether Bradley can manage this encounter on his own terms. Only when he establishes his identity and values can the relationship move to a new level. As we will see in *Cherry Reds*, this is the same problem confronting Lonnie. Gary is consistent, even though the plays are radically different in style, subject matter, and language. As he points out in the journal entries that follow, writing for a female voice gave him sufficient distance to engage the ideas dramatically, with a wider range of metaphor.

It is axiomatic that most writers tend to return to certain key themes in their work. Those who can create a continually expanding array of dramatic situations in which to explore these few themes are the playwrights who continue to grow.

6/25

My best friend Wendy and I had a talk today. I don't know how we got on the subject, but we began talking about how it seems that more straight women have had a sexual relationship with another woman, and feel comfortable about talking about it, then straight men ever admit to. Then I got to thinking about the number of straight women I know that have confessed to such an experience, whereas no straight man I know has ever admitted to having a consensual sexual relationship with another man. Okay, these are big issues, I know. And I don't know why this is striking me as more interesting today than yesterday, but it is. I think it's something I'd like to write about. Maybe I should write about that instead of *Rug Store Cowboy*.

6/28

Ditching *Rug Store Cowboy*. For whatever reason, I can't hook into it. And there's the deadline looming. BUT, I got really juiced today. I was riding the subway and all of these young girls (maybe sixteen, seventeen) were riding in the same car. They had the most gorgeous inner language among themselves: very street, very hip, sharp, edgy, nasty, funny. And these young women were very hot, very sexy, incredibly self-aware. They all had nicknames for each other (T-Bone, Zoo-Zoo, Deeky). They laughed, touched each other, giggled, sang. They were all very theatrical, very sharp. They got into a snapping contest, trying to one-up each other. Throwing nasty comments at each other, then snapping each other off. Looked like a young gaggle of drag queens, if I didn't know any better. I have an idea . . .

What follows here is a very useful exercise that Gary created for this project. As you will see, it's like a pyramid built from the top down. It begins with the most important central idea in the play: "Lonnie is unhappy . . ." and adds more depth and definition to that key element until the pyramid is complete. As the pyramid grows, each new idea is indicated in italics, which I've preserved here. This is an excellent exercise and exploration. It provides us with a useful tool for our own use, which can be varied in a number of ways. It clearly helped Gary find his way through to a play which works for him.

You will notice that there are portions of the exercise that are grammatically incorrect or awkward, but that is completely irrelevant to the task Gary set out for himself. This kind of brainstorming can only work if the writer is willing to relinquish worries about the exercise being "right" or "written correctly" or any other extraneous concern. The point is to get the ideas down as freely as possible. Corrections and adjustments can follow later. Keep in mind also that Gary did not write this for public scrutiny, but for his own work. As with all the other contributors, we're lucky to have his process made available in such a raw, unguarded condition.

Lastly, note how Gary keeps extending and complicating the initial idea of each sentence. In training for improvisational work for actors, the stress is often placed on the need for conflict in reactions—conflict which must escalate, or the improvisation stagnates. Actors are coached to respond with a "No, *and*—" or "Yes, *but*—" reaction so that the conflict isn't stuck at the "Is too," "Is not" level of circuitous argument. In this exercise, Gary uses conjunctions and simple transitional words or phrases as a way of furthering the complexity of Lonnie's situation, and digging deeper into her circumstances. This pyramid is followed by ideas, questions, and images that have spun out of the description of Lonnie's situation.

7/1—HOMEWORK

Lonnie is unhappy.

Lonnie is unhappy *and unsettled in her relationship*.

Lonnie is unhappy and unsettled in her relationship, *and thinks her unhappiness is a result of her problematic boyfriend, Fuzz.*

Lonnie is unhappy and unsettled in her relationship, and thinks her unhappiness is a result of her problematic boyfriend, Fuzz, *that everyone else seems to adore.*

Lonnie is unhappy and unsettled in her relationship, and thinks her unhappiness is a result of her problematic boyfriend, Fuzz, that everyone else seems to adore, *which causes even more unrest in the relationship.*

Lonnie is unhappy and unsettled in her relationship, and thinks her unhappiness is a result of her problematic boyfriend, Fuzz, that everyone else seems to adore, which causes even more unrest in the relationship. *Fuzz thinks the solution to Lonnie's unrest is to propose marriage.*

Lonnie is unhappy and unsettled in her relationship, and thinks her unhappiness is a result of her problematic boyfriend, Fuzz, that everyone else seems to adore, which causes even more unrest in the relationship. Fuzz thinks the solution to Lonnie's unrest is to propose marriage, *but his attempt to make it "funny" and "memorable" backfires on him.*

Lonnie is unhappy and unsettled in her relationship, and thinks her unhappiness is a result of her problematic boyfriend, Fuzz, that everyone else seems to adore, which causes even more unrest in the relationship. Fuzz thinks the solution to Lonnie's unrest is to propose marriage, but his attempt to make it "funny" and "memorable" backfires on him *which brings to focus for Lonnie their basic, intrinsic differences that to her mind cannot be resolved.*

Lonnie is unhappy and unsettled in her relationship, and thinks her unhappiness is a result of her problematic boyfriend, Fuzz, that everyone else seems to adore, which causes even more unrest in the relationship. Fuzz thinks the solution to Lonnie's unrest is to propose marriage, but his attempt to make it "funny" and "memorable" backfires on him which brings to focus for Lonnie their basic, intrinsic differences that to her mind cannot be resolved. *Lonnie decides that it's time to leave the relationship once and for all.*

Lonnie is unhappy and unsettled in her relationship, and thinks her unhappiness is a result of her problematic boyfriend, Fuzz, that everyone else seems to adore, which causes even more unrest in the relationship. Fuzz thinks the solution to Lonnie's unrest is to propose marriage, but his attempt to make it "funny" and "memorable" backfires on him which brings to focus for Lonnie their basic, intrinsic differences that to her mind cannot be resolved. Lonnie decides that it's time to leave the relationship once and for all, *but in the process of packing her belongings, relives memories that introduce the notion that maybe Fuzz isn't the real or only problem.*

Lonnie is unhappy and unsettled in her relationship, and thinks her unhappiness is a result of her problematic boyfriend, Fuzz, that everyone else seems to adore, which causes even more unrest in the relationship. Fuzz thinks the solution to Lonnie's unrest is to propose marriage, but his attempt to make it "funny" and "memorable" backfires on him which brings to focus for Lonnie their basic, intrinsic differences that to her mind cannot be resolved. Lonnie decides that it's time to leave the relationship once and for all, but in the process of packing her belongings, relives memories that introduce the notion that maybe Fuzz isn't the real or only problem. *As her past journey continues to unfold, Lonnie realizes that she's never been at rest, never been satisfied with what's in front of her, never been content to just be. But what is she running away from?*

Some ideas:

Lonnie collects shoes.

Lonnie's Puerto Rican.

Lonnie's been with Fuzz for eight years.

They live in the projects in Queens.

Lonnie's got a campy kind of street language.

Lonnie's got a secret.

Some questions:

Why does someone develop a sassy mouth? What's it to protect her from?

Lonnie's never satisfied: why? Why isn't something/anything enough?

She's a girl always on the move: I know this personally. If you don't settle, you don't have to think. What does she not want to think about?

Lonnie was a smart ass/tough mouth in high school. This is a very distinguishable type of kid. How do they become what they become? Why? Does different = more. In other words, a hundred different pair of shoes. But is it the difference in styles that attracts her, and or is it actually having 100?

Random thoughts:

I think if we see that throughout her life she can't settle down—that she's a girl always on the move—than marrying someone is the ultimate threat to the core of her existence.

Okay, now I'm hyped. I know *what* I'm writing about. I know *who* I'm writing about. So it's a woman. So sue me. I'm doing what I know I do best.

I asked Gary about the exercise, and where he'd gotten it. He told me he'd just made it up. I asked him to tell me a bit more about it, and he responded in an e-mail:

> I don't even know why I made it up other than it seemed like a cool train-of-thought thing and I thought if I just free-associated, I'd come up with something, and in fact, I think I did. Anyway, it's from my imagination . . . and now into your book.

Gary's journal continues the process on the play as it moves from an initial draft (first called *Old Soles*) toward the finished product.

7/3

Wrote the first 5 pages of *Old Soles* (which is what I think I'm going to call it). Got Lonnie D down on the first page. Rhythm, cadence, style of speaking, camp, sassy, flip. Her boyfriend's name is going to be "Fuzz." I just like the image of that. Lights up, and she's leaving, packing up. She's going to move out. We'll understand soon why.

To help establish the character for you, here is the opening sequence of the first draft. Note that the locale of the play is immediately identified as the stage, not a realistic environment, and that Lonnie's entrance is through the audience.

Excerpt from Initial Draft:

The front of the stage is lined with a variety of shoes—all different kinds from all different times of LONNIE D's life. We hear a door slam. LONNIE D storms towards the stage, carrying an empty cardboard box and a salami sandwich almost bigger than her hand.

LONNIE D: Oh, no! Uh-uh. No! Not in the middle of MY lunch. Not in the middle of MY fabulous salami sandwich! Oh, no, sweetheart, you're not going to start a fight with me when I barely got the mayonnaise on the bread, baby. I have had it, Fuzz! Do you hear me? Can't even eat my damn salami in peace without you getting noisy in my ear. And that's what you do, Fuzz. YOU MAKE NOISE! You think you make sense, but you just make noise.

LONNIE D *takes the stage, slings the box across the floor, takes a big bite of her sandwich and begins to pace. FUZZ enters the room. LONNIE D looks up—her eyes bulge. She's got plenty to say but her mouth is full of that damn salami. All she can do is chew and grunt, and say "Uh-huh."*

Uh-huh . . . uh-huh . . . uh . . . uh . . . UH! . . . UH-HUH. (*Finally swallowing*) Tell me you did NOT follow me in here to fight because I am not gong to fight, Fuzz. I am going to pack this cardboard box and leave, that's what I'm going to do . . . WHY? Look, sweetheart, I have been with you for eight years and two were good, two were bad, two were troubled, and two were sad. If Wall Street was brokering this relationship, baby, they'd be yellin', SELL, SELL, SELL! People would be jumpin' out of windows and shit.

This excerpt gives us an initial flavor of Lonnie's attitude and speech patterns. As Gary continues to define and develop the character, Lonnie's language gradually becomes more stylized until it accurately answers Gary's own question: "Why does someone develop a sassy mouth? What's it to protect her from?" As we will see, it protects her from Fuzz, but also from self-recognition, until she comes to connect with a key aspect of her identity.

7/4

Lonnie D collects shoes. To me, a choice a woman makes on shoes reveals so much about both her inner and outer character. So Lonnie D will collect shoes, or save shoes from different periods in her life. Some people collect baseball cards or PEZ dispensers; Lonnie collects shoes. She'll have all different kinds of shoes from different stages of her life. Most of the shoes will be hers; some maybe just keepsakes from friends, her mom, maybe her wedding? Or first date? Or first kiss? So the title, OLD SOLES, will be both about the shoes and the souls of the people connected to the memories they illicit. I'll use this somehow. I love the connection that I see my women friends make to their shoes. I want to explore that connection somehow.

I like Lonnie's character. Sassy, smart mouth, a real diva. I must be doing something right. This material has just come pouring out of me.

I've already written some cheap laughs. Got to go back and ground that stuff and stop doing that!

7/5

Lonnie's leaving her relationship. Maybe she doesn't even understand why, but she knows it's time to go; time for a change. She could easily stay in the relationship for years more, but it's not the right thing to do. She has to be the one to take the first step; Fuzz would never do it.

7/7

Got sidetracked. Wrote in a direction in which a pair of shoes that Lonnie has belonged to wise, sage old drag queen. Don't know where I was going with that. Interesting, but doesn't further the plot. Wrote a section that I titled, *My Patent Leathers*, which turned into *Lady K's Black Patent Leathers*; great monologue, but what the hell does it have to do with anything? Trashing it. Got to keep the conflict building. Why is Lonnie leaving? Where is she leaving to? Why is she unsettled?

Wait. Maybe she's not just unhappy with Fuzz, she's unhappy with men. Or she's done with men. Or she's had so many men in too little time. Or she's restless, and she doesn't know why, and all she knows is she's gotta get out.

Later this evening:

Back on the subway, saw a woman with a pair of open toed, red stiletto heels. Incredible. She was so goddamn sexy too. She worked those shoes. She knew their power. She was strong. She was incredible. I'm going to work that in somehow.

Although the Lady K monologue was dropped from the piece, it is an important transitional exploration that takes Gary deeper into Lonnie's world, and into the true heart of her internal conflict. It is crucial for playwrights to follow their instincts, even if the exploration takes them away from the main story for a time. Lady K's voice helps Gary develop Lonnie's speech and style a bit further, and examines the critical prop of the shoes in a way that is removed from the plot. This piece does not further the play, as Gary observes, but it is clearly responsible for what springs out next in his pursuit of Lonnie's reality.

Excerpt from the Lady K monologue

LONNIE D *becomes Lady K, a wildy flamboyant drag queen; she looks at a pair of black patent leather stiletto heels.*

LONNIE D: Yes, Diva. Look at these girls. Saw these cha-cha's from fifty feet away and ran like a school girl right to them. And wouldn't you know some poster child for Jenny Craig was reachin' for 'em when I arrived. I looked at her overly-mascaraed eyes and said, "Uh—huh, girlfriend. You put those on your big feet and it'll look like you're wearing a pair of fire hydrants. I wouldn't lie. Go soft, sweetheart. Something in a pastel." I musta scared the shit out of her (I wasn't in my drag) and she dropped them right into the palm of my hand. And don't they look grand, Diva? (*She puts the shoes on*) Oh, shit I can walk tall in these girls, prance, turn, vogue, work it. This is how you walk, girlfriend, to show you're sassy: Step, step. pause. Step, step, pause, turn and look. You know my philosophy, doll: How can you "step right up," "take a hike," or "walk on by" if you don't have the right shoes to do it in? It's a big question for small feet. Oh, and these shoes fit, honey. Tight. Snug. They're a skin—just the way I like 'em. Many a time I've been known to retort: "Baby, these aren't shoes, these are evening gloves for my toes." Learn your lesson from Lady K, baby. Shoes make the woman. You put the right shoe on your foot and, baby, you got a Broadway show happenin' up your leg. Let me tell you why Eve took a bite of that apple and screwed things all up. She got a look at her feet. Those feet were ugly. Nasty ugly. And you know, they didn't have shoes. So Eve knew she had to do something. She took one bite of that apple, and sweetheart, that alligator that was swimmin' in her swamp was on her feet in no time. Girlfriend was smart.

As we will see, this monologue helps to deepen Lonnie's sense of identity and memory of her past through her shoes—clearly central to the character—and establish the eventual importance of a particular pair, the "cherry reds." It also helps Gary decide to keep the piece a monologue. In the early draft, Fuzz could enter as an actual character. In the later and final drafts, Fuzz is created by Lonnie's reactions to him, as is the new character, Too-Too, who is introduced in the next journal segment.

7/8

Weird where writing takes you sometimes. I was writing a scene for Lonnie in which a pair of her shoes takes her back to her high school prom, where she first met Fuzz—I guess as a way of bringing some perspective into her reason for leaving him now. And out came this best friend of hers, Too-Too. Too-Too gets her name from doing everything over the top. She's too much of this and too much of that. She fucks too much. She wears too much make-up. She's grown up too fast. And I think she has a crush on Lonnie D. I don't know. Let me see how it plays out.

7/12

It played out. Too-Too has an unsuspecting crush on Lonnie D. And Lonnie, having been dumped by her latest boyfriend (this is back in high school), digs the idea of doing something, anything to remember her senior prom by. So they're gonna make out or something. I don't know. But this is taking me back to that place where young girls, or young women, or women more easily explore their options sexually than men.

7/13

I realize that I've been writing this as an extended monologue from the start. You don't see any of the other characters, though they're there. I like the idea of just staying focused on Lonnie; learning everything from her. Yeah, I like that.

7/14

Tried to work with some neighbors observing Lonnie from across the courtyard—Mrs. Cacciarelli; old, Italian, nosy, bossy. It's fun, but doesn't further the conflict; just adds color. I'll have to ditch it. Lonnie's reaction to her doesn't really advance the plot. Oh, well, it was a good idea for the moment.

7/15

I got it. Lonnie's leaving Fuzz; she's packing her shoes up. They bring back a flood of memories. One memory is Lonnie at her Senior Prom where she meets Fuzz for the first time. Her best friend, Too-Too is with her, and through the course of Lonnie dissing everyone, she discovers that Too-Too has a crush on her. She wants to remember her senior prom (and she's more than a little curious about kissing a girl), so she arranges with Too-Too to meet her somewhere and they'll make out. Back in the present, maybe Lonnie finally reasons that she's been restless all these years with Fuzz because he's not really who she wants to be with. She's at the beginning of a new sexuality—or something like that.

God, I have so many women friends that had this kind of experience. With a man for years, then finally touches a new part of sexuality and a whole new world opens up. Maybe this is where I'm going.

7/16

Okay, just to be straight: she's not leaving Fuzz because she's a lesbian. She's leaving Fuzz because she's unhappy in the relationship, and the memory of Too-Too is one possible reason why she's unhappy; not specifically Too-Too, but the idea of being with a woman instead of a man. Or maybe Lonnie is and always has been a lesbian that's taken cover in a relationship with a man all these years, and now wants to live the life she's meant to live. Hmmmmmmm.

I like the way it starts: lights up, BOOM, Lonnie with her cardboard box is on her way out. Right into the action. No question what's going on.

Love the pickle scene. Great image. Limp pickle for Fuzz's dick.

7/17

Alright. Lonnie's a sexual woman. Period. And the shoes are maybe an extension of that. And the red shoes, what she calls her "cherry reds" is a sexual image in and of itself. And that triggers the memory of her prom and Too-Too, which in turn, triggers her confirmation that she needs to get out of the relationship with Fuzz and explore other options—maybe women. She's at least okay with the idea of it.

Right now the ending's a little heavy handed. A little too much symbol and metaphor and image and sexuality and indicating.

7/18

Jesus, either I'm dead on or I'm la-la land. I look back over what I've written, and from the start, it's full of sexual images and phrases that weave throughout the story.

The name Fuzz
limp pickle
Lonnie's box
Lonnie's shoes
Cherry Reds
Ta-ta's and ass
"Sexed up"
The Shanita Sinclair story
curve and lift
Snatch to match
her "jane"
dick headed
Titty and Twat show
Coochie
Vaginarian
rose colored envelope

7/19

Finished a draft. I like it. Ending is still heavy handed. Don't know what to do. Is it too much?

I don't know. I can't be objective. I need to ask someone.

7/20

I think I'm short-shrifting the section in which Lonnie becomes aware that Too-Too's hot for her and she's curious herself. I do all this work to get there, and then it feels too "neat," too easy.

I'll work on it some more.

Gary ended up writing drafts dated 8/3, 8/8, and 8/10. When I told him the original deadline had been extended, he wrote a "final-final" draft in December, which is the draft presented here. I asked him how he felt about the end of the play in this last draft, and he responded in an e-mail:

Hmmmmmmmm. Now that's a good question. My worry is that it feels "gimmicky" that's she's reckoning with her sexual iden- tity, and that's why she's leaving Fuzz—an impulse she repressed years ago and now is allowing to surface. I don't know how woven into the fabric of the story it is. What I mean to say is that her journey leads her to a place where she calls into question something that's just below the surface—an impulse, desire, hidden desire, hidden wish, restlessness. Her friend Too-Too helps bring it to the surface back then, and her memory now makes it a pressing matter (emotionally) in her current circumstance with Fuzz. I guess the real question is— is her sexual restlessness what's responsible for leaving Fuzz, or, at the very least, being restless in her current relationship? Is any of this making sense? So to answer your question, yeah, I'm happy-er with it, but does it feel honest and right? I'm 50/50 on it.

The "final-final" draft of *Cherry Reds* follows. Keep in mind the initial scene and the Lady K monologue as you read it, and the useful comparisons to be made between this play and *Rug Store Cowboy*.

"Final-Final" Draft of *Cherry Reds*

The front of the stage is lined with a variety of shoes—tennis shoes, high heels, slippers, loafers, boots—all styles and kinds, each from a different time in LONNIE D's *life. We hear a door slam.* LONNIE D *storms towards the stage, carrying an empty cardboard box pinned under her arm. She wears a smart pair of mules. She yells back over her shoulder.*

LONNIE D: (*To off-stage*) Whatta you care where I got the box? I got the box, so forget about the friggin' box, because it ain't about the box. It's about what's going in it. And what's going in it is every ounce of my life that I can cram inside, then push through that front door. (LONNIE D *takes in the full stage*) This is not a threat, Fuzz. Oh, no, baby. This is the real thing. Lonnie D is on her way out. I'm packing it all up in my good, strong box, and I am blasting out of here so hard and so fast you're gonna swear you see NASA printed on my ass. And it's going to be a grand exit, honey. Oh, yes. I'm gonna make some loud noise, grunts and shit, 'cause I want every one of these loose-tongue, gossip-yappin', mama slappin' neighbors we got to hear and see my perky ass leave once and for all because I have had it, Fuzz! Capital Had, Capital It—Had It!

LONNIE D *drops the box and crosses back to the door.*

LONNIE D (*Cont.*): Do you hear me? Naw, you don't hear me. You never hear me when you need to hear me. Yeah, you get deaf to my drama! That's what you do. Well, go on. Get all Beethoven on me. (*Louder*) 'Cause I can get louder. Oh, yes, I can. I can get loud and mean, honey! I can growl and bite like your sister's nasty parakeet when I'm pissed, and I'm pissed, Fuzz because . . .

FUZZ *enters the room.* LONNIE D *looks up—her eyes bulge. She takes a few steps towards him and holds up her hand to stop him from talking.*

LONNIE D (*Cont.*): Uh-uh-uh. Don't say anything, Fuzz. Not a word. Your words mean nothin' to me, honey, 'cause whatta are you gonna say that'll make me forget what just happened?

LONNIE D. crosses to the cardboard box, picks it up. She then crosses to her closet, bends and picks up a pair of shoes and starts to put them in the box. She stands again.

LONNIE D (*Cont.*): Alright, maybe it couldn't be like I always pictured—fancy restaurant, a couple of Seagram's wine coolers on the table, big menu with fuckin' words I don't even know, ordering shit I can't even pronounce, chewing on a couple of bread sticks, then you sliding a ring box across the table and grinnin' that goofy ass smile of yours. I open it up, see the ring and cry, or moan, or some shit. Okay, maybe it couldn't be like that. (*Harder*) But who would have thought—in their right goddamn mind—that you would come in to the kitchen wearing your sagging Fruit of the Loom underwear, take a nasty, limp pickle out of that jar I told you throw away a year ago, put an engagement ring on the pickle, shake it at me and say, "Will you marry me?" (*Back to her box*) What were you thinkin, Fuzz? Nuh-uh. That shit's for the Jenny Jones show, but not for me. That's somebody else's nightmare. So we're not going to fight about it, Fuzz. We're just going finally face the cold, harsh truth, baby, that we are two people who do not belong together. Now, go on, 'cause mama needs to pack. (*LONNIE stops what she's doing, looks up*) I'm gonna pack, Fuzz, so don't try to stop me. Do you see this pair of shoes in my hand? See, they go in the box first. Then another. Then another. Pretty soon, the whole closet'll be empty and that's what you call "packing," and when I slide that box through that door, that's what you call "moving out."

LONNIE notices FUZZ hasn't left. She stands up, walks to the door and stands beside it.

LONNIE D (*Cont.*): Fuzz, I think we'll both feel better if you once and for all, throw that pickle jar out.

She watches him leave. LONNIE D stands for a moment, lost in thought, collects herself and pushes forward. Noticing shoes, quietly:

LONNIE D (*Cont.*): Now, which of you is going to be the pair that walks me out of here?

She tries on one pair, then another and another. After a moment she begins throwing shoes in the box and stops on a pair of red, high-heel step-ins. She puts the red high-heels on.

LONNIE D (*Cont.*): (*To herself*) Now they fit. First time I wore these, I had to cut one of my father's socks in half and stuff the toes. Look at that—they look brand new. Not even a scratch or a nick . . . (*The lights begin to fall to a single area*) Ohhh, I felt tall in these Cherry Reds. And grown-up. Ohhhhh, so grown up. Senior Prom and feeling forty, honey. Couldn't tell me nothing I'd listen to 'cause I knew I was the First Lady of P.S.138.

She stands and walks forward into her Senior Prom. A mirror ball begins spinning, sending dots of light across the room. The Fine Young Cannibals' "She Drives Me Crazy" begins playing in the background. She approaches her friend, TOO-TOO.

LONNIE D (*Cont.*): Child, what a night, Too-Too. What a crazy, messed-up, night. But at least we look good, girl. Yeah, honey, you look Too-Too Good. Swear. I wouldn't lie. You look complete, girl—hair, make-up, dress, style. S'right. Too-Too is Too-Too Hot. You're sexed up, girl. "Sexed up." It's a new phrase. Means you're built and ready for it. S'true. I overheard Jonquel said you gotta an ass just like Madonna. No lie—he said it had "curve" and "lift." I love that—"lift." The only lift I got is this under-wire, honey, and the bitch is killing me. But at least I got ta-tas, Too-Too, thank you very much. Yes, ma'am, mama's always had the ta-tas. These small, but perky girls are my calling card.

We hear lightning, then thunder. LONNIE D jumps, then calms.

LONNIE D (*Cont.*): Oh, shit, I hate lightning and thunder. Scares the pee out of me. That reminds me, Too-Too. Did you hear about Kenny Bennadito? Honey, blew a fart in chemistry class, right in front of one of those Bunsen burners and caught his drawers on fire. Yeah, ran down the hall with his ass blazin' and nobody would put it out 'cause they wanted to see how long it'd burn. I hear he's gotta big, black scorch mark back there. Scarred for life. Uhm! I hope it was worth all that. (*Dances a beat, then:*) Oh, Lord, it's Too-Too Bad you can't do shit about that big-assed storm outside 'cause I had big plans to lay in the grass behind the gym and make-out with my boy. (*A beat, then:*) See, I wanted a big-ass hickey tonight. I wanted my boy to suck on my neck hard and bruise the hell out of me so I could wear a v-neck tomorrow and show the world, Too-Too, how my night ended. 'Cause you know, people been saying I got cold after Biggie G dumped me. Yeah, that's the word. Saying I'm cold to the mens. Shit. They don't know Lonnie D, honey, 'cause all I wanted to do tonight is lay out in that grass and feel a pair of hands on me where a high school boy should never be. Fuckin' weatherman on t.v. with his big head saying' "Beautiful night tonight. Cool, clear skies and shit . . ." and look at the mutha fuckin' rain. You know that ain't right. He ain't never right. The bitch is never right, and I hear he wears a girdle, anyway. No shit. (*Jerking her head to the right*) Hey, Miss Rochelle! Sorry, MRS. Rochelle. And before you even ask, I ain't been drinking. Here, smell.

She takes a few steps forward and blows her breath out, then watches Miss Rochelle walk away.

LONNIE D: I shoulda burped right in her face. The women's got her nose in everybody's mouth. Damn, that's pitiful. That's what happens when you're uglier than a cat's ass. You're the one they ask to smell inside people's mouths. What kind of job is that? (*Looking at her watch*) It's late, and I should get my booty home, but I can't get this dress wet after I spent hours begging my poor mama to purchase my ensemble and then, and THEN, honey, had to promise my daddy I'd never say "mutha fucker" ever again in my life.

She stands for a moment, lost, looking in one direction, then another. When she turns back, a young geeky boy is standing in front of her.

LONNIE D (*Cont.*): Dance? (*Embarrassed, but okay*) Sure. I can dance.

Aretha Franklin's RESPECT blasts over the speakers. LONNIE D comes to life with Aretha's first, "What you want? Baby, I got it. What you need . . ." She dances for a moment, not looking at the boy, then finally:

LONNIE D (*Cont.*): I'm Lonnie and that's my new best-girlfriend, Too-Too. T-O-O, T-O-O. Too-Too. It's her nickname, 'cause the girl does everything, you know, way over the top. Eats too much. Sleeps too much. Weighs too much. Wears too much make-up, and if you repeat any of that to anybody, I'll cut you with a rusty knife, got it? (*A beat, then:*) Good. My friends call me Lonnie D. "Lonnie Deeeeeeeeeeee," they say. The "D" is a fill in the blank kind of thing, depending on what's happening. Like right now, it's a Lonnie Dancing. In a little while, it could be Lonnie Drinking.

The boy dances real crazy. Lonnie D is horror-stricken.

LONNIE D (*Cont.*): But right now, it's Lonnie's Done With You. So go on, now 'fore your sprain your neck or something. (*The young boy walks away*) Ohhhhh, Too-Too, did you see that? I think he was from the Special Ed class. (*Embarrassed again*) What the hell was I thinking? Honey, Lonnie D was Lonnie Dumb for that stupid move. (*Looking around*) Tell me nobody saw me, please! See, that's what happens when you are desperate and reckless and forced to dance with the biggest loser in the whole school because the tall, lame, ugly mutha-fucker you been dating for the last three years decided he couldn't wait to stick his tongue in the mouth of your ex-best girlfriend, who in my case, was Shanita Sinclair, who just happened to be at my house watching reruns of I *Dream of Jeannie* when the incident happened. (*Closer in*) Yeah, girl, I walked in to the t.v. room, he was laying on top of her—I'm not lying—with his hands all on her . . . (*She roughly grabs her own breasts and shakes them*) . . . and her hands were all on his . . . (*She roughly grabs her own butt and shakes it*) Oh, I love this part . . . (*She dances hard for a few moments, then sobers*) Yeah, I have to say it surprised me. I had gone upstairs to try on my new prom dress for them and when I came down, they were all over each other like a coat of paint. His tongue was about a foot inside her mouth and she was whimpering. Whimpering! In my own house! So I said, "Bitch, stop right there." Well, the fool tried to jump all the way back to my father's lazy chair, but I grabbed that half-breed by his bleached blonde hair and drug him out of my house, giving his ass one swift kick when I got him to the door. I slammed the door, I walked back inside, grabbed her silly ass, walked into the kitchen and beat her senseless with a spatula before I let her go . . . Yeah, well, it was the only thing I could find. It was between that and a week-old cucumber, so I thought I'd at least get a sting from the spatula . . . Yeah, I thought it was pretty cool. I mean, the bitch that I went to summer camp with for eight straight years and told all my trash to, AND lent her fifty dollars when she needed to get fitted for a diaphragm, AND gave her my own blood when she needed some after a bad car wreck that almost left her crippled—she wants to whimper, moan and groan all over my man in my house? I don't think so. What kind of shit is that? I'd slap a rabbi for less than that! They're over there, hiding. Been hiding out all night. (*She looks in their direction, then screams at them*) Don't look over here! There's nothing for you over here! You better keep your eyes on your own side or I'll kick your ass again. Hey, Shanita, you better stay out of your mama's closet. When are you going to learn her clothes don't fit you? That shit's nasty, girl. You look like Margaret Thatcher! Tell your mama to stop shopping at Caldor's, 'cause that looks lame, honey. Lame! You look over here again and I'll be up your ass so deep I can scratch your tonsils. Shit, I'd slap your blind grand-pappy for less than that. (*To* TOO-TOO) Five on that, Too-Too. That was cold, even for me. (LONNIE D *slaps her a high-five.*

She sobers) I hope my smell hasn't worn out. I'm wearing Chanel Number 5. I have a big bottle and it's expensive, but that's what I like, so that's what I have. Smell me.

She leans her head to the side so TOO-TOO *can get a good smell.* TOO-TOO *takes a good, long, involved smell.*

LONNIE D (*Cont.*): It's made in France, I think. I don't like France because, well, they have all those French people there. And they are rude, honey. I know. I worked at Taco Taco last summer, and these French tourists walked up and tried to order in French. I said, "uh-uh, honey, you want a burrito, you ask for a burrito in my mother tongue. Don't try any of that vous-le-vous burrito bullshit, with me 'cause that's when Lonnie D becomes "Lonnie Don't Fuck With Me" . . . Yeah, I can be pretty tough sometimes. You gotta be because people run all over you. Just like Shanita . . . (*Louder, for* SHANITA) . . . that SKANKY bitch that dyes her SNATCH TO MATCH. YEAH, I'M TALKING TO YOU! Go ahead. Take him. I don't want him. How long do you think it's going to be before you walk in and catch him with his tongue down someone else's throat?! . . . Right, right, right. One day with the man and you think you know him. Puh-lllleeeeeeeease. (*Turning back to* TOO-TOO) Too-Too, thank God we're new best girlfriends. 'Cause I know you'd never pull shit like Shanita did. Well, she can have him. She can have all of them. And believe me, she will before she graduates, if she hasn't already. Oh, she's loose, honey. Ask any boy around; he'll tell you. They say her Jane already has mucho mileage on it, and she's only seventeen. Pitiful. Fuckin' pitiful. (*Looking around*) She did me a favor. I'm tired of men, anyway. Most of 'em ain't got the sense God gave a park pigeon and don't know shit about how to treat a real woman. See, if men could be more like women, honey, there wouldn't be a problem one. Am I right? 'Cause, see, I think women are complex and shit. We got what they call fuckin' nuances, honey, and the men are too, you know, dick-headed to figure that out. Shit, I got pieces of me that no man has ever seen and never will 'cause they don't know where to look; don't want to look; don't know even know they should look. Thank God I'm a woman, that's all I got to say. Women are fierce, honey. We are the fierce gender. We got layers. God gave us clout, baby. (LONNIE D *notices* TOO-TOO *is looking at her long and hard*) Too-Too, what's wrong with you? Whatcha lookin' at? You lookin' at me a little Too-Too long, hon, and it's beginning to make me feel a little Too-Too weird. Do I got a booger, girl? Tell me I don't—I'll die. (*A beat, then*) Damn, girl. Whatcha lookin' at?

LONNIE D *gets lost in the memory.* FUZZ *re-enters; the lights change back to normal.* LONNIE *takes her shoes off quickly and places them to the side.*

LONNIE D (*Cont.*): (*On her guard*) What are you doing back in here, Fuzz? I don't want to argue, hon, 'cause there's nothing to argue about. We're just different people who want different things, and it's always getting us into trouble. (*A step closer in*) I mean, I am who I am, and you're the kinda guy who puts an engagement ring on a limp, mutha fuckin' pickle. That doesn't work for me, Fuzzy. But it's your way. It's always been your way. For eight years, it's been your way. No matter what damn year it was, what month, what day, what hour, what season, what holiday, what death in the families, what car was broken down or relative was locked up, there was one thing I could count on you having your tall, lanky, six-foot-two, never-put-a-comb-through-that-hair-of-yours, Puerto Rican ass sitting on that lame, lime green Jennifer Convertible sofa watching whatever gore and blood, titty or twat show you can find, with a jug of Mountain Dew in one hand and fiddling with yourself with the other. That's not what I want, Fuzz. That's not who I want. (LONNIE *crosses right up to him*) But right now, all I really want is some peace and quiet, baby. So go on, now. Go play with your pickles, or something.

FUZZ *doesn't move.* LONNIE D *steps up, folds her arms and bears down hard.*

LONNIE D (*Cont.*): Fuzz, don't make this hard, baby. You know it's the right thing to do. Okay, so maybe we could patch this up one—more—time. But for how long? How long will it be before I get all crazy again that all you do is sit? You don't do nothin' but sit. You go to work, you sit. You come home, you sit. You visit ya mama', you sit. We visit Donnita—who's got one chair in the whole house—you find it and sit. You live to sit, Fuzz. I've never seen anything like it in my life. You go to a basketball game, wedding, bar mitzvah or funeral 'cause you can sit and watch them. You sit through your whole life, Fuzz. But I'm a girl who's on my feet. That's why I've got all these shoes. Can't sit. Don't want to sit. Couldn't sit if I tried. If you don't believe me, just watch me now as I move these mules to my closet and start packing it up.

She bends down, picks up her cardboard box, then notices FUZZ *has not left the room. She holds her hand up, as if to stop him from speaking.*

LONNIE D (*Cont.*): Please, Fuzz, go clean out a closet, or comb your hair, or something.

LONNIE D *watches* FUZZ *leave the room. Satisfied that she's finally alone, she looks back to her shoes again, and quietly, almost secretly puts them back on. We're back in her high school prom with* TOO-TOO.

LONNIE D (*Cont.*): Now, Too-Too, you gotta stop staring at me, girl.
People are gonna talk. (LONNIE *notices something on* TOO-TOO's
face) Honey, I just said, "stop staring." I didn't say "fuck you and
get outta my life, worthless bitch." So why are you crying? No,
no, no, no, don't turn away. Talk to mama, honey. What's wrong,
sweetheart? (*No response*) You got something to say, say it. We're
new best girlfriends. I love you, girl . . . (TOO-TOO *turns and faces*
her) Was that the wrong thing to say? Was that the right thing to
say? Well, I do. I do love you, and . . . (*Realizing*) Oh. OH! But I
mean, love you, you know, love you like, you know, like, how a
friend should love another friend. But I don't want your coochie,
hon. I don't want any girl's coochie. (*Quickly*) I mean, there ain't
a thing wrong with that, if that's what you want. And alright, I
admit, I've been curious, but if you ever tell anyone I said that,
I'll slice you open with a rusty razor. But I mean the truth is,
shit, everybody I know's curious. Even Lisa Lowenstein, that
blonde and blue-eyed skank of a cheerleader who has fucked
every boy on the Varsity and Junior Varsity hockey team, honey,
I heard she's tried being a VAGINarian, but prefers her meat, if
you get my drift. Yes. Swear. So even Lisa Lowenstein's been
curious. (*A long beat, then softly*) Is that why you're looking at me?
You're like, you know, you're "curious" or something? 'Cause it's
alright if you are. Really. It's alright. It's cool. I mean, I'm not
shocked or anything. Nothing like that shocks me, except for
the time when Miss Sassoon touched me after gym class. Said
she was getting a piece of lint off my back, then proceeded to
pick at my sweater all the way down to the crack of my butt.
Then told me I missed class on the day she covered hygiene
and shit, and maybe she should catch me up in a one on one
session . . . at my convenience. Puh-leeeease, honey. How obvious was that? Now, that shocked me, but not the touching part.
If anything, I got the, uhm . . . (*Looking around*) . . . the, uhm,
uhm . . . tingles—which surprised the hell out of me. Tingles,
child. The same kind of tingles I felt when Rodney Burson felt
me up in the sixth grade . . . (*Quietly, giggling*) . . . and like now.
I'm getting the tingles all over now, like I'm about to do something I'm not supposed to. (*A beat, then:*) Too-Too, I want to do
something that's going to make me remember this prom night
forever. I want to do something we'll both remember a long
time from now, so that like ten years, way into the future, when
you least expect it, this night's gonna jump into your brain and
make something magical happen. (LONNIE D *looks around, then*
quietly and very direct) In her classroom, Mrs. Rochelle keeps a key

in her top left drawer in a rose colored envelope. That key unlocks that big closet in the back of her classroom where she keeps all those exercise mats. Maybe we should go there, and you know, get away from everyone and . . . and talk some more. Meet you there in five? (A *beat, then:*) And Too-Too, there's vents in the door. When I knock, look down and make sure you see these Cherry Reds I'm wearing before you open the door. Got it. Cherry Reds—open the door.

The lights brighten. We're back in the present. LONNIE D *looks down at the shoes on her feet. She calls out to* FUZZ.

LONNIE D (*Cont.*): Fuzz?! Mama's found her walkin' shoes and she's on her way out.

LONNIE D *looks around the space, picks up her box and exits out. The lights fade to black.* END

As this final draft shows, Gary has synthesized many of his ideas and concerns into a work that has gone through a thorough process. His voice and Lonnie's voice have been established effectively enough for the play to continue to evolve through further drafts without losing the key elements. Perhaps Gary's concerns about the ending will remain until the play has a reading. As a number of our writers have mentioned, it's only when actors give life to the words on the page that the playwright knows whether he has accomplished his goals or not. Regardless, Gary has provided a wealth of openly-evolved material which will serve as a paradigm of struggling through to one's truest voice.

5

CHAPTER

Velina Hasu Houston:
Mister Los Angeles
BRIDGES AND CONNECTIONS

VELINA HASU HOUSTON IS AN AWARD WINNING MULTI-
genre author. Her work includes plays, screenplays, teleplays,
cultural criticism, poetry, and prose. Her signature play, *Tea*,
has been produced internationally to popular and critical
acclaim. Other plays include *Kokoro (True Heart)*, *Cultivated Lives*,
Ikebana (Living Flowers), *Necessities*, and *Hula Heart*; recent work
includes *Sentimental Education*, *Shedding the Tiger*, and *Waiting for
Tadashi*. Velina's work has been produced by the Manhattan
Theatre Club, Old Globe Theatre, Syracuse Stage, and The
Pasadena Playhouse, among others.

Velina has also edited several anthologies of Asian
American drama: *The Politics of Life* (Temple University Press,
1993), and *But Still, Like Air, I'll Rise* (Temple, 1997). She is also
an associate professor and director of the playwriting program at the University of Southern California School of
Theatre.

Velina's credentials are clearly exceptional, and the material she submitted for this book shows the quality of artistic
and analytical skills she is able to bring to any project she
undertakes. Her journal and plays serve as models of meticulous work, and have been reproduced in a completely
unedited form so that the reader will be able to follow the
journey Velina took in her work without interruption.

Before moving into Velina's work, however, there are a few

observations to be made about craft, and the connections between her work and that of our other playwrights.

First, I have placed Velina's work in this particular position in the book because it serves as a natural bridge between Parts II and III. This is purely coincidental, of course, like the connections within the groupings themselves, but a lucky accident nonetheless.

Like the other playwrights in Part II, Velina began with one play—*This Is A Key*—and finished with another: *Mister Los Angeles*. However, Velina's work also bears some similarity to that of Guillermo Reyes and Julie Jensen, the playwrights in Part III: *Mister Los Angeles* seems as if it arrived in one piece, completely intact from first word to blackout. As we will see from the plays in Part III, the key word in that sentence is "seems." Each play appears to have arrived in one piece, but each is the result of years of experience in theatre combined with a lifetime of observation, consideration, and reaction. The plays represent a nexus of these and other factors.

Velina's work spans these two parts of the book. It presents a combination of thinking on paper to find the truest piece and producing material that flows directly out of inspired and compound thought.

This combination brings me to the second point: it addresses our ongoing interest in the "personality of process." Velina's two plays serve as excellent reminders that every playwright must use their own techniques, and be faithful to their own vision. That Velina's work has a foot, so to speak, in each grouping makes clear once again that there is no single methodology for writing a play—or even for one playwright. It is crucial to know one's own nature, sense of theatre, and metaphor, and many other elements in order to understand when a leap or turn seems in order. It takes a trusting heart to actually make the leap.

Both Gary Garrison and Elena Carrillo speak of this in their journals. Gary observes some young women on the subway and suddenly feels a connection to the voices and attitudes he witnesses. Elena remembers an early image she found provocative—the "glass bats"—but bypassed. She returns to it when her first plays aren't working to discover it was the crucial image for a play that is exactly right for her. As we will see in Velina's journal, a simple event—the loss and return of some keys—provided the springboard from her first play into the second play. That this occurrence involved actual keys in an envelope is one of those fantastic poetic moments that life sometimes provides. The playwright's awareness of what he/she is observing and ability to react to a given stimulus are critical to finding one's truest expression.

Third, good work requires patience and can be assisted by the passage of time. When there is the luxury for the writer to have some distance from the original work, a maturation occurs in the work. Writers don't always have this luxury, of course, but when it happens the results can be very rewarding. The writer has encountered new events in his/her life, focused on many other things as the days progress, and yet the play lingers in the mind. There is a sort of tandem growth that goes on in this situation: both the writer and the play continue to evolve. When sufficient time has gone by, the playwright can return to the material refreshed and renewed, ready to bring the recent accumulation of perspectives to bear on the work. Sometimes this break occurs as the playwright's choice, and sometimes it is imposed by external factors.

As I've mentioned in previous chapters, I asked all of the playwrights in December 1999 if they wanted to write a further draft, since my deadline had been pushed back a bit. I had not planned initially to give the writers this kind of time for their plays to ripen on the vine, but my delay created dividends for the writers in a number of ways. Gary Garrison wrote his final-final draft, David Crespy had a chance to hear his work read and reacted to, Elena Carrillo wrote some retrospective notes for her journal, and so on. Velina wrote a play that seems very different from her first play, and yet *Mister Los Angeles* was born directly out of the work Velina did on *This Is A Key*.

As she explains in her journal, when Velina sat down to work on another draft of *This Is A Key*, ". . . it mutated into something entirely different . . ." The something different, *Mister Los Angeles*, is a play that addresses concerns Velina had explored in the first play, and springs as well from her experiences at the time of taking up a further draft. All of these steps are detailed in Velina's journal in a way that I could never capture, so I won't try to describe them here. The point is that time is a tool at the writer's disposal.

Playwrights, especially young ones, often feel they must rush through to the completion of their work. I have observed many times that student playwrights will start a new play with a verve and energy that generates some amazing material. However, when the original compelling inspiration to write the play begins to fade, the play often ends up aborted. This is where a lack of craft and patience will create problems every time. Having strong technical abilities combined with a willingness to grow and evolve with one's work is a combination all playwrights need to develop.

As we will see with Velina's work, the steps she takes are steady and well thought out. Even though *Mister Los Angeles* seems to leap into being fully grown, there is a wealth of craft and experience involved. Pay careful attention to Velina's journal throughout—this is a writer who knows her own work methods and creativity very well.

Fourth, and finally, there is a relationship between the approaches taken by Gary Garrison, Julie Jensen in Part III, and Velina: letting the voices of the characters emerge. As we think about our work at any stage of development, the characters tend to talk in our minds, and give us a sense of who they are. Velina's initial entries show us her process of thinking about and finding the voice of Ella, the main character in the first play. This provides a useful comparison/contrast to approaches used by other writers in this book.

At this point, it's time to read Velina's material and track her process. Velina's journal and plays follow here exactly as she gave them to me. This affords us the opportunity to encounter her work directly, and to virtually enter her mind as we follow her sequence of thoughts from start to completion.

March 17

The following are my writing notes and worksheets for a new one-act play that I hope will be approximately ten minutes in length when I complete it. I am embarking on this project based on a stimulus provided to me by Michael Wright, which is as follows, "There is a key in an envelope in a desk drawer." The first thought that comes to mind today is about the openings and closings in relationships, and what can be locked up and what cannot. It is a very vague idea at this point, but I shall give more thought to it and see what characters come knocking at my door in the midst of my deliberative wanderings.

March 18

A young woman named ELLA has appeared in my thoughts. She is sixteen years old. An introspective individual, she is academically gifted and formerly an "ugly duckling" who is pretty close to being a swan, but not quite there yet—and not even close as seen through her own self-critical eyes. ELLA is a philosophical sort, prone to deep contemplation, sensitivity, and a caution about all that occurs around her. She is wise for her years, an old soul who has been around the universe several times. She dresses like a flower child, but it is not a designed look. She simply throws on the long, faded flower-print dresses and there it is: a certain old-fashioned style that works for ELLA. And she would not really care if it did not. She just is. Usually, ELLA is even-tempered, but, when pushed to the limit, she turns into fire. Even when she does, there is something interesting about that fire, something very provocative. Some of it is just her age—a wildflower teenager, bittersweet sixteen. Some of it is just her unique and strangely attractive temperament. Everybody wants to look at that fire when it rages. Some even want to pass their fingers through it to see whether or not they will burn.

ELLA'S mother does not have a face yet; that is to say, her physical look has not taken shape in my mind. I do sense that she is a doting housewife who is lacking in the psychological tools needed to finesse (or even recognize, absorb, and process) the tempest of female adolescence. ELLA'S father is even less clear at this point, perhaps because, in terms of his role in ELLA'S life, that is the most that can be said about him—that he is her father. He appears to me now as a communications manager for a mortgage company, a communications manager who cannot manage to communicate well at home.

March 20

ELLA is growing quite active in my thoughts. Today, she starts to move.

ELLA has placed her house key in an envelope and put it into the catch-all drawer in her mother's kitchen, that drawer into which her parents throw things that do not have a specific place to be in the house, that are hard to categorize and therefore simply placed into the catch-all drawer as miscellany, perhaps to be placed into a more appropriate site at a later date (when a place merges for them or when they can be seen in a new light thereby suddenly being easy to categorize and earning that very American and often suburban "privilege").

ELLA has put the key in the drawer, but takes it out. She rifles through the drawer. These are initial images.

Now I see ELLA opening the mail and finding a letter from a clinic telling her that her pregnancy test is positive. She puts the key in the drawer for good and takes out her backpack, empties it and begins to re-pack it for departure. A young man arrives. She has not told him anything about her situation. She wants him to leave because she wants to depart on her own. When he refuses, she is forced (?) to tell him her news or she does so in order to make him leave. She needs to leave because she feels that her parents will make her keep her baby. She manages the departure. A car comes and she gets in. The driver tries to discern her dilemma. Magical cab? Driver says he is her son from the future? End?

A big chunk of action is bouncing around in my head. I keep thinking that I ought to stop and give more thought to ELLA, but she seems so clear in my head now. I can feel her energy, see her eyes, sense her pain, sense secrets about her that I cannot articulate, but know with clarity. She is confused. She is not sure what to do. She trusts her mother, but does not trust her father. She loves the young man, but thinks that he does not love her—and perhaps he does not. She feels she has to manage her own problems, that she cannot burden others with them. She feels she has disappointed her mother and she does not know how to face her. She is disappointed in herself. She wants to make her life right again, but the path to that objective is muddled with questions of morality, emotional welfare, capability, and a myriad of other critical issues. Her instinct is to run and hide, but, deep down inside, she knows that there is no sanctuary for the fears with which she is struggling.

I am going to let ELLA begin to talk and see where it leads me. I am going to attempt this in a rough first draft of the play.

March 20 Draft
THIS IS A KEY
Scene One

Spotlight on ELLA LANG with a key on a string that she swings back and forth in front of her like a pendulum. She watches it, seemingly hypnotized. Throughout, the sound of jangling keys unlocking a door that creaks open and then shuts are heard. These sounds repeat, with intervals of time that grow shorter with each cycle until it is a rapid succession, culminating as such at the end of ELLA'S speech:

ELLA: Mom does the laundry and ironing on Mondays and Thursdays. On Tuesdays and Saturdays, she does the floors and dusts everything. She gets up at five every day to make breakfast for my father. Then she makes my lunch and takes me to school. Her mornings are spent on putter-putter cleaning. She allows herself one talk show at lunch time, except on Fridays, which is a bridge party instead. She used to listen to Dr. Laura Schlesinger at lunch time, until those pictures of her—Bully in the Buff—showed up on the 'Net. Mom hates hypocrites. But there are all kinds of hypocrites. Like a woman who says she became a housewife because she wants to stay home and give me the attention I deserve, but who really did it because she just isn't all that. In fact, she never was. And, after the cleaning and cooking and talk-showing and bridging, very little's left of her attention. We don't talk. Dad either. He's a communications manager at work, but can't manage to communicate at home to save his own life. Or ours. And so I'm waiting for the mail. At least the mail talks to me. Sometimes. I mean the real mail. The kind you can feel in your hands: texture, words, better than poetry. Sometimes I get a letter from Blossom. We were friends in kindergarten and, when her family moved away, she said she'd keep in touch. And she does. Maybe three letters a year. She lives in Santa Barbara.

A letter spins onto the stage like a Frisbee. ELLA grabs the key with her fist to make it stop swinging. She stares at the letter. Finally, she approaches it, reaches for it tentatively, and then picks it up. She opens it and reads it. As she reads, she projects dark amusement. But the key drops to the floor as if she is stunned.

ELLA: (*A whisper as though to herself*) Positive. (*ELLA tears up the letter into little pieces with an eerie calmness and tosses the pieces up into the air like confetti*) Congratulations, Ella Lang, you're a positive girl. "O" positive blood, "A" positive grades. And now this. All this positiveness is positively going to make me sick.

ELLA *picks up the key, removes it from its long chain, puts it into the envelope that the letter came in, tries to put some of the letter confetti into it, and approaches a drawer suspended in mid-air. She stares at the drawer for a moment and then at her key envelope.*

April 5

I discussed the stimulus for the process with friend and fellow playwright Elizabeth Wong. She asked if I was incorporating the stimuli into the play as a plot point or simply using it as a jumping-off point to start her play. I shared with her that I was doing a little bit of both. The stimulus is sort of a springboard for the play, a point of departure for it, but also a plot point that figures in the action of the play. The latter is not necessarily because the stimulus is introduced later in the play, but because the protagonist is both aware of it (the key) and actively, complicitly connected to its presence. Elizabeth and I never discussed the details of our stories—character, through-line, etc.—but the effect of the stimulus and the way is in which we chose (and are still choosing) to utilize it were of interest to us. I noted to her that my application of the stimulus might shift as I continue the process over the next few weeks.

The discussion with Elizabeth provided its own creative stimulation for me because it returned my mind to thinking about the process, and the character and situation that I began developing a little over two weeks ago. I have not been able to give much thought to the play's dramatic elements because I have been preoccupied writing revisions for another play of mine (a full-length, *Cultivated Lives*) which opened on April 2 in San Diego. I was quite vigilant in that rewriting process, challenging myself to take that play to a higher artistic level, burning the midnight oil, pushing myself, challenging myself to find some answers that at least satisfy me. I am still not satisfied even though it has opened. The theater has been gracious enough to consider putting my post-opening revisions into the play. Thus, my mind has been and is very much on that play and that production. I welcomed the distraction of ELLA and her dilemma. In fact, in talking to Elizabeth, I began to worry about ELLA and where I had left her, disintegrating letters and starting to shift from her steady pensiveness to being frayed around the edges. My chat with Elizabeth was useful in distracting me from one sector of creative vigilance so that I can focus on another budding sector vis-à-vis this new play, which does not even have a title yet. But the young man, the only other character who I feel will appear on stage, is emerging in my thoughts. His name is CHANDLER. He is quiet, not introspective like ELLA, but quiet in an intense way. He is even more confused than she is and he does not yet know that deeper, entangled confusion is right around the corner. He has not yet lost all of the innocence of boyhood yet, despite the fact that he is definitely a man. He is eighteen years old. He, like ELLA, has no sense of his good looks, but she is keenly aware of them. He is vulnerable, but conceals it well. He is bright, but not intelligent. Maybe he earns straight "Bs" in school. He plays tennis. He is quite good at this. He likes the Steve Miller Band and likes to think of himself as the Space Cowboy, but he is far from it, maybe because he is too nice to be the Space Cowboy.

April 7

I have just re-read what I wrote on March 20 and am contemplating it. More scene work is taking shape in my head. I have to reflect on it a bit more, take it apart and put it back together again a few more times, before I commit it to paper.

April 8

Today, I am ready to write more of the play and to introduce CHANDLER EVANS.

Scene One (Continued)

ELLA *opens the drawer and puts her key envelope in it. Slowly, she closes the drawer. As she does, she hears a snippet of "Rock-a-bye Baby" sung by a little boy. Startled, she opens the drawer and examines the key envelope. She closes the drawer quickly. She hears radio distortion, as though someone were scanning frequencies. Just a snippet. Then a door chime. She opens and closes the drawer, but the door chime continues. Confused, she opens and closes the drawer rapidly. Still, the chime. Then the sound of a door opening and closing. ELLA is frayed from the sounds. Enter CHANDLER, a handsome young man who is not aware of his good looks. On the young side of eighteen with some innocence left, he stops and stares at ELLA. She fights the fact that she enjoys him staring at her. She wins.*

CHANDLER: Hi.

ELLA: Hi.

CHANDLER: Taxi?

ELLA: Taxi?

CHANDLER: Outside.

ELLA: Oh.

CHANDLER: You call it?

ELLA: What are you doing here?

CHANDLER: I was driving by.

ELLA: Just driving by.

CHANDLER: I saw the taxi and figured that if somebody in your house needed a ride, I'd give it.

ELLA: Didn't I already take a ride with you?

CHANDLER: (*Hands her pink panties, embarrassed*) You left your . . . in my car.

ELLA: Thanks.

She does not take the panties. Feeling awkward, he looks at them squashed up in his hand, tightens his fist around them, and stuffs them back in his pocket.

ELLA: You can keep them. Somebody ought to keep something.

CHANDLER: You going somewhere?

ELLA: Me?

CHANDLER: You're the only one in this house without a drivers' license so I figured . . .

ELLA: Santa Barbara.

CHANDLER: You never said.

ELLA: Santa Barbara. Santa Barbara. I'm saying it.

CHANDLER: Okay. Uh, sorry about the car.

ELLA: The car's a piece of fiberglass, okay? The car can get smashed, cracked, torn, even impaled by a unicorn and all you've got to do is take it to the shop. It's good as new.

CHANDLER: Almost.

ELLA: Go to hell.

CHANDLER: I didn't mean the car anyway. Just sorry, period. I meant for us to go to the movies, that's all.

ELLA: I have to catch a train to Santa Barbara, okay?

CHANDLER: You're the one who ran out of the car before I could tell you.

ELLA: Tell me what?

CHANDLER: And I've called, too.

ELLA picks up her backpack. The taxi's horn blows.

ELLA: Gotta go.

CHANDLER: When you coming back?

ELLA: (*A pause, then:*) When I'm finished.

CHANDLER: Let me take you to the train station.

ELLA: Go home, Chandler.

CHANDLER: What's in Santa Barbara?

ELLA: What's here?

CHANDLER: That's what I've been trying to find out.

ELLA: Look, my mom'll be home from the market soon, so see ya, okay?

CHANDLER: Let me drive you to Santa Barbara.

ELLA: It's five hours, Chandler. Seven, the way you drive.

CHANDLER: So give me those seven hours.

ELLA: It won't take you that long to tell me where you've been for six weeks.

CHANDLER: College interviews.

ELLA: Where're you going?

CHANDLER: (A pause, then:) Boston.

ELLA: Boston?

CHANDLER: Yeah. But I thought about staying here.

The taxi's horn blows again. ELLA gives CHANDLER the once-over and walks out, dragging her backpack.

CHANDLER (Cont.): Ella!

April 9

I am continuing the scene work, leaving off at the same place at which I ceased writing previously.

Scene One (Continued)

ELLA reappears.

ELLA: Come on, Chandler. I need to lock up.

CHANDLER: Why are you in such a hurry?

ELLA: Weren't you in a hurry six weeks ago at around 8:30 p.m.?

CHANDLER: Let me check my calendar.

ELLA: Loser.

CHANDLER: Oh, you're so beautiful, Ella.

ELLA: Blah, blah, blah. Get out.

CHANDLER: I'll follow you to the train station then.

ELLA: No.

CHANDLER: Why are you so angry?

ELLA: Why are you so calm? Are you dead? Is that what happens? You take girls, you make girls, and then you die?

CHANDLER *escapes by studying the confetti.*

CHANDLER: What's this?

ELLA: My life.

CHANDLER: Your life?

ELLA: It doesn't fit anywhere. Not even in there. The catch-all drawer can't even catch me. (*Points to the drawer*)

CHANDLER: A drawer? (*He does not seem to see it*)

ELLA: Catch-all. Isn't there one in your house where everybody throws the things that they don't know where else to put? You know, the stuff that seems to belong nowhere, that doesn't fit in with anything in the house?

CHANDLER: Like old nails, rubber bands, matchbooks from places you only visited once, or never.

ELLA: Stuff that's hard to figure out.

CHANDLER: Sooner or later, you find a place for it though.

ELLA: Yeah. The garbage can.

CHANDLER: No. It's like you're walking around the house one day and you see something that reminds you of the things in the drawer and you run and go get the thing and put it in its place.

ELLA: People don't ever really look at all the stuff they throw in those drawers. They just throw it away to make room for more stuff that has no important meaning or place in their lives.

CHANDLER: I cleaned out my parents' drawer once.

ELLA: Yeah. Once. We never clean ours out. Never.

CHANDLER: No, more than that. I was looking for an Allen wrench and I kinda remembered my mom throwing one in there one day. Another time, I was looking for a paper clip.

ELLA: You use paper clips?

CHANDLER: Sure. To keep things together.

ELLA: But stuff always gets loose and the thing falls apart.

One last blast from the taxi and then the sound of it driving off.

ELLA (*Cont.*): Damn.

CHANDLER: Want me to clean out your parents' junk drawer?

ELLA: Junk drawer? You call it junk?

CHANDLER: What'd you say? "Catch-all." Sounds better I guess. Where is it?

He wanders around looking and almost collides with the suspended drawer.

ELLA: NO!

Curious, he reaches out and "feels" the drawer, as though he were a blind person.

CHANDLER: Is this the drawer?

ELLA: You don't know a drawer when you see it?

CHANDLER: Ella, I don't see a drawer. (*He holds onto it as if in "Charades"*) This is it, isn't it? I can tell by your face. (*He fiddles with the drawer and tries to open it. She tries to stop him, but can't. He manages to open it. He finds the envelope and looks inside, holds up the key.*) I thought there was nothing there, but there is something. Here's something. This is something.

ELLA: You found it. How did you do that? If you couldn't see it, how could you do that?

CHANDLER: You. You told me.

ELLA: I didn't say anything.

CHANDLER: You didn't have to say anything to tell me. What is it? (*He observes her silence*)

This time you have to say something.

ELLA: Key.

CHANDLER: Yeah, but to what?

ELLA: House.

CHANDLER: This one.

ELLA: Duh.

CHANDLER: Your key?

ELLA: I could've been halfway to the train station by now.

CHANDLER: So this (*Notes confetti*) is for your mom?

ELLA: A . . . gift.

CHANDLER: Don't, Ella. Who was that letter from?

ELLA: Providence.

CHANDLER: Who, Ella?

ELLA: Doctor.

CHANDLER: Doctor? You sick?

ELLA: Oh yeah.

CHANDLER: Then why Santa Barbara?

ELLA: Because it's there. It talks to me.

CHANDLER: I talk to you. Tell me what's wrong.

ELLA: I belong to a different universe, Chandler.

CHANDLER: You mean like writing poems and writing in your journal, all that kind of stuff?

ELLA: You think the world revolves around a bouncing yellow-green ball that gets slammed back and forth over a net. That's a world of nets, balls, and slamming. I have to believe that there's more. If you could even believe there was more . . . if you could.

CHANDLER: (*Softly*) Ella, are you sick? Really sick? You don't have some terrible disease or something, do you?

ELLA: Look, this isn't Valentine's Day, okay? Go home. Go get interviewed again. Go to Boston.

CHANDLER: You're pregnant.

ELLA: (*Takes the key from him*) This is a key. A piece of metal cut to fit a certain lock. It can lock you out or let you in. This is the key that locks my parents in this house and that locks me out; that can't ever really let me in, only out. This is a key. I can even make a copy of it, lock other people in this house where I used to live or be or something like that. And I am still on the outside. I can go. I can travel. I can put this away and say '*you are in there and I am out here and this is good-bye*', this is '*I don't need this anymore*', this is "*throw this in your catch-all drawer because it didn't/couldn't catch me*', this is '*you're off the hook*'. This is a key.

She stares at him. He looks as though he might cry, which stuns her, but she tries to manage her feelings.

ELLA (*Cont.*): Good luck in college.

CHANDLER: Thanks.
ELLA: Boston or whatever.
CHANDLER: Probably. (*Exits*)
ELLA: I thought so.

> ELLA *puts the key in the drawer and closes it. Wind chimes tinkle and sound of breezes as lights strobe. A magical aura. Lights out on the house, fading up on the representation of a vehicle, some sort of whimsical, neo-romantic riksha/chariot. No passengers.* ELLA *studies it for a moment, throws in her backpack, and them climbs in. A YOUNG MAN enters, looking just like CHANDLER, but simpler, much more innocent, in long white robes.*

YOUNG MAN: Did you call a cab, Miss?
ELLA: Uh, yeah. Uh, is this a cab?
YOUNG MAN: Where're you headed?
ELLA: A place where I fit.

> He *gestures to his vehicle and helps her get in.*

YOUNG MAN: That's easy, especially if you know you want it. Look how nicely you fit in my chariot.
ELLA: I thought you said it was a cab.
YOUNG MAN: I knew you'd have a sense of humor.
ELLA: You don't know me.
YOUNG MAN: But I do.
ELLA: But how? Why?
YOUNG MAN: Where is Chandler Evans?

> At first, ELLA *is startled, then sad, then resolute.*

ELLA: Not in this universe. (*Studies the* YOUNG MAN *pensively*) You know what's wrong with me, don't you? (*He nods*) And there isn't really anything wrong with me. (*He nods*) You know who I am, don't you?

> He *approaches, takes her hand, which she tries to pull away. But something about his nature makes her relax. He takes her hand, kisses it. Then he prepares to lead the vehicle. He stops to look back at her solemnly.*

YOUNG MAN: Yes, I know who you are.
ELLA: Who am I? (*Searches her own soul*) Just who am I . . .
YOUNG MAN: You're my mother.

> *Black-out. The End (I think.)*

April 9

Having read what I wrote in the last sitting, I am concerned that the piece is too long and that the ending is a bit too strange. I have to think about it a little longer before I start being the artistic vigilante again.

April 15

Am adding a new line in the play for ELLA: I belong to a different universe. At end, add: Where's Chandler? ELLA: Not in this universe. Rewrites will be placed in text above.

In returning to the text to add the few lines mentioned above, I found myself rewriting a bit more than intended. Rewrites included about the last third of the play.

January 4

I have returned to the play after communicating with Michael. I am re-reading it today in the hope of refining it a bit further and giving it a name. Many leap into my mind, such as *Chariot* (which sounds too historically Greek) or *This is the Key* (which feels too postmodern) or *Mother* (which is too to-the-point). My colleagues always tell me that I have the "title-genie" magic, which implies some ability to create interesting titles. I do not always feel so certain about this in the midnight hour when a play has not yet been named. Sometimes titles come easily and fit well. At other times, however, I simply wait for the right title to come along. Right now, I am waiting. Perhaps re-reading the play will inspire me. Part of the issues weighing in at present is that I am overloaded with writing. I am in pre-production (at different stages of pre-production) with two full-length plays, *Ikebana* (*Living Flowers*) at The Pasadena Playhouse and *Kokoro* (*True Heart*) at Sacramento Theatre Company. Furthermore, I am completing revisions on my dissertation for my Ph.D. at the University of Southern California's School of Cinema-Television. I also am working on another play with Loy Arcenas and Brava Theatre, San Francisco. So it is a rather wild and wonderful time, but keeping my muses and me quite busy.

January 8

All right, now things are getting lunatic. I re-read the play a couple of days ago and chose a title, inserting it in the text. Then I made some minor revisions in the text. THEN I lost the keys to my car, and this is when things began to be creatively lunatic.

I am not certain if I can explain the nature of events as they affected me, but it is something like this . . . My key chain has an emblem of the flag of Japan on it with the word "Japan" printed under the emblem. I happened to be at my university office when I lost the keys. I gave up looking for them and went to get a cup of tea. While I was away, a student found the keys in the hallway and returned them to me—in an envelope. She commented on the emblem and notation of "Japan," by saying, "I figured these keys were yours because of the Japan thing and you are always the Japan green tea thing." Several things began to happen as I thought about my keys, the envelope in which they were returned; and the fact that my transnationalism (and multirace and multiculture) are such an organic and primary part of who I am not just personally, but also in my professional life as an artist. I believed that the fact that my keys were returned in an envelope were in some way tied to my efforts to write a play with a key as an impetus. Ella and Chandler began to fade away in my mind because their dilemma was not enough. It was not enough for Ella simply to be pregnant. In a colored and cultural life, a woman can be pregnant, but it is often much more compli-cated than that because about assumptions made about her (in a sociopolitical/class vein) that bring to bear upon her reproductive condition a whole panoply of third-party attitudes, behaviors, and expectations that challenge her condition. For a woman of color never can be just a woman. She is first and foremost a racialized woman and even a majority of white liberals will view her through the filter of her color and ethnicity first, no matter how much her individuality illuminates her as a Human Being. This being deliber-ated in tandem with my keys and their Japanese emblem inside of an envelope, I sat down to revise *This Is A Key* (the name I have given to the Ella play), but it mutated into something entirely different; and more in keeping with my transnational self. (Granted, I live as an individual and as a Human Being, naming myself as an American playwright who is writing American plays, but what it means to be "American" is changing, so my drama of Japanese Amerasian magic realism is just as "American" as the work of any white playwright writ-ing in the United States.) Ella's face fades into a mask and re-emerges in a reincarnation that intensifies her with personal politics and more urgent needs beyond, and yet inclusive, of maternity. Interestingly enough, in this new play, *Mister Los Angeles*, the key in the envelope is not in the play per se, but is entirely responsible for the play coming into being as a mutation of *This Is A Key*. Perhaps, how-ever, the infant in the drawer is the "key" in the drawer. Here we go:

MISTER LOS ANGELES
Cast of Characters
JOE AMERICA
SEIKO GRACE

Time and Place
Los Angeles. Now.

> JOE, *dressed in muscle T-shirt, leotards, and big sneakers; sits in the posi-tion of The Thinker staring at a drawer on the floor out of which cooing*

emanates. Enter SEIKO, *elegantly dressed.* JOE *jumps up with enthusiasm and embraces her. She is friendly, but does not engage in the embrace with the same enthusiasm.*

JOE: Seiko, Seiko. You've come back. I knew you'd come back. You've been gone three years, but I knew—

SEIKO: Joe, it's only been three weeks.

JOE: Oh. Well, the important thing is: you've come back. Time disintegrates in this city. City of Angels, hell. City of ravenous angels, that's for sure. Everything disintegrates into plastic and the politics of the dollar. Did you know nobody cares about race anymore? There's only one color: the color green.

SEIKO: Nice to see you, too, Joe.

JOE: So, uh, well, yeah. Thank goodness. Look. Look at our child. Isn't she beautiful? Rainbow across the Pacific, ay?

SEIKO: (*She looks, smiles with a maternal glow*) Yes. (*To the infant*) Hi baby girl.

JOE: She looks like you.

SEIKO: (*Relieved*) Yes.

JOE: That's what I been sitting here thinking about: looking at her and seeing your face and hoping and praying that you'd come back.

SEIKO: Okay, Joe.

JOE: Now we can get married. You'll take me out of this place, take me out before I get killed, suffocated by plastic people, road rage, and rudeness; save me before it's too late to be normal. Get me out of here, Seiko. It's a war zone. Take me to a place where dreams can really come true. (*A quick pause*) Did you, baby? Did you?

SEIKO: *Nani?*

JOE: *Yubiwa.* Did you buy me a ring?

SEIKO: Joe, there's something I have to tell you.

JOE: Oh no. You're not pregnant again are you? I can't take care of two.

SEIKO: Joe, you haven't even been taking care of one. I pay the nanny to care for her sixteen hours a day.

JOE: Yeah, well, there's the other eight.

SEIKO: You mean the eight hours that she's sleeping?

JOE: Yeah well. . . . Gee, Seiko, you look so great. Did you change your hair or something? Oh my god, Seiko, you cut your hair!

SEIKO: Yeah, Joe. Listen, Joe.

JOE: Yes, my sweet lotus blossom; my hibiscus honey, my pineapple. To listen to your voice is like swimming in a lake of green tea, mountains made of mochi to the north and cherry blossoms to the . . .

SEIKO: Joe, I have something to tell you.

JOE: It's okay. I forgive you for leaving me. I know you didn't have a choice. The earthquake was so bad. You would have come for us if you could. I know you tried. Don't apologize.

SEIKO: Joe, I got married.

JOE: What?

SEIKO: Married, Joe. I got married.

JOE: No, Seiko Grace.

SEIKO: Yes, Joe America.

JOE: But you could have been Mrs. America. How? Why?

SEIKO: I fell in love, Joe.

JOE: But you loved me, too.

SEIKO: But you didn't want to get married, Joe.

JOE: You know what that therapist told me: I was afraid. That was just my fear talking.

SEIKO: No, that was just your mom talking, telling you you're too good to marry an "Oriental." What was that she called me? Your rice queen?

JOE: But I want to get married now, Seiko.

SEIKO: Too late, Joe.

JOE: But you shouldn't have tried to rush me. You know what else the therapist told me? He told me you were trying to make me feel guilty for getting you pregnant. He told me that women always try to get pregnant to tie a guy down and force him to make a commitment that he isn't ready to make. He told me that it isn't really my fear, but your insecurity.

SEIKO: So now you admit that this therapist was a man.

JOE: I'm not admitting anything! He was a woman.

SEIKO: "He" was a woman.

JOE: I'm not telling you what he was.

SEIKO: You don't have to. The picture is clear. A white American male who was summarily dumped by an Asian woman at some other moment in time and is taking out his frustrations through you. And your head is buried too far in the ground to know that he's plucking your tail feathers. I mean, do you even know your penis from your pituitary. *Mendokusai ne.*

JOE: What does that word mean? I haven't learned that word yet.

SEIKO: Look, Joe, my husband wants to adopt the baby and I think that would be for the best, don't you?

JOE: But Seiko, I love you.

SEIKO: Trivial and tardy at this point, Joe. Besides, it isn't me you love. It's just the golden light. Guys like you flock to it, fluttering and buzzing around it until adoration disintegrates into annoyance.

JOE: Wait a minute! It sounds like you're talking about a moth!

SEIKO: And then when you've sucked one golden light dry, you move on to the next one and the next one. It's how you stay alive. I've cleaned the dust from your wings, Joe. The lights are out for you, but perhaps they have been for some time.

JOE: That's what I am to you? A butterfly?

SEIKO: No. A moth.

JOE: And what exactly does that mean?

SEIKO: You figure it out, Joe.

JOE: Well, you can't take my baby.

SEIKO: She's mine, too.

JOE: I'm her father, her Great White Hope, okay? Everybody knows that I'm much more capable of providing a life for her than you are. I can give her power that you never can.

SEIKO: I'm Japanese, Joe. I know all about overachieving and power. And, if I don't, I'll just watch what you do, co-opt it, improve upon it, and make it my own.

JOE: She's not going anywhere.

SEIKO: Joe, this is the part where you concede that it is better for our baby to have her mother and a surrogate father than to be raised by a single white guy who puts her diaper on backwards, makes her sleep in a drawer, and can't even recognize Japanese rice—much less cook it, or afford it.

JOE: Chinese rice tastes better.

SEIKO: Well, after all of your visits to the golden light, I'm sure you're an expert in every type of Asian rice available.

JOE: Who is he?

SEIKO: You don't want to know.

JOE: WHO IS HE?

SEIKO: The King of Siam. Now give me the baby.

JOE: I knew it! You're shacking up with some Oriental guy.

SEIKO: Yes, Joe. I'm a governess for his son. Give me the baby.

JOE: An Oriental guy? You had to choose an Oriental guy? Over me? You call that an upgrade?

SEIKO: I call that home improvement, Joe. Now give her to me.

JOE: No.

SEIKO: Yes, Joe. It's the only way. What are you going to do? Kill yourself?

She grabs the baby. (It is a stuffed doll that looks like a real infant.) He grabs the baby. They struggle with it and it begins to rip apart in shreds. SEIKO tries to save it, but JOE grows excited and finishes ripping up the baby all on his own, reveling in his power as SEIKO unsuccessfully tries to stop him.

SEIKO: Stop, Joe! Stop!

JOE: Now tell me again who's more powerful.

> SEIKO *stares at her baby, kneels beside her, and starts to cry.* JOE *towers over them; he looks sad.*

JOE (*Cont.*): Look what you've done. Just look what you've done. You're so greedy. You people are so greedy. Just had to try to have the whole world, didn't you.

SEIKO: (*Bitterly*) I learned it from you.

JOE: Shut up, Madam Butterfly.

SEIKO: (*Looks at him with incredulity*) So witness the beast. This is the beast, unmasked.

> JOE *takes a gun from the drawer and points it at her.*

JOE: Shut up. Where's your kimono anyway?

SEIKO: I don't own any kimono, Joe. I never did.

JOE: But you had one of your mother's. Where is it? Why aren't you wearing that? That's what you're supposed to look like.

SEIKO: Joe, put the gun down.

> He draws near to her as if trying to be intimate; but then yanks her close to him and forces the gun into her hand, forces it towards her temple as she struggles.

JOE: Sayoonara.

> He forces her to shoot herself. She crumples into a heap by the remains of the baby. He stares at them for a moment.

JOE (*Cont.*): Dear God. I vow to kill every Oriental girl I meet until the day I die. I will visit the golden light. I will suck it dry and glow golden myself, more powerful, more luminescent; more like you, good fella.

> He looks at the bodies again. A bit of remorse settles in. He wipes away tears that are not truly apparent and crouches beside the bodies. SEIKO slowly rises in a ghostly fashion and swathes herself in a long black silk shroud that she pulls from her sleeve in choreographed movement. Lights fade to that of twilight and sounds of night fade up: the buzzing of insects, distant cars. He suddenly discovers her as she pulls the shroud over him.

JOE (*Cont.*): Hey! What the!

SEIKO: (*As light fades into blue on her, with* JOE *in semi-darkness*) I have caught you, my pretty little moth. Caught you as you suck the energy out of one golden light after another, feeding on our glow so that you can live. I will spread your wings and dry them. I will put you in the museum, that tomb that you always believed you deserved. Good-night.

Black-out. END OF PLAY.

January 9
I just re-read the mutated play. I feel peace.

* * *

Velina's work clearly spans Parts II and III, as the next section will reveal. Her work provides us with a potent study in process which combines a variety of techniques and creative efforts. As we have already observed with Elena Carrillo and Gary Garrison, the ability to jump from one play to another involves a willingness to take large risks. The best work comes more often from such risks than from taking the easier route. There are no guarantees the risk will work, of course, but there is so much to learn that it is always worth it.

As I mentioned at the start of this chapter, it is just a lucky happenstance that Velina's work forms a bridge, but one which affords us many opportunities to compare and contrast her work in several contexts. I will leave this chapter with two suggestions: 1) if possible, read the next two chapters immediately—both as their own individual work and as reflections on Velina's material to see what conclusions can be drawn, and 2) be certain to revisit all of the chapters once the book has been read completely, in order to gain perspectives on how the playwrights match up and diverge, and which processes have the most value.

III

PART

Cut from Whole Cloth

"Simplicity is the natural result of profound thought."
—Anonymous

"We have to look at our own inertia, insecurities, self-hate, fearing that, in truth, we have nothing valuable to say. When your writing blooms out of the back of this garbage compost, it is very stable. You are not running from anything. You can have a sense of artistic security. If you are not afraid of the voices inside you, you will not fear the critics outside you."
—Natalie Goldberg

"This above all—to thine own self be true,
And it must follow, as the night the day,
Thou canst not then be false to any man."
—Polonius, in *Hamlet*, by William Shakespeare

OUR FINAL TWO PLAYWRIGHTS, GUILLERMO REYES and Julie Jensen, present work that gives the appearance of arriving intact, like a garment cut from whole cloth. This is not true, of course. Both writers made many changes in their texts as they rewrote and refined, as will be evident in their chapters. What is true is that experience can often make a vast difference in one's approach, and in one's certainty about the approach. Ideas for plays do arrive intact occasionally, though this doesn't mean they automatically write themselves. All work requires evolution, time to mature, and patience. Julie Jensen comments on this in her chapter: "I used to say about full-length plays that it took me 20 minutes to think up the idea and 3 years to write it."

The plays by Guillermo and Julie present us with a feast of subtleties in the art of rewriting. The choices they make are often delicate and fine, yet each adjustment deepens the texture of the work. Their plays represent a synthesis of the three quotes above: seeming simplicity achieved through a sense of personal truth, artistic security, and careful, maybe even profound, process.

CHAPTER

Guillermo Reyes:
Bitter

"THE PROCESS REDEFINES THE NEED
FOR THE WORK"

CHILEAN-BORN GUILLERMO REYES IS A PROLIFIC playwright with numerous productions, including *Chilean Holiday* at the Actors Theatre of Louisville, and *Men on the Verge of A Hispanic Breakdown*, which won Theatre L.A.'s Ovation Award for Best World Premier Play, and the 1996 Emerging Playwright Award in New York. His work is political on several fronts, covering issues such as life during and after the repressive regime of the dictator Pinochet in Chile, and the problems of maintaining an identity as a man who is both gay and Hispanic in a culture that leaves little room for either reality.

Like Julie Jensen, Guillermo does little in the way of formal explorations prior to beginning a play. He described his initial process in an e-mail:

> It's rare for me to do a full outline of anything. At best, I will try to blurb it into existence, although that happens when I feel stuck and I need to know what is this play about so I may do something like this: "Young Man decides to marry into wealthy family and tries to seduce young daughter of the family, and ends up getting more than he bargained for, and learns such and such about himself." I would then try to define what it is that he learns, what does it mean for him to get more than he bargained for, what are the specific adventures he could undergo trying to get himself into this family, and so forth. I

am more likely to do that with a full-length play than with a ten-minute play. Maybe that's because I feel I can afford to get lost in a ten-minute play.

This approach slightly echoes the technique used by Gary Garrison, in which a simple statement is compounded more and more until the full story has emerged. The purpose of Guillermo's approach, however, certainly reflects the work of all the other playwrights as he focuses on the key elements of objectives, obstacles, character qualities, and so on.

Since *Bitter* is short, it's possible to reproduce all three drafts. Draft One and Two were written approximately one month apart, in June and July 1999, respectively; Draft Three was written nearly six months later, in the first week of January 2000. Guillermo's rewrites are very deft as he steadily moves toward a refinement of the play that reflects the evolution of his thinking and process. His observations on the changes are a record of subtle shifts in a play that is highly political and very theatrical.

Notes on the First Draft of Bitter

In choosing a topic, I tend to follow my instincts. What's bothering me? What's on the back of my mind? What is being played in that sick 24-hour showcase called my imagination?

The recent bombing of Yugoslavia has brought back plenty of anxieties. I tend to be anti-war and anti-military, especially after my bitter memories of the Pinochet dictatorship which troubled me as a Chilean-born teenager. By the same token, I was feeling relieved that the Serbian strongman Milosevic was finally being faced with retribution (no matter how tentative), after the many atrocities his henchmen have committed. Ethnic cleansing indeed. For me to get a vicarious thrill over a bombing is already guilt-inducing; that I actually welcomed the bombing was even more overtly shocking.

That's because, as I've gotten older, I think I've evolved some priorities. As ugly as war may seem, there's something uglier still, the blind eye toward human rights violations. That Clinton finally decided to take a stand was a welcome change of priorities after turning a blind eye to similar atrocities (among the Kurds, or the Hutus and the Tutsis in Rwanda, the Tamil rebels in Sri Lanka and other places).

Ethnic cleansing is nothing new and in my recent readings of California and Native American history, I've discovered the US government used to practice it with a missionary spirit called Manifest Destiny. It was the way of the world at the time perhaps, and the way Indians were removed, their culture obliterated, their language and customs expunged from the national consciousness inspired Hitler's methods later in our century.

I was born in a country that committed itself to the "extermination" of Marxist ideology. Soon enough, anyone suspected of being Marxist, whether or not he was, became vulnerable to elimination.

In the writing of *Bitter*, I wanted to bring all these thoughts together in the short format of the 10-minute play. Which meant the ideas would work best through allusion. I didn't want anyone even mentioning the words "ethnic cleansing." In fact, I wanted the characters to have no names and to be part of an alternate reality. The play could be happening anywhere on earth, I assumed, and wrote it accordingly. I present two characters who aren't different from one another. I didn't want a literal representation of ethnic or other differences. The Rep Guy is slightly older just because I wanted him to have a pretentious intonation like that of a British butler, and the Man who's being removed would then react accordingly to the Rep's highfalutin' style. Their relationship as it lives on stage seemed more important than any ideas behind the scenes. They are the ones who bring the action alive and they have to take precedence over what I, as the playwright, would be thinking.

The first draft presented the basics of this relationship. Again, nothing should be over-explained, everything alluded to. The key became a symbol of entrance. A key allows you to go in and out of your private dwelling, which signifies ownership and sovereignty. As given to the Man, the Rep reassures him he will control the key to the place he's being removed. An old trick, mind you, something I learned from history. The key is part of the empty promise of removal—the reassurance that everything's going to be alright, that it's for the Removed One's own good, and that the new land will be plentiful. All lies, of course, but delivered charmingly and convincingly by the smooth-talking Rep. I borrowed it from the books I've read about the many empty promises made to Native Americans as they were being removed.

The first draft of *Bitter* introduces us to the nightmare world Guillermo describes. It effectively sets the tone and lays down the groundwork for the more finished play that evolves from this initial effort.

First **Draft** *of* **Bitter**
MAN, man in his 30s
THE REP, older man, official sounding bureaucrat

> *Two men in a room, modern dress, modern times. It's important that they are NOT cast to look as if they were from separate groups or race, or any other feature that makes them seem distinct. They should ideally even look alike or be dressed alike, to further the mystery. The Rep hands the man a key in an envelope.*

THE REP: There's the key, sir. I'm sure you'll find the accommodations quite suitable.

MAN: Suitable?

THE REP: Nothing luxurious, you understand, but clearly up to par.

MAN: With what?

THE REP: With what, you say? (*Laughs*) Tricky. Very good, sir. Keep up the spirits.

MAN: Where exactly am I going?

THE REP: Oh, the bus will take you there, sir. A good bus, new shock absorbers.

MAN: But where am I going?

THE REP: Going?

MAN: Where is the bus taking me?

THE REP: If you'd like to speak to a representative.

MAN: You are the representative.

THE REP: But I don't have all the answers.

MAN: Not all the answers, just one answer will do.

THE REP: I know it's difficult, sir. I have kids myself, two boys, and a wife. Rather ill. Terminal, I'm afraid—

MAN: I don't give a shit!

THE REP: Sir!

MAN: Tell me what you know or shut up.

THE REP: My job is to put you on the bus along with the others.

MAN: The others. Who are the others?

THE REP: Look, sir. I really must go—

MAN: No, don't go! Please. Don't leave me here.

THE REP: I will be back.

MAN: I know you will, but don't leave. I don't like this place, no windows, no air in here.

THE REP: It is rather bleak, isn't it?

MAN: I'm—I'm scared.

THE REP: Yes, yes, it can be frightful, this whole thing, but it's really for the best.

MAN: Whose idea of the best?

THE REP: For your people really.

MAN: What people would that be?

THE REP: Your people, so badly treated around here, it's for their protection really.

MAN: Whose protection?

THE REP: You'll be better off removed.

MAN: Is that so?

THE REP: You will have a key, of course.

MAN: But who'll own the home?

THE REP: You will have sovereignty. The key assures you of it. Otherwise, why hand over a key? It will let you enter and leave at any time.

MAN: A key.

THE REP: A key, sir! Regular good ole chrome.

MAN: Which you can take back any time, is that right?

THE REP: Not me personally, sir.

MAN: Not you. Your government.

THE REP: Well, it's not exactly my govern . . .

MAN: Answer yes or no.

THE REP: I really don't know the answer. If I were you, I'd be grateful for the key.

MAN: Would you?

THE REP: Huh?

MAN: Would you be grateful for the key if you were me?

THE REP: I said as much, I believe.

MAN: What did I do?

THE REP: You? Don't take it personally.

MAN: I'm being removed.

THE REP: Relocated, sir. You really are taking this personally. It has nothing to do with you, it's your . . . your group.

MAN: What did my group do?

THE REP: I don't know.

MAN: You don't know.

THE REP: But it's really for the best. For your protection. Really.

MAN: Alright, go.

THE REP: What?

MAN: You have no answers, nothing constructive to say, go! Get the hell out of here and don't come back until you're ready to take me.

THE REP: I find this treatment uncalled for, reprehensible really.

The Rep gets up. He goes to the door. It's locked. He knocks on it once, then again, but there's no answer.

THE REP: Hello! Hello!

The Man gets up and watches him.

MAN: Alright . . . you've had your fun.

THE REP: For a minute there, I thought I could, I could get up and walk away.

MAN: Here's your key. Nice little prop, very theatrical.

THE REP: I was an actor after all.

MAN: We are nothing now.

THE REP: Nothing at all.

MAN: We'll start again. All of us. The human race, all from scratch.

THE REP: Yes. That's how it was meant to be.

MAN: That's how it is.

Lights go down as the two men feel cold and snuggle up against the wall to keep themselves warm. The key lies on the floor inside the envelope, neglected, untouched.

Guillermo's second draft incorporates additions that he describes as "minimal." In my view, these changes manage to generate an even darker quality than we find in the first draft. With this particular play, Guillermo's process is focused on maintaining the critical balance between allusion and overt statement. The second draft offers some additional hints to the real meaning of the piece while attempting to stay on the tightrope between the theatrical truth and the real truth.

Notes on the Second Draft of Bitter

The second draft has minimal changes in it, and that's because when I rewrite I usually need a year or so to do a substantial rewrite. I probably won't change much until I see it staged or as I begin working with actors. I've been known to alter major moments in any given play. People who've read *Chilean Holiday* in the *Humana Festival '96* anthology would find the play has changed considerably since (three years have gone by, you see). As things stand, I did not have time yet to rethink the entire play. I kept an eye out on a tight construction that culminates on a trick ending that may or may not work in production. I would change it then, and given some input by audiences and friends, the play would then go in some other direction perhaps. I only added a couple of lines in which the character says, "Why do you get to stay?" It's not a sincere question, I think. The character is trying to test the Rep in answering a question using the ideology that has been battered into him by the Leaders, whoever they might be. The Rep falls for it and mentions something about "civilization." That's all. I almost went off into heavy ideological discussion and pulled back. I do miss the line from the first draft, "You have no answers, nothing constructive to say, go!" In this draft, the Man does have some answers, nothing too thorough, but I felt the need to give more hints. I hope they don't violate the spirit of maintaining the mystery. If I find a better approach in some future rewrite, I will use it.

A note on the title. *Bitter* seems ironic considering that I'm trying to maintain a dark comedic tone throughout. I wouldn't want the play to be performed with full solemnity. If there's a tone to be struck, the one Jean Paul Sartre uses in *No Exit* seems fitting. Dark and haunting, yet filled with sarcasm, seems to be the right tone.

The cast and opening stage directions remain the same as in the first draft. Most of the opening sequence is identical as well, and I thought at first there would be little value in reproducing it. However, because the play is so compact and tightly constructed, omitting the first third of the dialogue would interrupt the flow of the piece.

Second Draft of Bitter

THE REP: There's the key, sir. I'm sure you'll find the accommodations quite suitable.

MAN: Suitable?

THE REP: Nothing luxurious, you understand, but clearly up to par.

MAN: With what?

THE REP: With what, you say? (*Laughs*) Tricky. Very good, sir. Keep up the spirits.

MAN: Where exactly am I going?

THE REP: Oh, the bus will take you there, sir. A good bus, new shock absorbers.

MAN: But where am I going?

THE REP: Going?

MAN: Where is the bus taking me?

THE REP: If you'd like to speak to a representative.

MAN: You are the representative.

THE REP: But I don't have all the answers.

MAN: Not all the answers, just one answer will do.

THE REP: I know it's difficult, sir. I have kids myself, two boys, and a wife. Rather ill. Terminal, I'm afraid—

MAN: I don't give a shit!

THE REP: Sir!

MAN: Tell me what you know or shut up.

THE REP: My job is to put you on the bus along with the others.

MAN: The others. Who are the others?

THE REP: Look, sir. I really must go—

MAN: No, don't go! Please. Don't leave me here.

THE REP: I will be back.

MAN: I know you will, but don't leave. I don't like this place, no windows, no air in here.

THE REP: It is rather bleak, isn't it?

MAN: I'm—I'm scared.

THE REP: Yes, yes, it can be frightful, this whole thing, but it's really for the best.

MAN: Whose idea of the best?

THE REP: For your people really.

MAN: What people would that be?

THE REP: Your people, so badly treated around here, it's for their protection really.

MAN: Whose protection?

THE REP: You'll be better off removed.

MAN: Is that so?

THE REP: You will have a key, of course.

MAN: But who'll own the home?

THE REP: You will have sovereignty. The key assures you of it. Otherwise, why hand over a key? It will let you enter and leave at any time.

MAN: A key.

THE REP: A key, sir! Regular good ole chrome.

MAN: Which you can take back any time, is that right?

THE REP: Not me personally, sir.

MAN: Not you. Your government.

THE REP: Well, it's not exactly my govern . . .

MAN: Answer yes or no.

THE REP: I really don't know the answer. If I were you, I'd be grateful for the key.

MAN: Would you?

THE REP: Huh?

MAN: Would you be grateful for the key if you were me?

THE REP: I said as much, I believe.

MAN: What did I do?

THE REP: You? Don't take it personally.

MAN: I'm being removed.

THE REP: Relocated, sir. You really are taking this personally. It has nothing to do with you, it's your . . . your group.

MAN: What did my group do?

THE REP: I don't know.

MAN: You don't know.

THE REP: But it's really for the best. For your protection. Really.

MAN: Why do you get to stay?

THE REP: To do the work of civilization.

MAN: In what way?

THE REP: You know . . .

MAN: I don't know.

THE REP: To bring the True God to this land. There's no point in resisting the True God, is there?

MAN: And those who do?

THE REP: Those who do must die.

MAN: I see. Alright, go.

THE REP: What?

MAN: Get the hell out of here and don't come back until you're ready to take me.

THE REP: I find this treatment uncalled for, reprehensible really.

The Rep gets up. He goes to the door. It's locked. He knocks on it once, then again, but there's no answer.

THE REP: Hello! Hello!

The Man gets up and watches him.

MAN: Alright . . . you've had your fun.

THE REP: For a minute there, I thought I could, I could get up and walk away.

MAN: Here's your key. Nice little prop, very theatrical.

THE REP: I was an actor after all.

MAN: We are nothing now.

THE REP: Nothing at all.

MAN: We'll start again.

THE REP: Yes. That's how it was meant to be.

MAN: That's how it is.

Lights go down as the two men feel cold and snuggle up against the wall to keep themselves warm. The key lies on the floor inside the envelope, neglected, untouched.

The third draft of *Bitter* was undertaken in the first week of January. In December, I extended an invitation to all the playwrights to write a further draft or modify their work one last time, and Guillermo took me up on it. His commentary does a wonderful job of clarifying his work on the final draft. Again, the changes are not major, but the script is clearly stronger for them.

Notes on the Third Draft of Bitter

I hadn't looked at the script since July and I decided I needed something else to happen, a new approach to the story.

I added a twist to it. The "man" has been defined as a potential leader for "the people" being relocated. It's a powerful temptation. He was a former mayor, voted out of office, now he has the opportunity to start again. But there's enough conscience in him to know he'd be a puppet, yet there's always the temptation. . . . I was thinking of the Vichy France government, or any other collaborational government. Surely, people have been tempted constantly to sell out their own people for something in return.

I took out some of the earlier lines about "doing the work for civilization" and "to bring the true God to this land." Maybe they were more important in the earlier version where I was trying to define this relocation being done for a greater good. The story has gone in a different direction, and I no longer need to be so exact. I've let the reasons remain more mysterious. Governments have managed to relocate people and remove them for various reasons, all of them excuses for the real thing, which is land and sovereignty, also racial or religious or ideological purity. I decided not to pin down this situation so neatly. Let it remain a parable of all these situations.

I didn't set out to write this type of story. It became this in the course of three drafts. I'm setting a bad example! The student is constantly being lectured about having an outline and knowing his ending—I've been guilty of doing that in class. But when push comes to shove, the process redefines the need for the work. Your personal need for it. It still remains a personal rediscovery of certain anxieties I've felt about the abuse of power (very relevant still for Chileans or Chilean-born types like myself who still haven't come to terms with dictatorship and the former dictator is sitting under house arrest in England of all places until the courts decide whether or not to extradite him to Spain to see whether he'll be tried for crimes against humanity—as of 1/4/00 anyway). Combine that with my research of Native American relocations and the recent ethnic cleansings in the former Yugoslavia, and I keep seeing the same patterns of behavior. People exhibit a certain aversion to the Other, and their governments react accordingly. It's scary to realize that under any given circumstances, any of us can be removed for what might appear to be perfectly legitimate (or legitimatized) reasons. So the thinking process may remain the same, but the approach to the characters had to change for better or for worse to give the play a greater depth of character. I've redefined the Man as having greater complexity as a victim and potential victimizer. He could be lured into becoming a puppet, and while I leave that hanging, it's perfectly feasible that he could just as he could just as easily have been making up the whole thing (as the ending suggests role playing borne out of this anxiety). I made a choice early on to leave the questions unanswered, but to suggest all sorts of possibilities within ten minutes.

Again, not much changes in the first set of beats, but the continuity is needed to realize the impact of the changes when they do arrive. The cast and opening stage direction remain the same.

Third Draft of Bitter

THE REP: Your key, sir. I'm sure you'll find the accommodations quite suitable.

MAN: Suitable?

THE REP: Nothing luxurious, you understand, but clearly up to par.

MAN: With what?

THE REP: With what, you say? (*Laughs*) Tricky. Very good, sir. Keep up the spirits.

MAN: Where exactly am I going?

THE REP: Oh, the bus will take you there, sir. A good bus. Modern. Video monitors, new shock absorbers and such.

MAN: But where am I going?

THE REP: Going?

MAN: Where is the bus taking me?

THE REP: If you'd like to speak to a representative.

MAN: You are the representative.

THE REP: But I don't have all the answers.

MAN: Not all the answers, just one answer will do.

THE REP: I know it's difficult, sir.

MAN: Do you?

THE REP: 'Have my own responsibilities. Kids, two boys, and a wife. Rather ill. Terminal, I'm afraid . . .

MAN: I don't give a shit!

THE REP: Maybe you'd like to be alone!

MAN: Tell me what you know or shut up.

THE REP: My job is to put you on the bus along with the others.

MAN: The others. Who are the others?

THE REP: Look, sir. I really must go—

MAN: No, don't go! Please. Don't leave me here.

THE REP: I will be back.

MAN: I know you will, but don't leave. I don't like this place, no
windows, no air in here.

THE REP: It is rather bleak, isn't it?

MAN: I'm—I'm scared.

THE REP: Yes, yes, it can be frightful, this whole thing, but it's
really for the best.

MAN: Whose idea of the best?

THE REP: For your people really.

MAN: What people would that be?

THE REP: Your people, so badly treated around here, it's for their
protection really.

MAN: Whose protection?

THE REP: You'll be better off removed.

MAN: Is that so?

THE REP: You will have a key, of course.

MAN: But who'll own the home?

THE REP: You will have sovereignty.

MAN: Really now? Sovereignty?

THE REP: Otherwise, why hand over a key? It will let you enter and
leave at any time.

MAN: A key.

THE REP: A key, sir! That key. Regular good ole chrome.

MAN: Which you can take back any time, is that right?

THE REP: Not me personally, sir.

MAN: Not you. Your government.

THE REP: Well, it's not exactly my govern . . .

MAN: Answer yes or no.

THE REP: I really don't know the answer. If I were you, I'd be grateful for the key.

MAN: Would you?

THE REP: Huh?

MAN: Would you be grateful for the key if you were me?

THE REP: I said as much, I believe.

MAN: What did I do?

THE REP: You? Don't take it personally.

MAN: I'm being removed.

THE REP: Relocated, sir. You really are taking this personally. It
has nothing to do with you, it's your . . . your group.

MAN: What did my group do?

THE REP: I don't know really.

MAN: You don't know.

THE REP: But it's really for the best. For your protection. Really.

MAN: Why do you get to stay?

THE REP: I'm sure our Leader will clarify the purpose soon
enough. You'll get to work the land—
MAN: Whose land?
THE REP: Your land. Reap the benefits of your own labor, that type
of thing.
MAN: Without interference?
THE REP: None whatsoever, that's been promised.
MAN: When? How was it promised?
THE REP: I'm sure our leader made a declaration of some kind, I
don't keep up.
MAN: And he promised sovereignty, land, a key.
THE REP: A chance to start again. You must help your people
understand that.
MAN: My people—? So that's what this is about, you think that I
would—?
THE REP: You're highly regarded among . . .
MAN: A former mayor, I was voted out of office . . .
THE REP: It was a close election and the new mayor is dead.
MAN: Dead?
THE REP: Suicide, we believe. Your people require new leadership,
and who else could—?
MAN: They won't listen to a puppet.
THE REP: A puppet, sir? A rather unfortunate choice of —?
MAN: Shut the hell up!
THE REP: No, . . .
MAN: Get the hell out!
THE REP: You will lead your people towards a new land! A touch of
Biblical resonance there! How could you not, a man of your intel-
lect and temperament? In times of crisis! You will be listened to,
you will be respected, and we will guarantee it. Your people will
have land, and you will be their leader, if you cooperate.
MAN: Otherwise . . .
THE REP: Otherwise, they will be set loose upon the world, with-
out a leader, without guarantees of land—
MAN: Unless I . . .
THE REP: Unless you . . .
MAN: I see.
THE REP: Isn't respect important in a man's life? Especially a man
of your talents and wisdom?
MAN: I thought so, once.
THE REP: You will get a chance to prove yourself again in difficult
times. Great heroes are born in times like these.
MAN: Heroes? Yes, heroes. Well . . .

THE REP: You will be the leader again.

MAN: Yes, that would be something. Alright, go.

THE REP: You will think about it.

MAN: Get the hell out of here and don't come back until you're ready to take me away for good.

THE REP: If you come around—

MAN: Some other time!

THE REP: That's the spirit, there will be some other time! Take all the time . . .

MAN: Fine! Just go! Leave me alone!

The Rep gets up. He goes to the door. It's locked. He knocks on it once, then again, but there's no answer.

THE REP: Hello! Hello!

The Man gets up and watches him.

MAN: Alright . . . you've had your fun.

THE REP: For a minute there, I thought I could, I could get up and walk away.

MAN: I commend you for believing it.

THE REP: Amateur though I may be at these things . . .

MAN: Amateur? Professional? What difference does it make? We are nothing now.

THE REP: Nothing at all.

MAN: We'll start again.

THE REP: No, don't fall for the illusion.

MAN: That's all I've got left.

THE REP: I commend you for thinking it.

MAN: Thank you. I will continue to think it. And you?

THE REP: I will be here by your side, waiting for it to happen.

MAN: Yes, waiting.

Lights go down as the two men feel cold and snuggle up against the wall to keep themselves warm. The key lies on the floor inside the envelope, neglected, untouched.

As we have seen, *Bitter* arrived in a relatively complete form in Guillermo's process, then evolved through fine shadings of meaning in the rewrites until it reached the point of the third draft. For Guillermo, the only step remaining is to have the play read, and receive feedback from various perspectives. His concern, as he points out in the quote below from an e-mail, is which elements transfer successfully from the page to the stage as he has imagined them.

For *Bitter*, I am still trying to decide whether the reversal at the end works. Sometimes I get so tired of stories where it turns out it was all a dream at the end. I think this is different in that the two characters have been role playing, and there's something potentially compelling about all that. I don't know yet if it's the right ending. I'm certainly much more interested in the third draft's new twist, that the Man is being asked to become a collaborator. That added a couple of pages to the script because it gave me something more to play with. I did not plan for that to happen. It really just happened after six months of letting the script rest. I felt I needed more possibilities, and this was one of them. It also helped bring out yet another issue in the complex psychological game of removing people while making them think it's for their own good. Collaborators among the removed people are needed to make that acceptable.

I can't say I have a more structured process than that. My next step would be to read the play out loud with actors and solicit responses, which mirrors what I usually do with a full-length play. After that first reading, I will find new things to rewrite, whether it's dialogue or a character that needs to be fleshed out. Even after a performance, I will do considerable rewrites, depending on whether the production has inspired something, or at least highlighted a deficiency that needs to be removed.

Guillermo's willingness to keep working on a play even after it has been produced is inspiring. It is a strong reminder that the relationship between the playwright and his or her play can continue far beyond a "final" draft. Each play we write is not just an artistic effort, but a personal one as well. The act of writing challenges us to find ways of expressing new ideas and perspectives, and often opens up parts of us that we have not come into contact with previously. The writer working on a current play is finding applications for techniques and views he learned while writing previous plays. The prior work and current work then combine to inform the next play, and so on. When the playwright continues to refine the work even after production, he redefines his own process and artistic maturity. Although making art is never easy, it has the asset of being a lifelong pursuit: as we work we grow; as we grow we mature in our work, and the cycle continues. As Guillermo puts it so aptly, "The process redefines the need for the work."

7

CHAPTER

Julie Jensen:
Give Us This Day
"NOTES IN DIALOGUE FORM"

JULIE JENSEN HAS AN EXTENSIVE LIST OF PRODUCTIONS at such venues as Arena Stage, Capitol Rep, the Women's Project, Mark Taper Forum, and the Edinburgh Fringe Festival in Scotland. Julie has worked in Hollywood as a screenwriter and a writer for television. She has also taught playwriting at five colleges and universities and, most recently, in the graduate playwriting program at University of Nevada, Las Vegas.

Julie's submission provides us with an excellent examination of her particular manner of working on a script. Her approach is very straightforward, something that is as much an inheritance of working in television as it is part of Julie's innate personality. As I discussed in the introduction to this section, there is no mandate on craft—some writers need lots of exploratory work before committing to a play, some need little or none. Julie does not do a great deal of prewriting, but tends to trust her instincts with the story. Also, Julie doesn't worry about the meaning of the play as she develops it. Her view is to let the story and characters evolve through basic, random explorations, which she calls "notes in dialogue form." As she describes it, the meaning or central issue in the play did not surface until she had worked on it for a while:

> By the time I got to the end of the last draft, I realized that the play is about loss. The old guy is going to die, and the young

girl is going to lose her father. But she also is something of a failure socially. Sheila, her friend, is not going to show up. The girl covers up her sense of betrayal and loss. But she feels it. We can see it. That makes for an interesting piece.

I asked Julie to describe her prewriting process. I was interested that *Give Us This Day* seemed to arrive to her in a rather complete state. As you will see from the drafts, there are many refinements in the texture of the characters and in the dialogue, but the essential plot changes very little.

> I used to say about full-length plays that it took me 20 minutes to think up the idea and 3 years to write it. With this piece, far from a full-length play, I was simply intrigued by the idea of my father and my sister. He had a no-nonsense attitude toward farm animals, and my sister had a much more indulgent attitude. That conflict, however, stands for more than just an attitude toward a horse. So I thought that it was worth exploring. Besides all this, I've never seen a play about shoeing a horse, and any play that ain't ever been written is inviting.

After spending time with Julie's work, I was intrigued by her approach, and asked Julie for further amplification on her choices. Why, I wanted to know, did she choose to utilize dialogue exploration rather than plot outlines or other story-oriented efforts?

> In early exploration work, it's true that I try to get characters to talk. Because I am interested in their sound, their voice. But that part is easy for me. I can usually hear characters early and easily. The harder part for me is conflict. So in the preliminary explorations, I try to write characters who are pursuing something, wanting something, needing something.
>
> Often it happens that one character's needs are stronger than the other's. In the early drafts of this play, for instance, the old man has much stronger needs than the young girl. That didn't bother me. I wrote those needs as strongly as I could. I knew that later I would have to strengthen the young girl's needs, because in the early drafts, she was just an unwilling partner in what's going on. That does not make for very good conflict; it's not sharp enough, not interesting enough. It's more like bickering, yammering, yes you did, no I didn't. In

subsequent drafts, therefore, I tried to clarify the young girl's needs, and that inevitably made the contrast between the two characters stronger and made the conflict more dynamic. Ultimately it resulted in a better plot.

When I began work on the play, I knew there were a couple of things the old man was going to discuss with his daughter: the caskets and her behavior in school. That's all I knew about the content of the beats. The rest evolved out of those two topics, those beginnings.

The needs, desires, wants of the characters are clearly critical here, and certainly to all strong playwriting. Julie's description of the young girl as an "unwilling partner" is an excellent reminder to us that plays work best when both characters have an active agenda. Two-character plays in particular often suffer from an imbalance, where one character dominates the other because the other is passive. Playwrights do best when they keep in mind that a dramatic situation is a negotiation: each character wants something and attempts to obtain it from, through, or with the other character. As we read Julie's drafts, we can see the young girl emerge from this state of passivity into a far more assertive and at-risk condition, which improves the play immeasurably.

Julie's work provides us with a solid example of meticulous rewriting. She provided me with what I have reproduced here: samples of preliminary dialogue followed by drafts of the play with her changes recorded directly in the text to demonstrate where she made decisions about the piece. Julie's way of showing these changes is very visual, almost like a road map through her rewrites. Deleted lines are shown with a strike-through: ~~This line is cut~~; new lines are shown with an under-line: <u>This line has been added</u>. This is very helpful to the reader because you will be able to see her choices right on the page, rather than having to compare drafts.

Since her touch seems so certain throughout the drafts, I asked Julie if she had a quote or mantra or any particular thing that inspired her or kept her in focus as she worked. She answered in an e-mail with her usual delightful candor:

I don't have a quote, really, that keeps me going. But I do have to keep reminding myself that I am brilliant. That's a lot of fantasy, but necessary to finish a draft. As long as I think I am brilliant and this is a great play, I can manage the work. Later, the editor in me comes along, grumbles and says I'm really flawed and this play is really in need of help. So it's something of a two-headed approach I have. The writer is brilliant, a genius. The editor knows better, so she fixes things.

Julie was very organized in the material she submitted. The dialogue explorations and drafts include astute observations from her as well, making my job very easy, indeed.

PART ONE: JOURNAL

This is the early work on the play, consisting of the idea, the characters, and preliminary scenes. I try to do as much of this work as I can in scene form. Anything else, such as writing outlines, biographies, or discussing the play with others all seem to dissipate the idea. Each working day, I try to write at least three or four scenes. They are unedited, unchallenged. Some of them are repetitious of other scenes, others clearly will not fit into the play; none of that matters. I'm just trying to get the characters to talk to one another and to go after their needs.

Initial Idea

This is what I think the play will be about. It has something of a plot, or at least some goals for the characters. It's just a beginning. Much will change.

The piece has two characters, an older man, and a young adolescent girl, his daughter. The old guy is shoeing a horse. The young girl has to hold the horse.

The old guy does most of the talking. He is a natural born-teacher, after all. The girl is a reluctant listener. She'd rather be doing almost anything else, but no one wants to do it with her.

The old guy lives for work. He turns everything into a little job or a big one. He cures diseases by getting to work. He fixes injured limbs by working them a little. He reroutes wayward children by giving them a job. All anyone needs is enough work.

At this point, the old guy is scared. He's not worried about the cancer, and he ain't scared of dying. He's scared of not working.

The young girl doesn't get it. She's practicing beauty standing in her mother's high heels. Besides, she's heard all this before, and he ain't dead yet.

Characters

Here is some preliminary work on the subject of the two characters in this piece. Just a little focusing, adding of detail.

The Old Guy only lives because he works. He turns everything into a little job or a big one.

Once during the Depression he applied for a job. He didn't get it, but he decided to show up for work anyway.

Boss: You didn't get the job.
Old Guy: I know. But I thought I'd come down and give you a hand anyway.
Boss: We can't pay you.
Old Guy: I'd rather work for nothing than not work at all.

The Adolescent Girl does anything to avoid her father's agenda. She's rather lazy, according to her father. And she does not believe her father is dying. Bored with most things, she's most bored with her father. She's heard everything too many times.

The material that follows is a continuation of the journal, where Julie moves into preliminary scene work. I've chosen to edit it for reasons of space, since many of these trial scenes show up intact in the piece itself. The scenes I have included are key explorations that will help ground the reader in the essentials of the character and plot in order to follow the evolution of the piece. One thing of particular interest is that the female character's name changes from "Adolescent Girl" to "Girl" to "Sister." Lastly, note that the lines (————) which separate each snippet of dialogue are in Julie's original journal.

Preliminary Scene Work

These are merely trial scenes with the two characters going after some of their needs. I do not censor these, do not edit them, do not care if they are on or off the subject, do not care what order they come in, do not care that some of them are repetitious. They're notes in dialogue form.

Old Guy: All he needs is a job.
Adolescent Girl: That's not the cure for everything

Old Guy: Damn right it is. Hand me that rasp.

––––––––––

(*The horse rears up.*)

Old Guy: For god sake, get a hold of those reins.

Girl: I got em. I got em.

Old Guy: What's your job here?

Girl: Holding her head.

Old Guy: That's right. And you don't sit on the ground to do that
job. And you don't let go of the reins to do that job.

Girl: But it's boring, Dad.

Old Guy: Oh, for god sake. I hope that's the worst thing ever happens to you. Now stand up there and pay attention here.

Girl: But she doesn't want to do what I say.

Old Guy: It does not matter what she wants. I expect her to
behave. And that's your job. Okay?

Girl: Okay. But the next time you poke her with the point of that
rasp, she'll rare up again.

Old Guy: Well, if she does, we'll tie her head up to that stump.

Girl: No. Don't.

Old Guy: Then you're gonna have to do the job. (He *hands her something*)

Girl: All right. But don't be mean to her.

Old Guy: It's not mean. Jesus. I'm putting shoes on her. How long
you suppose she'd last this summer without them.

Girl: I know. But you're doing it mean.

Old Guy: I am not having a crazy horse.

Girl: You're the one that's crazy. Makes her crazy.

––––––––––

Old Guy: Well, get up here then. Stand right in front of her head.
Closer.

Girl: No.

Old Guy: What's the matter with you?

Girl: She gets spit on me.

Old Guy: Oh, she does not. Now stand up there. And take a hold
of that pair of reins. (*She does*) That's right. Now pay attention.
(*Old Guy returns to rasping the hoof*) There's one thing about working with a horse. You have to be smarter than it is.

Girl: I'm smarter than this horse.

Old Guy: Course you are. But you gotta let *her* know it.

––––––––––

Old Guy: Okay, here's what you wanted to know about the nails.
You bend the nail like that, see. Put the nail in that hole right
there and bend it. Now come around here so you can see.

Girl: What about her head?

Old Guy: She's not going anywhere. She'll stand there.

Girl: (*She lets go of the horse's reins. It stands there*) Then how come I've been holding her?

Old Guy: Jesus, it's a job. You needed one.

Old Guy: I went down to the undertaker's this afternoon.

Girl: You don't have to talk about this.

Old Guy: I want you to know some things before I die.

Girl: I already know some things. And you ain't gonna die.

Old Guy: Course I am. Now listen up. They got this blue one. Made out of metal. Get that one.

Girl: I thought you wanted something with nice wood.

Old Guy: It's all this prefab stuff. Nothing with good wood working. Might as well get metal.

Girl: Is it good metal working?

Old Guy: Looks like a car metal. Molded like that. They probably come out of Detroit.

Girl: I can bury you in the ole Chevy, Dad. Put you in the back seat and drive you over the edge of Wild Cat Gulch.

Old Guy: Hand me that rasp. Now this is how you finish the job. Take that foot like that, on your knee. Then you rasp down the hoof. Like that. You got ahold of her head?

Girl: Yeah I got her.

Old Guy: Jesus Christ, what you got them kind a shoes on for?

Girl: That's what I had on when you yelled.

Old Guy: Oh for god's sake. Your mother's gonna have both our hides.

Girl: I ain't gonna hurt them, Dad.

Old Guy: Get inside and change them things.

Old Guy: Now you're clear about the funeral?

Girl: Yes. I'm clear, Dad.

Old Guy: Don't let the Church run it. They always want to run it.

Girl: I won't. I won't let the Church run it.

Old Guy: And I don't want anyone speaking that's long-winded.

Girl: And don't let any of those long-winded ones speak.

Old Guy: None of those long-winded ones.

Girl: You mean you don't want Wallace Yardley?

Old Guy: No, I do not want Wallace Yardley.

Girl: How 'bout Joseph Manzione?

Old Guy: Hell, no, now listen to me here. There's some people that can do a better job than that.

Girl: Okay, Dad. Who should we have?

Old Guy: Have anyone you want. But don't let them run on. The whole thing shouldn't last more than an hour. Beginning to end.

Girl: Okay, but you're not dying, Dad.

Old Guy: Of course I am. We've talked all about it.

Girl: You're not dying, Dad.

Old Guy: But I'm gonna in the next while here.

Girl: You have to be real sick to die, Dad. You ain't real sick.

Old Guy: And that's lucky. But that fact doesn't change things.

Girl: All right, Dad.

Old Guy: And I don't want you making a fool of yourself in Mrs. Griffith's class. After I'm dead, I'll come back and haunt you if you act up Mrs. Griffiths' class.

The next step in Julie's process was to work toward a draft. As I observed earlier, Julie provides us with a very visual display of her process with the use of strike-throughs and underlines. Her introduction to the draft reveals a highly focused, disciplined process, and the draft itself is very illuminating. We can see lines which have been cut, then reappear in a later beat sequence; whole beat sequences that have been relocated; and lines that have been newly added then immediately cut. As Julie characterized it before: ". . . it's something of a two-headed approach I have," where the writer side and the editor side of her struggle with each other, then come to closure on choices.

PART TWO: DRAFT

This is the draft of the play. It is taken from the scene work. In other words, it is an attempt to make some sense of the scene work. The underlined parts indicate material that was added to what I'd written in the scenes. And the strike-thru parts indicate material that was deleted. Some parts, as you will see, were added and deleted both. This draft represents no less than twenty passes through the play, trying for economy, sharper conflict, an agenda for each of the characters, clear dialogue differences in the characters, clean transitions between beats, and naturalness of speech rhythms.

GIVE US THIS DAY ~~OUR DAILY WORK~~

OLD GUY *is assembling tools.*

OLD GUY: Sister, get out here and give me a hand. ~~will you?~~

SISTER: (*Off*) Can't, Dad, I'm busy.

OLD GUY: ~~I need you to take a hold this horse for me.~~ Well, if you are, ~~busy, it's~~ that's a first.

SISTER: (*Appearing in the screen door*) ~~I'm busy, Dad.~~ I am busy, Dad.

OLD GUY: ~~Fine, but Listen,~~ I need you to hold this horse. ~~for me. Well if you are, it's a first. Take a hold of those reins.~~

SISTER: What for?

OLD GUY: I gotta finish putting these shoes on her.

SISTER: Oh ~~no~~, Dad, I hate that job. Ask Buddy.

OLD GUY: No. Now I'm asking you. Get on out here.

SISTER: I haven't got time. I gotta be to the swimming pool by 4:30. ~~I gotta be someplace by 4:30.~~

OLD GUY: ~~Won't take us half that amount of time. All right. Better get on out here, then.~~ Let's get started, then.

SISTER: ~~Oh, Dad. That~~ Shoeing that horse takes all day.

OLD GUY: Not if you do *your* half of the job.

She reluctantly comes out the door.

SISTER: ~~But Hey, Dad, But~~ Hey, wait a minute, ~~here, Dad~~ you ain't supposed to be doing ~~them kinda things.~~ that kinda stuff.

OLD GUY: ~~Oh, to hell with that.~~ The hell I'm not.

SISTER: Doctor says you wasn't supposed to . . .

OLD GUY: Doctor says I was SUPPOSED to do any damn thing I CAN do.

SISTER: Snap your bones like toothpicks. ~~I heard him say that.~~ That's what they told you.

OLD GUY: Work never hurt anyone.

SISTER: ~~Except kill em.~~ Nah, it just kills ~~em.~~ you.

OLD GUY: Work doesn't kill you. It's NOT working that kills you.

~~SISTER: Work is work, nothing more or nothing less.~~

~~OLD GUY:~~ Hell, if it wasn't for work, we'd all be crazy.

SISTER: Work ain't the cure for everything, Dad.

OLD GUY: ~~Damn right it is.~~ The hell it ain't. Hand me that rasp.

SISTER: I'll hold the horse if you'll take me to the swimming pool by 4:30.

OLD GUY: You do a job because it needs to be done, not because you get something in return.

SISTER comes outside and hands him the rasp.

SISTER: ~~All right, I'll hold her. But I need to be done by 4:30. I'm going someplace.~~ Where do you want me to stand?

~~SISTER comes out, and takes hold of the reins.~~

OLD GUY: ~~All right. That's good, now stand right~~ In front of her
 head, <u>where else?</u> (SISTER ~~comes out,~~ *takes hold of the reins.*) Closer.
SISTER: I don't want to.
<u>OLD GUY: Closer!</u>
<u>SISTER: No.</u>
OLD GUY: <u>What's the matter with you?</u> ~~Why not?~~
SISTER: She gets spit on me.
OLD GUY: ~~Oh, she does not~~. <u>Oh, for God's sake.</u> ~~Now~~ Stand up
 there. And take a hold of that pair of reins. (*She does*) That's
 right. Now pay attention. (OLD GUY *picks up the horse's hoof and
 begins rasping it.*) There's one thing about working with a horse.
 You have to be smarter than it is.
SISTER: I'm smarter than this horse.
OLD GUY: Course you are. But you gotta let *her* know it. (*He contin-
 ues rasping*) <u>I gotta talk to you about something.</u>
SISTER: ~~What's that, Dad?~~ <u>I ain't talking about dying, Dad.</u>
OLD GUY: I went down to the undertaker's this afternoon.
SISTER: ~~You don't have to talk about this.~~ <u>Not that subject, please,</u>
 ~~Dad.~~
OLD GUY: I want you to know some things before ~~I die.~~ <u>it happens.</u>
SISTER: I already know some things. And you ain't gonna die.
OLD GUY: Course I am. Now listen up. <u>We're talking caskets here.</u>
 They got this blue one. Made out of metal. Get that one.
SISTER: I thought you wanted something with nice wood.
OLD GUY: It's all this prefab stuff. Nothing with good wood work-
 ing. Might as well get metal.
SISTER: Is it good metal working?
OLD GUY: Looks like ~~a~~ car metal. Molded like that. They probably
 come out of Detroit.
SISTER: I can bury you in the ole Chevy, Dad. Put you in the back
 seat and drive you over the edge of Wild Cat Gulch.
OLD GUY: Hand me that rasp. <u>(*She does*) Now then, listen to me.</u>
 They'll try to sell you one with ~~some kinda~~ <u>a</u> seal. I don't want
 one with a seal.
SISTER: Seal for what?
OLD MAN: Seal for whatever. Water.
SISTER: What's wrong with a seal for water?
OLD MAN: Gees, you're no smarter than the damn salesman.
 ~~down there.~~ <u>at the undertaker's</u>. Think about it.
SISTER: Okay, but I still don't see what's wrong with a seal for water.
OLD MAN: First of all I'll be dead. I don't have to be dry when I'm
 dead. Second, how long's it gonna last? Sooner or later the
 damn seal's gonna rot <u>or disintegrate</u>. ~~something. Don't matter~~

~~what it's made out of.~~ Then the water comes in anyway. ~~Third,~~ And finally, how you gonna tell whether ~~it~~ the damn thing works or not? You gonna dig me up?

SISTER: No seals. Okay, I got it. (SISTER *sits down.* ~~while holding the reins~~) But you ain't gonna die, Dad.

OLD MAN: Yes I am, and I want everything in order when I do.

SISTER: You have to be real sick before you die. You ain't one bit sick.

OLD MAN: And that's lucky. ~~a lucky thing~~. But I'm still gonna die. All of em said so. And I know so, too. I can tell it.

SISTER: ~~You'll outlive us all.~~ Whatever you say, Dad.

OLD GUY: Now what's this thing with Mrs. Griffiths?

SISTER: Oh no. That's why you got me out here, isn't it? I ain't talking about that.

OLD GUY: ~~All right, but I bet~~ The hell you ain't. ~~I can out last you.~~ ~~(Pause)~~ ~~I got the rest of my life. You only got till 4:30.~~ ~~(Pause)~~ Oh yes you are, sister. (*Pause*) I mean business here.

SISTER: She's really dumb, Dad.

OLD GUY: She might be. But I want you to get along with her.

SISTER: What did she tell you?

OLD GUY: Less than half of what you really did, I'm sure.

SISTER: She is so dumb, Dad.

OLD GUY: I don't care if she is, sister.

SISTER: Well, I do. ~~Dad~~.

OLD GUY: I want you to behave. I don't care what the circumstances are. (*Silence.*) Do you need another job?

SISTER: No.

OLD GUY: Cuz I can give you more work if you haven't got enough to do.

SISTER: I got enough to do.

OLD GUY: Then why you crawling around under the tables?

SISTER: Did she tell you that? I wasn't crawling around under the tables.

OLD GUY: What were you doing?

SISTER: Sitting under the table.

OLD GUY: I don't want you sitting under the table either.

SISTER: I wasn't hurting nothing.

OLD GUY: (*He looks at her.*) ~~Don't be sassing me. Now, sister.~~ I mean business here, sister.

SISTER: I know, but she's lying about me. She hates me, Dad.

OLD GUY: I don't blame her. I'd hate you too.

SISTER: But she's lying, Dad. You can't believe a thing she says.

~~OLD GUY jabs the horse with the rasp~~. *The horse rears up.*

OLD GUY: FOR GOD SAKE, GET A HOLD OF THOSE REINS!

SISTER: I got em. I got em.

OLD GUY: What's your job here?

SISTER: Holding her head.

OLD GUY: And you don't sit on the ground to do that job. And you don't let go of the reins to do that job.

SISTER:But it's boring, Dad.

OLD GUY: ~~Oh, for god sake.~~ Jesus Christ, I hope that's the worst thing ~~ever happens to you~~ you ever have to suffer through. Now stand up there and pay attention.

SISTER: But she doesn't want to do what I say.

OLD GUY: It does not matter what she wants. I expect her to behave. And that's your job.

SISTER: Okay. But the next time you poke her with the point of that rasp, she'll rare up again.

OLD GUY: Well, if she does, we'll tie her head to that stump.

SISTER: No. Don't, <u>Dad</u>.

OLD GUY: Then you're gonna have to do the job.

SISTER: All right. But don't be mean to her.

OLD GUY: It's not mean. Jesus. I'm putting shoes on her. How long you suppose she'd last ~~this summer~~ without ~~them?~~ shoes?

SISTER: I <u>don't</u> know. But you're doing it mean.

OLD GUY: I am not having a crazy horse.

SISTER: You're the one that's crazy. Makes her crazy.

OLD GUY: <u>And I'm not having a crazy daughter either.</u> Now then, <u>pay attention here</u> <u>and I'll show you a few things.</u> This is how you drive these nails <u>in</u> so <u>the horse</u> ~~don't~~ <u>doesn't turn up lame.</u> ~~they don't hurt her foot.~~ Remember, you ~~remember you~~ <u>asked me about that the other day.</u> ~~wanted to know that.~~

SISTER: I wanted to know that a long time ago, Dad. I don't need to know it now.

OLD GUY: First off, you pick up her foot like this. (*He pushes the horse so that it shifts its weight.*) So. So.

SISTER: I know how you pick up her foot.

OLD GUY: Well, maybe you do. <u>Maybe you don't.</u>

SISTER: I do.

OLD GUY: ~~Well, I thought I'd try to teach you something. Beats staring at the head of a horse.~~

(*He lifts up the horse's foot.*) So. So. Then rasp ~~this~~ her hoof flat like this. Then you take this shoe, and you fit it right there. Like ~~so~~ <u>that</u>. And you take a nail and you bend it a bit like that, see. <u>A horse-shoe nail is soft. You can bend it easy.</u> And then you drive it in ~~like~~ so and it comes up through there. Just like that, see there.

SISTER: <u>Yeah, Dad. I know how to shoe a horse. I've watched you do it ten million times. And you ~~have to go through~~ repeat the same stuff every time.</u>

OLD GUY: <u>That's the only way you learn.</u>

SISTER: <u>It's useless information. No one needs to know how to shoe a horse. Who's gonna call on me to shoe a horse in this world or the next?</u> ~~I ask you who?~~

OLD GUY: <u>Hand me that pair of pliers. (SISTER does not move. OLD GUY gets the pliers himself) I thought you could learn something. Beats staring at the head of a horse.</u>

SISTER: <u>Are we done, Dad?</u>

OLD GUY: <u>No, we are not done.</u>

OLD MAN: I don't want you misbehaving in Mrs. Griffiths' class.

~~SISTER: She hates me, Dad. I have to defend myself.~~

~~OLD MAN: Oh for god's sake. She's the one that has to defend herself.~~

~~SISTER: She hates me. You gotta admit that.~~

~~OLD MAN: Of course she hates you. Wouldn't you hate you? You are to behave yourself, is that clear.~~

~~SISTER: She's dumb, Dad.~~

~~OLD MAN: Yes, she's dumb. But you still have to behave yourself. And I don't want you making a fool of yourself. in Mrs. Griffiths' her class.~~ After I'm dead, <u>so help me,</u> I'll come back and haunt you if you act up in Mrs. Griffiths' class.

SISTER: <u>Now are we done, Dad?</u>

OLD GUY: <u>No, we are not done.</u> This is how you finish the job. Take that foot like that, on your knee. Then you rasp down the hoof. Like that. <u>So her foot fits the shoe. You got her head?</u>

SISTER: Yeah, I got her head. (*He rasps the horse's foot.*)

OLD GUY: <u>There now. That ought to last her the summer.</u>

SISTER: Good, are we done?

OLD GUY: <u>Yes, we're done. But I got one other thing to tell you.</u>

SISTER: <u>Hurry up, cuz I'm in a hurry.</u>

OLD GUY: ~~(OLD GUY thinks about it.)~~ There's an envelope in the top drawer of the dresser. That's where the key is to the safety deposit box. You remember that, don't you.

SISTER: Yes, Dad. Now ~~will~~ how about you take me up to the swimming pool?

OLD GUY: <u>What's wrong with your bike?</u>

SISTER: <u>I'm gonna be late.</u>

OLD GUY: <u>Jesus, you sure can work an old man.</u> ~~Give me that pair of reins.~~

SISTER: Work's good for you, Dad. ~~(She does.)~~

OLD GUY: ~~All right. Here. Hand me that pair of reins. (She does.)~~ Go get in the car.

SISTER: Thanks, Dad. ~~I'll go get my stuff. Where shall I put these reins.~~

OLD GUY: You're a good girl. Here, give me that pair of reins. (SISTER *hands him the reins. She runs off.* He watches her go) Here you old son of a bitch. Stay there till I get back.

He ties up the reins and with effort moves off. —END—

Part Three of Julie's journal is the same draft as we just read, only with all the cuts and additions in a clean script. This draft really reveals the economy and rhythm which Julie indicates she was working toward in the introduction to Part Two. Again, spatial considerations only permit me to show a fragment of the script so I can include Part Four, which is another rewrite.

From Part Three: Fragment of Give Us This Day

OLD GUY *is assembling tools.*

OLD GUY: Sister, get out here and give me a hand.

SISTER: (Off) Can't, Dad, I'm busy.

OLD GUY: Well, if you are, that's a first.

SISTER: (*Appearing in the screen door*) I *am* busy, Dad.

OLD GUY: I need you to hold this horse.

SISTER: What for?

OLD GUY: I gotta finish putting these shoes on her.

SISTER: Oh no, Dad, I hate that job. Ask Buddy.

OLD GUY: No. Now I'm asking you. Get on out here.

SISTER: I haven't got time. I gotta be to the swimming pool by 4:30.

OLD GUY: Let's get started, then.

In the next section, Julie develops the character of Sister further. She also continues to sharpen lines, deepen the texture of the piece. The delicacy of Julie's touch is evident here as she carefully shapes and adds to the material without losing any of the quality of the original draft.

PART FOUR

This draft occurred three or four months later. The piece worked well, I thought, up through the casket stuff. But then it sagged a bit.

And finally the end didn't have the punch I wanted. I decided that Sister needed a bigger stake in this whole afternoon. So I decided she was in the process of getting stood up by a girlfriend she likes. Perhaps the Old Guy knows it, perhaps not. By the end of the play, though, he certainly knows what's happened. She's been humiliated. He's trying to make that better.

Fourth Draft of Give Us This Day

OLD GUY *is assembling tools.*

OLD GUY: Sister, get out here and give me a hand, <u>will you</u>?

SISTER (*Off*): Can't, Dad, I'm busy.

OLD GUY: Well, if you are <u>busy</u>, ~~that's~~ <u>it's</u> a first.

SISTER: (*Appearing in the screen door*) I <u>am</u> busy, Dad. I'm waiting to go someplace.

OLD GUY: I need you to hold this horse.

SISTER: What for?

OLD GUY: ~~I gotta~~ Finish putting these shoes on her.

SISTER: ~~Oh, no,~~ Dad, I hate that job. Ask Buddy.

OLD GUY: No. ~~Now~~ I'm asking you. <u>Now</u> get on out here, <u>please</u>.

SISTER: I haven't got time. ~~I gotta be to the swimming pool by 4:30. ready by 4:30.~~ <u>Sheila's picking me up thirty-eight minutes ago.</u>

<u>OLD GUY: Sheila who?</u>

<u>SISTER: Sheila Sidney.</u>

<u>OLD GUY: Sheila Sidney is a junior in high school.</u>

<u>SISTER: I know. She just got her license.</u>

<u>OLD GUY: And she ain't got a brain in her head.</u>

<u>SISTER: She's real funny, Dad.</u>

<u>OLD GUY: She's too damn old for you.</u>

<u>SISTER: We're going up to the pool together. She's supposed to be</u> here . . . <u>thirty-nine minutes ago.</u>

OLD GUY: <u>Well,</u> let's get started, then.

<u>SISTER: But, Dad, I'll get all dirty.</u>

<u>OLD GUY: You won't get dirty.</u>

SISTER: Shoeing that horse takes all day.

OLD GUY: Not if you do your half of the job.

She reluctantly comes out the door.

SISTER: Hey, wait a minute, you ain't supposed to be doing ~~that~~ <u>this</u> kinda stuff.

OLD GUY: The hell I'm not.

SISTER: Doctor says you wasn't supposed to . . .

OLD GUY: Doctor says I was <u>supposed</u> to do any damn thing I <u>can</u> do.

SISTER: Snap your bones like toothpicks. ~~That's what they told you.~~

OLD GUY: Work never hurt anyone.

SISTER: ~~Nah,~~ It don't hurt you, it just kills you.

OLD GUY: Work doesn't kill you. It's <u>not</u> working that kills you. Hell, if it wasn't for work, we'd all be ~~crazy~~ in the hospital or the nut house.

SISTER: Work ain't the cure for everything, Dad.

OLD GUY: The hell it ain't. Hand me that rasp.

~~SISTER: I'll hold the horse if you'll take me to the swimming pool by 4:30.~~

~~OLD GUY: You do a job because it needs to be done, not because you get something in return.~~

SISTER *comes outside and hands him the rasp.*

SISTER: Where do you want me to stand?

OLD GUY: In front of her head, where else?

SISTER *takes hold of the reins.*

SISTER: <u>I gotta go, soon as she comes, now remember that.</u>

OLD GUY: Closer.

SISTER: I ~~don't want to~~ am closer.

OLD GUY: Closer!

SISTER: No, <u>Dad</u>.

OLD GUY: What's the matter with you?

SISTER: She'<u>ll</u> get~~s~~ spit on me.

OLD GUY: Oh, for God's sake. Stand up there. And take a hold of that pair of reins. (*She does*)

That's right. Now pay attention. (OLD GUY *picks up the horse's hoof and begins rasping it*)

There's one thing about working with a horse. You have to be smarter than ~~it~~ <u>she</u> is.

SISTER: I'm smarter than this horse.

OLD GUY: Course you are. But you gotta let <u>her</u> know it. (*He continues rasping*) <u>Now then,</u> I gotta talk to you about something.

SISTER: <u>Not about your funeral, Dad. We done that yesterday.</u> ~~I ain't talking about dying, Dad.~~

OLD GUY: I went down to the undertaker's this afternoon.

SISTER: Not that subject, please.

OLD GUY: I want you to know some things before it happens.

SISTER: I already know some things. And you ain't gonna die.

OLD GUY: Course I am. Now listen up. We're talking caskets here. They got this blue one. Made out of metal. Get that one.

SISTER: I thought you wanted something with nice wood.

OLD GUY: It's all this prefab stuff. Nothing with good wood working. Might as well get metal.

SISTER: Is it good metal working?

OLD GUY: Looks like car metal. Molded like that. They probably
come out of Detroit.

SISTER: I can bury you in the ole Chevy, Dad. Put you in the back
seat and drive you over the edge of Wild Cat Gulch.

OLD GUY: Hand me that rasp. (*She does*) Now then, listen to me.
They'll try to sell you one with a seal. <u>They'll even tell you it's
guaranteed. But</u> I don't want one with a seal.

SISTER: Seal for what?

OLD MAN: Seal for whatever. Water.

SISTER: What's wrong with a seal for water?

OLD MAN: Gees, you're no smarter than the damn salesman.
Think about it.

SISTER: Okay, but I still don't see what's wrong with a seal for water.

OLD MAN: First of all, I'll be dead. I don't have to be dry when I'm
dead. Second, <u>the damn thing ain't gonna last forever.</u> ~~how
long's it gonna last?~~ Sooner or later <u>it's</u> ~~the damn seal's~~ gonna
rot or disintegrate. Then the water comes in anyway. And finally,
~~how you gonna tell whether the damn thing works or not? You
gonna dig me up?~~ <u>the damn guarantee is a crock. They</u> gotta dig
me up to <u>prove anything.</u> ~~find out if it works.~~

SISTER: No seals. Okay, I got it. (SISTER *sits down*) But you ain't
gonna die, Dad.

OLD MAN: Yes I am, and I want everything in order when I do.

SISTER: You have to be real sick before you die. You ain't one bit
sick.

OLD MAN: ~~And that's lucky. But I'm still gonna die. All of em said
so. And I know so, too. I can tell it.~~ This thing is gonna get me.
They're all telling me that, and I know it's true. ~~it too.~~

SISTER: Sure you ain't turning into Lucille Beeson? Dying every
day for the last sixty years of her life.

OLD GUY *stops his work, waits, starts it again.*

OLD GUY: Now what's this thing with Mrs. Griffiths?

<u>SISTER: I gotta go now.</u>

<u>OLD GUY: Not yet.</u>

<u>SISTER: Sheila's forty-one minutes late already. She'll be here any
minute.</u> ~~Oh no. That's why you got me out here., isn't it? I ain't
talking about that.~~

OLD GUY: ~~Oh yes you are, Sister. (Pause.)~~ I mean business here,
<u>Sister.</u>

<u>SISTER: But Dad. . . .</u>

<u>OLD GUY: You heard me.</u>

   Pause.

SISTER: ~~She's~~ Mrs. Griffiths is really dumb, Dad.
OLD GUY: She might be <u>dumb</u>. But I want you to get along with her.
SISTER: What did she tell you?
OLD GUY: Less than half of what you really did, I'm sure.
SISTER: She is so dumb, Dad.
OLD GUY: I don't care if she is a cretin, Sister.
SISTER: Well, I do.
OLD GUY: I want you to behave. I don't care what the circumstances
   are. (*Silence*) Do you need ~~another job?~~ more <u>work</u> to do?
SISTER: No.
OLD GUY: Cuz I can give you more work if you haven't got enough
   to do.
SISTER: I got enough to do.
OLD GUY: Then why you crawling around under the tables?
SISTER: Did she tell you that? I wasn't crawling around under the
   tables.
OLD GUY: What were you doing?
SISTER: Sitting under the table.
OLD GUY: I don't want you sitting under the table <u>neither</u>.
SISTER: I wasn't hurting nothing.
OLD GUY: (*He looks at her*) I mean business here, Sister.
SISTER: I know, but she's lying about me. She hates me, Dad.
OLD GUY: I don't blame her. I'd hate you too.
SISTER: But she's lying, Dad. You can't believe a thing she says.

   The horse rears up.

OLD GUY: FOR GOD SAKE, GET A HOLD OF THOSE REINS!
SISTER: I got em, <u>Dad</u>. I got em.

   <u>*After some fussing the horse settles down.*</u>

OLD GUY: What's your job here?
SISTER: Holding her head.
OLD GUY: And you don't sit on the ground to do that job. And you
   don't let go of the reins to do that job.
SISTER: But it's boring, Dad.
OLD GUY: Jesus Christ, I hope ~~that's~~ <u>this is</u> the worst thing you
   ever have to suffer through. Now stand up there and pay atten-
   tion <u>to this horse</u>.
SISTER: But she doesn't want to do what I say.
OLD GUY: It does not matter what she wants. I expect her to
   behave. And that's your job.
SISTER: Okay. But the next time you poke her with the point of

that rasp, she'll rare up again.

OLD GUY: Well, if she does, we'll tie her head to that stump.

SISTER: No. Don't, Dad.

OLD GUY: Then you're gonna have to do the job. _(He notice her shoes)_ Good, god, what you doing with them shoes?

SISTER: They're what I had on.

OLD GUY: You do not wear high heels to shoe a horse.

SISTER: I ain't gonna be shoeing a horse. I am going someplace with Sheila Sidney.

OLD GUY: Take them damn things off and stand up there like a person.

SISTER: All right. But don't be mean to her.

OLD GUY: It's not mean. Jesus. I'm putting shoes on her. How long you suppose she'd last without shoes?

SISTER: I don't know. But you're doing it mean.

OLD GUY: I am not having a crazy horse.

SISTER: You're the one that's crazy.

OLD GUY: And I'm not having a crazy daughter either. Now then, pay attention here and I'll show you a few things. This is how you drive these nails in so the horse doesn't turn up lame. ~~Remember, you asked me about that the other day.~~

SISTER: ~~I wanted to know that a long time ago, Dad. I don't need to know it now. I don't need to know that, Dad.~~ I know that already, Dad.

OLD GUY: First off, you pick up her foot like this. (He _pushes the horse so that it shifts its weight_) So. So.

SISTER: I know how you pick up her foot.

OLD GUY: Well, maybe you do. Maybe you don't.

SISTER: I do.

He _lifts up the horse's foot._

OLD GUY: ~~So. So.~~ Then rasp her hoof flat like this. Then you take this shoe, and you fit it right there. Like that. And you take a nail and you bend it a bit, like that, see. A horseshoe nail is soft. You can bend it easy. And then you drive it in so and it comes up through there. Just like that, see there.

SISTER: Yeah, Dad. I know how to shoe a horse. I've watched you do it ten million times. And you repeat the same stuff every time.

OLD GUY: That's the only way you learn.

SISTER: ~~It's useless information. No one needs to know how to shoe a horse.~~ Except I don't need to know how to shoe a horse. Who's gonna ~~call on~~ want me to shoe a horse—in this world or the next?

OLD GUY: Hand me that pair of pliers. (SISTER _does not move._ OLD

GUY *gets the pliers himself*) I thought you could learn something. Beats staring at the head of a horse.

SISTER: Are we done, Dad? I gotta go.

OLD GUY: No, we are not done. ~~I don't want you misbehaving in Mrs. Griffiths' class.~~

~~After I'm dead, so help me, I'll come back and haunt you if you act up in Mrs. Griffiths' class.~~

~~SISTER: Now are we done, Dad?~~

OLD GUY: ~~No, we are not done.~~ This is how you finish the job. You take the foot like that, on your knee. Then you rasp down the hoof. Like that. So her foot fits the shoe. You got her head?

SISTER: Yeah, I got her head.

He rasps the horse's foot.

OLD GUY: There now. That ought to last her the summer.

SISTER: Good, are we done?

OLD GUY: Yes, we're done. But I got one other thing to tell you.

SISTER: Hurry up, cuz I'm in a hurry.

OLD GUY: There's an envelope in the top drawer of the dresser. That's where the key is to the safety deposit box. In there is your mother's wedding rings and those wheat pennies your grandfather collected. You remember that, don't you?

SISTER: Yes, Dad.

OLD GUY: Now where you off to?

SISTER: The swimming pool. With Sheila Sidney. For the fiftieth time.

OLD GUY: Well, she's late.

SISTER: She might have tried to call, and I been out here.

OLD GUY: How late is she?

SISTER: I don't know. Fifty-two minutes late.

OLD GUY: Girl ain't got a brain in her head.

SISTER: But she's funny. You have to be smart to be funny.

OLD GUY: Where you think she is?

SISTER: Something probably come up.

OLD GUY *looks at his daughter. Pause.*

OLD GUY: Something probably did.

SISTER: We get along real good, Dad. You wouldn't think so with the difference in our ages. But we do. It's probably because I'm old for my age, more mature than other kids her age. So then the two of us, we get along.

OLD GUY: Well, that's real nice.

SISTER: Yeah, you'd think so if you ever saw us together.

OLD GUY: I'm sure I would.

SISTER: You should see her up at the swimming pool. She does this cut-away off the diving board, and when she's coming down, she hits it with her hand. Everyone thinks she's hit her head. Then she floats up with her face in the water. Everyone thinks she dead. Roaring around and yelling. Pretty soon she just starts swimming like nothing happened. Real funny.

OLD GUY: Yeah, it sounds like it.

SISTER: Yeah.

OLD GUY: You wanna give her a call?

SISTER: Nah.

OLD GUY: Why don't you go get your bike.

SISTER: Nah. I'm too old for that now. ~~Now how about taking me up to the swimming pool?~~

~~OLD GUY: What's wrong with your bike?~~

~~SISTER: I'm gonna be late.~~

~~OLD GUY: Jesus, you sure can work an old man.~~

~~SISTER: Work's good for you, Dad.~~

OLD GUY: Here. Hand me that pair of reins. And go get in the car.

~~SISTER: Thanks, Dad~~. Nah, it's all right, I'll wait for Sheila.

OLD GUY: When she comes, I'll tell her where you are.

SISTER: She's usually pretty reliable with me.

OLD GUY: I'm sure she is.

SISTER: She's real funny.

OLD GUY: All them Sidneys are funny.

SISTER: I want to grow up to be funny.

OLD GUY: You're a good girl, Sister. Go get in the car.

SISTER *hands him the reins. She* ~~walks~~ *shambles off. He watches her go.*

OLD GUY: Here you old son of a bitch. Stay there till I get back.

He ties up the reins and with effort moves off. END.

As we can readily see, Julie Jensen is totally in command of her craft in this piece. Her observations and progressive draft work reveal a capacity to hone an idea carefully from something relatively rough to a polished final piece.

The last question I asked Julie has to do with an element we haven't touched on before in the book: production considerations. After reading through her work a number of times, I began to step outside of the writing process to consider the play from a director's perspective. This is when, however belatedly, it suddenly dawned on me: wait, there's a *horse* in this play. I didn't want to assume that Julie meant the horse to be literal, so I asked her if she thought about production issues when she was working. As usual, Julie's thoughts about her work go far deeper than my basic question, and serve to conclude this chapter with useful insights about craft and how the playwright sees her/his own play.

> Well, yes, of course I always think about sets and technical requirements. I can't imagine not thinking of them. With something like a horse, though, I know full well there will be no horse, and in fact, I wouldn't want a horse. I'm not entirely sure all the business will be clear all the time, since shoeing a horse is fairly arcane, foreign to most folks. That's part of the reason the old guy explains some of it. But finally, the shoeing is less important to the old guy than seeing to it that his daughter is in line. He just doesn't do anything that's not hooked up to work. Unthinkable.

Afterword

FANTASIES, DREAMS,
IMPRACTICALITIES, IMPROBABILITIES

IN THE LATE 70S, I MET A WONDERFUL WRITER/SCHOLAR named Arthur Feinsod, who was (and still is) chair of the Theatre Department at Trinity College in Hartford, Connecticut. Through various conversations, we came up with the idea to do a journal devoted to playwriting at the college/university and professional levels. We would call it *The Playwrights' Quarterly.*

The quarterly never happened, of course, for a variety of reasons having to do with money, time, and lack of other resources. Even so, it was a great dream.

One of the things we wanted to do, besides publish the best plays from college/university and professional writers, and brilliant articles on playwriting, was invite some writers of note to contribute drafts of a play-in-progress, or even write their idea of a "bad" play. The point was to talk about craft through craft, to address playwriting through the act of writing a play, and not through retrospective analysis of work which had already achieved commercial acceptance. *Playwriting Master Class* has achieved this fantasy in many ways, so that item on the list of dream projects can be checked off.

Here are some others on my list, some of which are impractical and/or improbable, but it is a dream list, after all:

- To see sequential drafts of major plays published. I mentioned *Angels in America* already, and there are many other important works that could be presented in this fashion. Established plawrights ought to ransack their files for us and share their material (keep in mind, this is fantasy).

- To have more documentation on new work in a recorded form—video would be best, but even audio could be useful. The Bravo Network presented a piece on *Moon Over Buffalo* that had some interesting things in it, for instance. PBS did a special on *Angels in America*. We need more of this kind of documentation on plays which are not already successful, on material which is raw and where "failure" is a real possibility. We also need a great deal more documentation of non-naturalistic work, to encourage those visions which fall outside story-driven theatre. There are an increasing number of videos available, but most focus on recording the production and rarely address the writing/development process.

- To see a festival of the plays in this book. I assume all the writers will have a reading in their home environments, and maybe even a production, but wouldn't it be wonderful to see an evening of these seven plays, all linked to the "key" prompt?

- To have more publications dedicated to printing plays. *American Theatre* is doing an excellent job in collaboration with A.S.K. Theatre Projects, *TheatreForum* publishes international new work, etc. But we need more, simply because we need to ensure that new work gets done.

That's the short list. I could go on and on—as we all could. My dreams include festivals of original short plays starting at the elementary school level and up, seasons at every theatre from community to LORT which include new work, and even an increase in original work on Broadway.

The bottom line is that if more new work is seen and done,

new work will become what's normal in theatre. In educational theatre, one often hears conversations which go something like this:

"Hey, have you done (a recent hit from New York) yet?"

"Yep. We also did (another recent hit from New York)."

And I always wonder: What was learned from this? That something already "worked" doesn't mean it's any good.

This is not to blame educational theatre directors for doing what's already been measured by the questionable yardstick of success in New York. The arguments are all familiar: everyone has to please their audiences; audiences come to plays they've heard of. But I do wonder why these seasons can't include new work as well. I know, it's pie-in-the sky, but I guess I'm flying pretty high at the moment on the completion of this book.

It took more than fifteen years to realize one of the dreams that Arthur Feinsod and I shared in our plans for *The Playwrights' Quarterly*, but in the face of an art form as old as theatre, that's a drop in the bucket. Just think what the next fifteen years can bring.

CONTRIBUTORS

Elena Carrillo received an MFA in Creative Writing from the University of Texas at El Paso. She writes fiction and poetry, and her plays have had readings and productions at the Frontera Fest in Austin, Texas, the University of Texas–El Paso, The Border Book Festival in Las Cruces, New Mexico, the WordBRIDGE Playwrights Lab in St. Petersburg, Florida, and the New Salem Center in Springfield, Illinois. She is co-editor of *The Student's Guide to Playwriting Opportunities, 2nd Ed.*, a Core member of Austin ScriptWorks, and was also the editor of *The Rio Grande Review*. Her play *Call the Serpent God to Me* received an honorable mention in the 1996 21st Century Playwrights Festival in New York and was honored by the 1998 Kennedy Center/American College Theatre Festival. Her plays have been published by Heinemann in *The Elvis Monologues* and *Monologues from the Road*. Elena currently has fiction appearing in the *Indiana Review* and is working on a new play called *Embrujada*.

For further information and permission, contact Care of Heinemann.

David Crespy is Assistant Professor of playwriting in the University of Missouri-Columbia's Department of Theatre. He serves as the artistic director of MU's Missouri Playwrights Workshop and is the faculty advisor to Loose Change Productions, MU's friendly guerrilla theatre. His play *Men Dancing* received the 1996 21st Century Playwrights Award, and has been developed at Jewish Repertory Theatre, HB Playwrights Foundation, and Ensemble Studio Theatre in New York. David is the founder and former artistic director of The WaterFront Ensemble, Inc., a professional non-profit organization dedicated to the development of New American plays. He is currently under contract with BackStage Press to write a book on New York's off-off-Broadway in the 1960s entitled *The Off-Off Broadway Explosion*. He is currently working on a new play, *William & Bettie*, a Civil War romance taking place in Keytesville, Missouri.

For further information and permission, contact Robert Duva, Duva-Flack Associates, Inc., 200 W. 57th St., Suite 1008, New York, NY 10019, telephone: (212) 957-9600, fax: (212) 957-9606.

Gary Garrison is a member of the full-time faculty of the Dramatic Writing Program at NYU's Tisch School of the Arts and producer for all of its productions of student original work. He has produced the last 14 Festival of New Works for NYU, working with over three hundred playwrights, seventy-five directors, and hundreds of actors. At NYU, he annually produces the Marathon Festival of One-Act Plays, The Ten-Minute Play Festival, and The Annual Festival of New Works. Garrison's plays include *We Make A Wall* (Open Door Theatre, Expanded Arts), *The Big Fat Naked Truth* (Brooklyn Playworks, Circle Rep Lab, Pulse Ensemble Theatre, Spectrum Stage, Manhattan Punchline, Alice's Fourth Floor, Second Generation Theatre Company, The Miranda Theatre), *Scream With Laughter* (Expanded Arts, Pulse Ensemble Theatre, Sienna Theatre), *Gawk* (Pulse Ensemble Theatre, Turnip Theatre Festival), *Smoothness With Cool* (Expanded Arts), *Empty Rooms* (Miranda Theatre, Sienna Theatre), *Does Anybody Want A Miss Cow Bayou?* (New York Rep), and *When A Diva Dreams* (Miranda Theatre, Hedgerow Theatre Company, MetroStage, African Globe Theatre Works). Scenes and monologues from *We Make A Wall* and *When A Diva Dreams* were included in the *Best Men's Monologues of 1997*, *Best Women's Monologues of 1997*, and *Best Stage Scenes of 1997* (Smith & Krause, Inc.) *Gawk* was recently published in *A Grand Entrance: Scenes and Monologues for Mature Audiences* by Dramatics Publishing Company. In 1999, Heinemann Press published a collection of his essays on playwriting under the title, *A Playwright's Guide to Survival: Keeping the Drama in Your Work and Out of Your Life*. He is a member of the Dramatists Guild and a regular contributor to its member publication, *The Dramatist*.

For further information and permission, contact Fifi Oscard, Fifi Oscard Talent and Literary Agency, 24 West 40th Street, 17th Floor, New York, NY 10018; telephone: (212) 764-1100.

Velina Hasu Houston's plays have been commissioned by The Mark Taper Forum, Manhattan Theatre Club, Asia Society, Honolulu Theatre for Youth, and the Lila Wallace-Readers Digest Foundation New Generations Play Project, among others. She is an artistic associate of the Sacramento Theatre Company, a member of the Women's Project and Productions (New York), and on the Board of Advisors of Sand Diego Asian American Repertory Theatre. Her plays appear in anthologies published by Vintage Books-Random House, Applause Books, Smith & Kraus Books, University of Massachusetts Press, University of Illinois Press, Rowman & Littlefield, and University of Texas Press. Houston's honors include Japan Foundation Fellow, James Zumberge Fellow, Remy Martin New Vision Screenwriting Award from Sidney Poitier and the American Film Institute, Japanese American Woman of Merit 1890-1990 by the National Japanese American Historical Society, Rockefeller Foundation fellow, and others. Houston's works and personal papers are archived in The Huntington Library, The Velina Hasu Houston Collection. She is a member of the Dramatists Guild and the Writers Guild of America, west.

For further information and permission, contact Mary Harden, Harden-Curtis Associates, 850 Seventh Avenue, Suite 405, New York, NY 10019, maryharden@aol.com (theatre); Merrily Kane and Maggie Roiphe, The Artists Agency, 10000 Santa Monica Boulevard, Los Angeles, CA 90067, merrily01@sprynet.com (film and television); Betsy Amster, Betsy Amster Literary Enterprises, 2151 Kenilworth Avenue, Los Angeles, CA 90039, amsterlit@com-puserve.com (prose).

Julie Jensen's first full-length play, *Cisterns*, premiered at the Attic Theatre in Detroit. Early one-acts were produced in New York at the Negro Ensemble Company, the Quaigh Theatre, and the Women's Project. Jensen's *Stray Dogs* won the CBS/Dramatists Guild Prize and opened at Arena Stage in Washington, D.C.; it is published by Dramatists Play Service. Other works include *Thursday's Child*, *White Money* (winner of the 1990 Award for New American Plays), *The Lost Vegas Series* (Joseph Jefferson award-winner), *Last Lists of My Mad Mother* (commissioned by Mark Taper Forum, nominated for best play of the year by the American Theatre Critics Association, selected as Critic's Choice by *American Theatre*), and *Two-Headed* (commissioned by A.S.K. Theatre Projects). Her most recent play, *Cheat*, was commissioned by Geva Theatre in Rochester, NY, where it was workshopped in 1999. It was a part of the fall reading series at the Working Theatre in New York City and will be workshopped by Playwrights Theatre of New Jersey.

For further information and permission, contact Karin Wakefield, Epstein Wyckoff & Associates, 280 Beverly Drive, #400 Beverly Hills, CA 90212; telephone: (310) 287-7222.

Guillermo Reyes's plays include *Chilean Holiday*, *Men on the Verge of A His-Panic Breakdown*, *Deporting the Divas*, *Miss Consuelo*, *Allende by Pinochet*, *The West Hollywood Affair*, *The Seductions of Johnny Diego*, an adaptation of the novel *Ramona*, and others. *Chilean Holiday* was produced at Actors Theatre of Louisville, and published in *Humana Festival '96: The Complete Plays* (Smith and Kraus). *Men on the Verge . . .* won Theatre L.A.'s Ovation Award for Best World Premiere Play and Best Production 1994, and has since played across the country including New York City where it also won the 1996 Emerging Playwright Award, and received an Off-Broadway production at the 47th Street Playhouse. *Deporting the Divas* premiered at Celebration Theatre of Los Angeles. It was subsequently produced by Borderlands Theatre of Tucson, and Theatre Rhinoceros in San Francisco where it won the 1996 Bay Area Drama-Logue for Playwriting and was nominated for best original script by the Bay Area Critics Circle. Mr. Reyes won the 1997 National Hispanic Playwrights Contest with his play *A Southern Christmas*, and the Nosotros Theatre of Los Angeles' 1998 Playwriting Award with *The Hispanick Zone*. He received his Master's degree in Playwriting from the University of California, San Diego. He is currently Assistant Professor of Theatre at Arizona State University in Tempe and head of the playwriting program. Mr. Reyes is a member of the Dramatists Guild.

For further information and permission, contact Guillermo Reyes, Theatre Department, Arizona State University, Box 872002, Tempe, AZ 85287-2002; telephone: (480) 965-0519; e-mail: Reyes@asu.edu.

Elizabeth Wong is a winner of ATHE's Jane Chambers Award for her play *China Doll*, which tells the tragic story of Hollywood movie icon Anna May Wong. Her latest play *Boyd & Oskar*, premieres March 2000, and was commissioned by Cincinnati Playhouse in the Park and the Lazarus Foundation. Her play *Prometheus*, an adaptation of Aeschylus' *Prometheus Bound*, was commissioned by Denver Center Theatre, and premiered January 1999 under the direction of Luanne Nunes. Miss Wong's plays include *Letters to a Student Revolutionary*, *Kimchee & Chitlins*, *Let the Big Dog Eat*, *Alice Downsized*, *The Happy Prince*, and *Punk Girls* (Omaha Magic Theatre, working with Megan Terry). Miss Wong is a Walt Disney Writer's Fellow, a Petersen Emerging Playwright Fellow, and a former editorial columnist for the Los Angeles *Times*. She serves on the Theatre Emory board along with Wole Soyinka, Wendy Wasserstein, and Alfred Uhry. She is a member of PEN WEST, the Dramatist Guild, and Writers Guild West, and her papers are archived at the Davidson Library, University of California–Santa Barbara where she teaches playwriting. Wong was honored to serve as a 1999 National Selection Team adjudicator for the Kennedy Center/American College Theatre Festival with the late John Lion.

For further information and permission, contact John Buzzetti, 130 W. 42nd Street, Fourth Floor, New York, NY 10036; telephone: (212) 997-1818; e-mail: JBuzzetti@GershNY.com.

Michael Wright has extensive professional credits in writing for performance, as well as twenty years teaching experience in under-graduate and graduate theatre. He is Applied Associate Professor of Creative Writing and Theatre at the University of Tulsa. He is the former head of Playwriting and Directing at the University of Texas at El Paso; creator of the UTEP PlayWorks Festival, a new play devel-opment program; past Playwriting Chair of Region VI of the Kennedy Center/American College Theatre Festival; and a Resource Artist for the WordBRIDGE Playwrights Laboratory in St. Petersburg, Florida. Michael is a National Advisor to Austin Script Works Theatre, in Austin, Texas; and the Coordinating U.S. Representative for the World InterPlay Europe 2000. His books include *The Student's Guide to Playwriting Opportunities, 2nd Ed.* (Theatre Directories, Inc.) and *Playwriting in Process: Thinking and Working Theatrically* (Heinemann). His plays *Payments* and *Debts* are published by Palmetto Play Service; other plays, poems, fiction, articles, and photography have appeared in *The Elvis Monologues, Scenes and Monologues for Mature Actors, Monologues from the Road, Rio Grande Review, Dramatics Magazine, and Voces Fronterizas*, among others. Michael has conducted playwrit-ing workshops across the U.S. and in Australia, Poland, and Sweden; he has consulted on scripts for MGM, American Playhouse, Circle in the Square, and the Mississippi, Ohio, and Tennessee Arts Councils. He served as Artist-in-Residence at the University of Arizona in February–March, 2000 on a Bank One Visiting Artists Fund grant. Wright is a member of the Dramatists Guild

For further information and permission, contact Michael Wright, Applied Associate Professor of Creative Writing and Theatre, Kendall Hall 100E, The University of Tulsa, 600 S. College Avenue, Tulsa, OK 74104-3189; telephone: (918) 631-3175; e-mail: myquagga@yahoo.com.